SCALPED

INDIAN COUNTRY

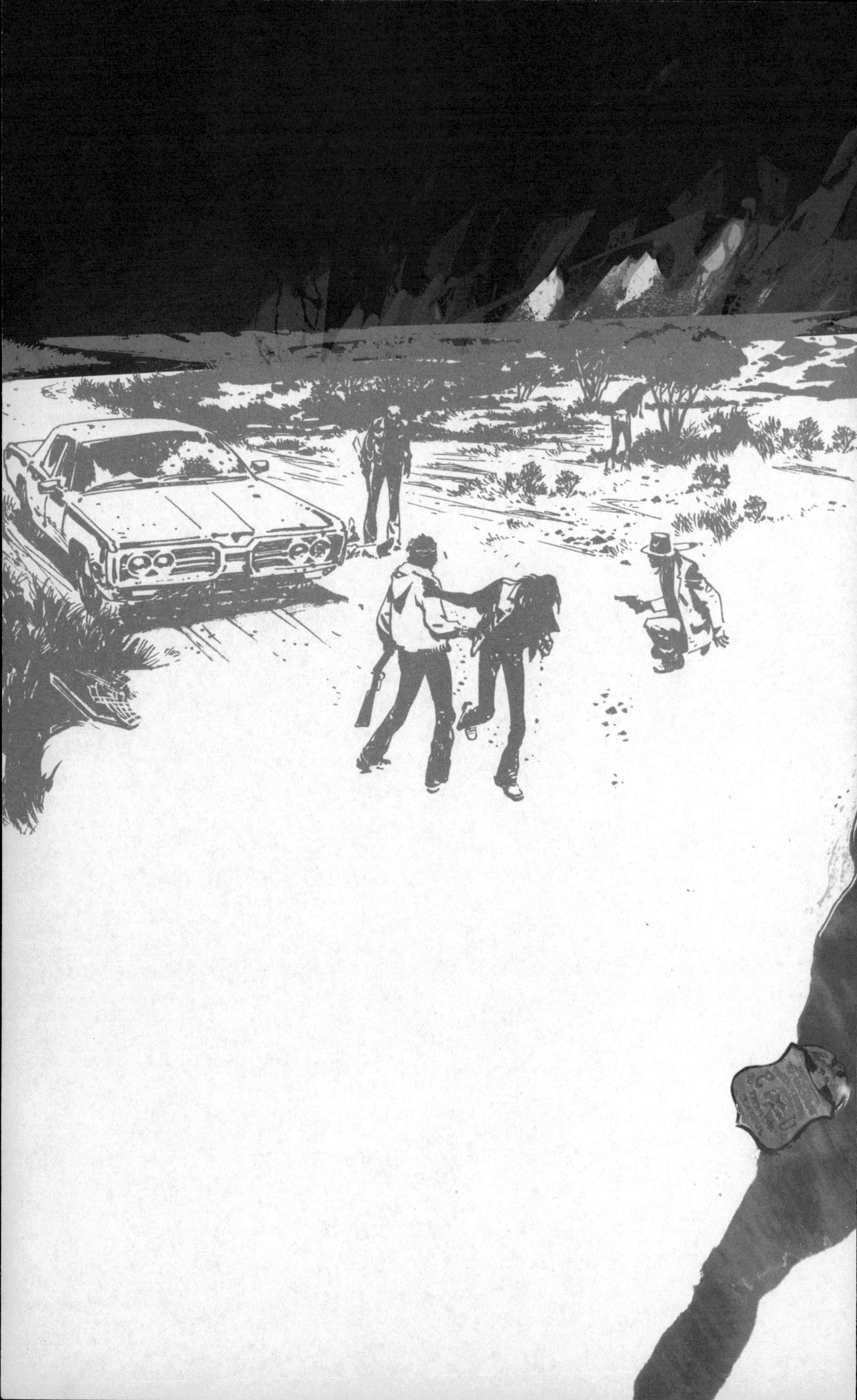

JASON AARON WRITER   R.M. GUÉRA ARTIST

LEE LOUGHRIDGE COLORIST   PHIL BALSMAN LETTERER

SCALPED

INDIAN COUNTRY

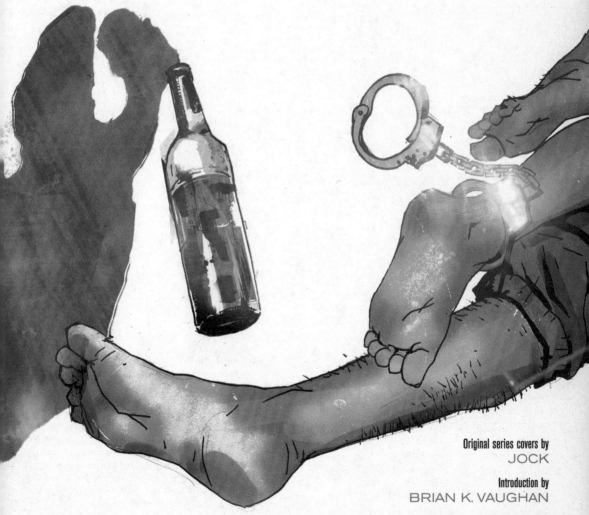

Original series covers by
JOCK

Introduction by
BRIAN K. VAUGHAN

SCALPED created by
JASON AARON and R.M. GUÉRA

KAREN BERGER
Senior VP-Executive Editor

WILL DENNIS
Editor-original series

CASEY SEIJAS
Assistant Editor-original series

BOB HARRAS
Editor-collected edition

ROBBIN BROSTERMAN
Senior Art Director

PAUL LEVITZ
President & Publisher

GEORG BREWER
VP-Design & DC Direct Creative

RICHARD BRUNING
Senior VP-Creative Director

PATRICK CALDON
Executive VP-Finance & Operations

CHRIS CARAMALIS
VP-Finance

JOHN CUNNINGHAM
VP-Marketing

TERRI CUNNINGHAM
VP-Managing Editor

ALISON GILL
VP-Manufacturing

HANK KANALZ
VP-General Manager, WildStorm

JIM LEE
Editorial Director-WildStorm

PAULA LOWITT
Senior VP-Business & Legal Affairs

MARYELLEN MCLAUGHLIN
VP-Advertising &
Custom Publishing

JOHN NEE
VP-Business Development

GREGORY NOVECK
Senior VP-Creative Affairs

SUE POHJA
VP-Book Trade Sales

CHERYL RUBIN
Senior VP-Brand Management

JEFF TROJAN
VP-Business Development,
DC Direct

BOB WAYNE
VP-Sales

LOGO AND COVER ILLUSTRATION BY JOCK
PUBLICATION DESIGN BY BRAINCHILD STUDIOS/NYC

SCALPED: INDIAN COUNTRY

DC Comics, 1700 Broadway, New York, NY 10019
A Warner Bros. Entertainment Company.
Printed in Canada. First Printing.
ISBN: 1-4012-1317-0 ISBN 13: 978-1-4012-1317-6

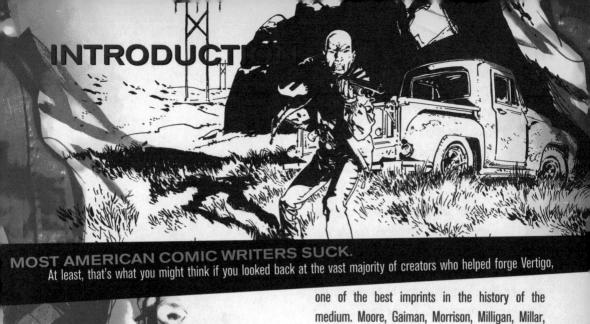

INTRODUCTION

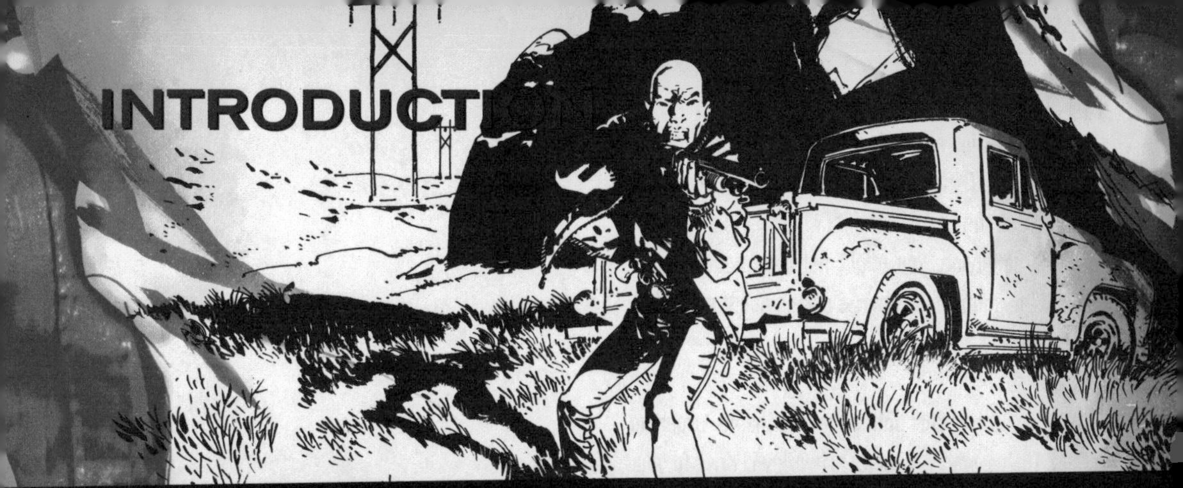

MOST AMERICAN COMIC WRITERS SUCK.

At least, that's what you might think if you looked back at the vast majority of creators who helped forge Vertigo, one of the best imprints in the history of the medium. Moore, Gaiman, Morrison, Milligan, Millar, Ellis, Ennis...dirty foreigners, every one of them. This U.K. invasion had already moved on to innovative new adult fiction while we lowly Yanks were still trying to figure out how they beat us at our own superhero game.

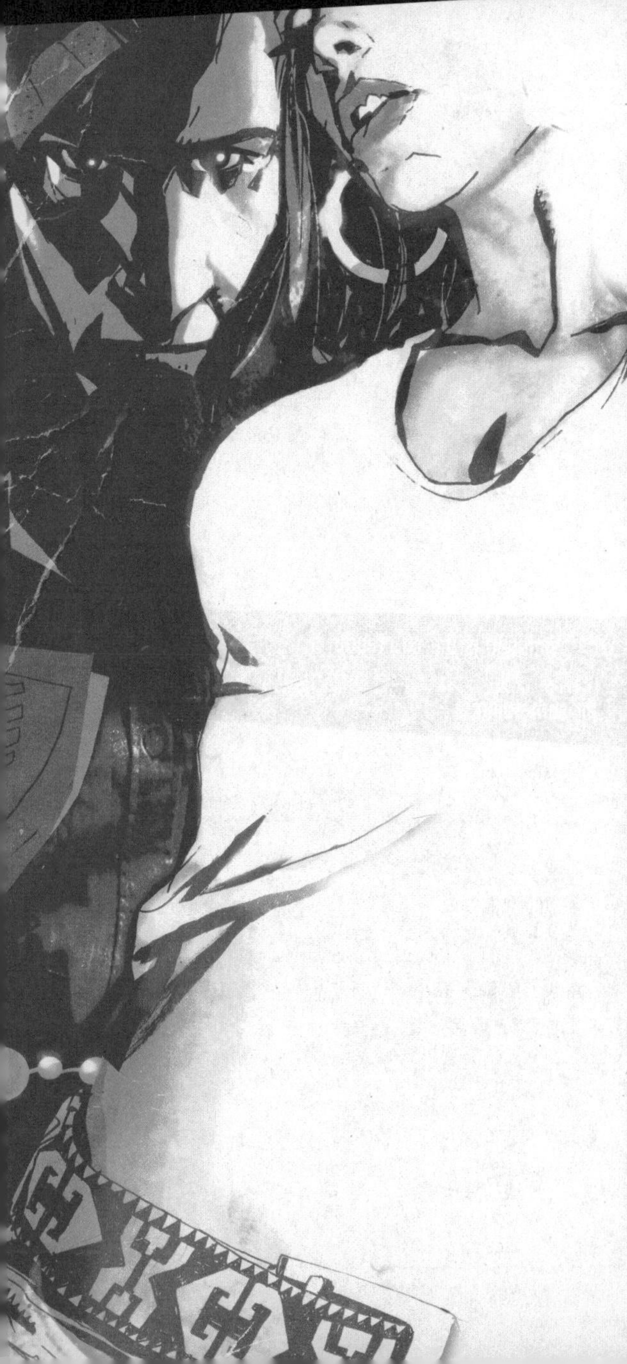

And while the scales have started to even out over the last few years, it was still a particular thrill for a U.S. citizen with a nasty inferiority complex like mine to discover the work of a young guy named Jason Aaron. See, Jason isn't just a great writer who happens to be American, he's a great writer largely because he *is* American.

And before all the international readers out there start tucking their Euros back into their wallets, let me be clear that I'm not talking about rah-rah jingoistic bullshit. If you've read **THE OTHER SIDE**, Jason's staggeringly brilliant Vietnam story, you know that he's able to write about the United States with both the burning passion and the uniquely vitriolic rage that's difficult to balance if you didn't gestate inside the loving belly of this cruel beast.

And speaking of natives, **SCALPED** is Jason's distinctly American Western-slash-crime story about the people who had this country first. Starring Dashiell Bad Horse, the rare film noir protagonist who's actually as cool as his name, this is the riveting tale of one mean cop with a big damn secret.

It's about a lot more than that, of course, but the skeleton in Dash's closet (which you'll meet for yourself at the end of the first chapter) is so perfect and so satisfying, you might not even notice all the tough questions this comic is asking about race, vice, class, family, and sex.

Okay, you'll probably notice the sex, thanks largely to R. M. Guéra, whose visceral artwork will drive to your house, throw you into the back of a pickup, and haul your ass straight onto the reservation. This book has got some of the best cliffhangers on the stands, and Guéra nails every one of them. Just awesome.

Well-researched yet imaginative, funny but serious, political and politically incorrect, **SCALPED** is further proof that the most exciting new writer in comics is an American.

Don't hold it against him.

BRIAN K. VAUGHAN
May 2007

Along with writing for the television series **LOST**, Vaughan is the co-creator of **Y: THE LAST MAN**, **EX MACHINA** and **PRIDE OF BAGHDAD**. He was born and raised in the States but married a Canadian, which has got to count for something.

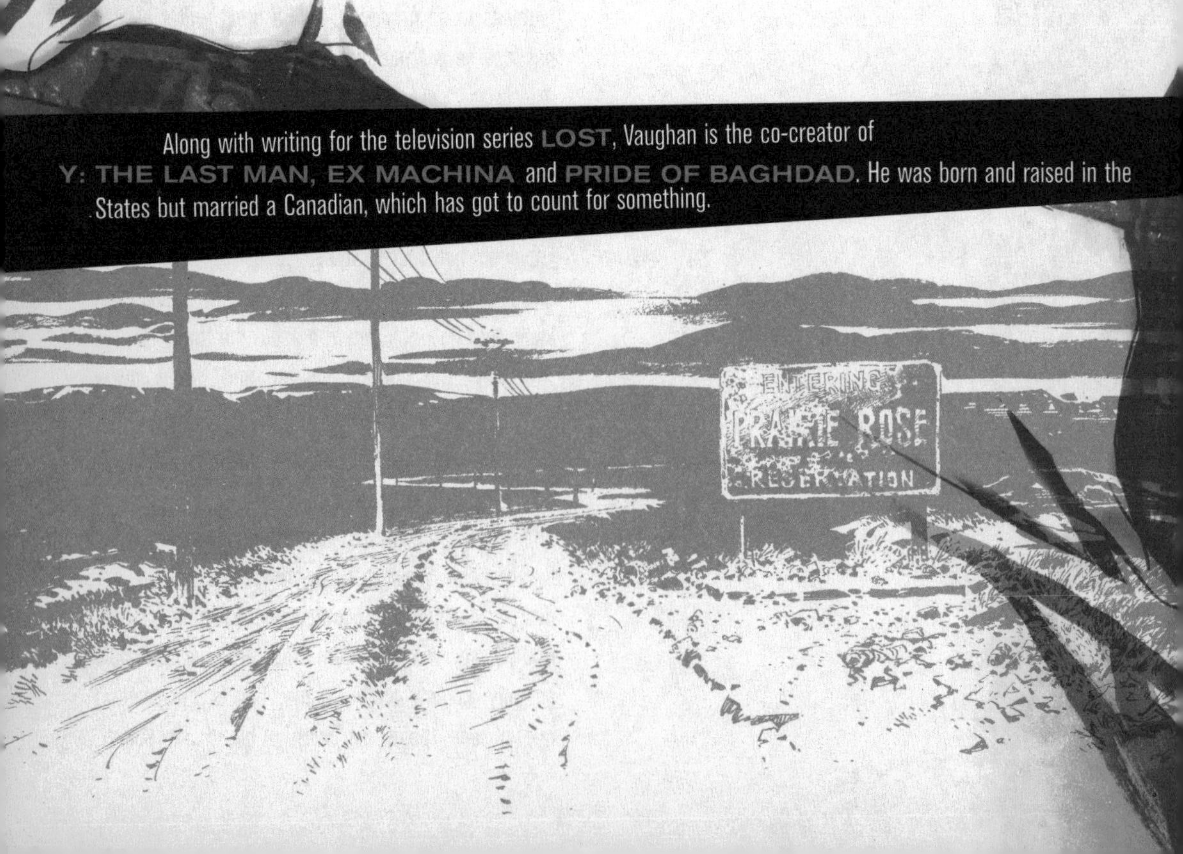
ENTERING
PRAIRIE ROSE
RESERVATION

INDIAN COUNTRY
CHAPTER ONE

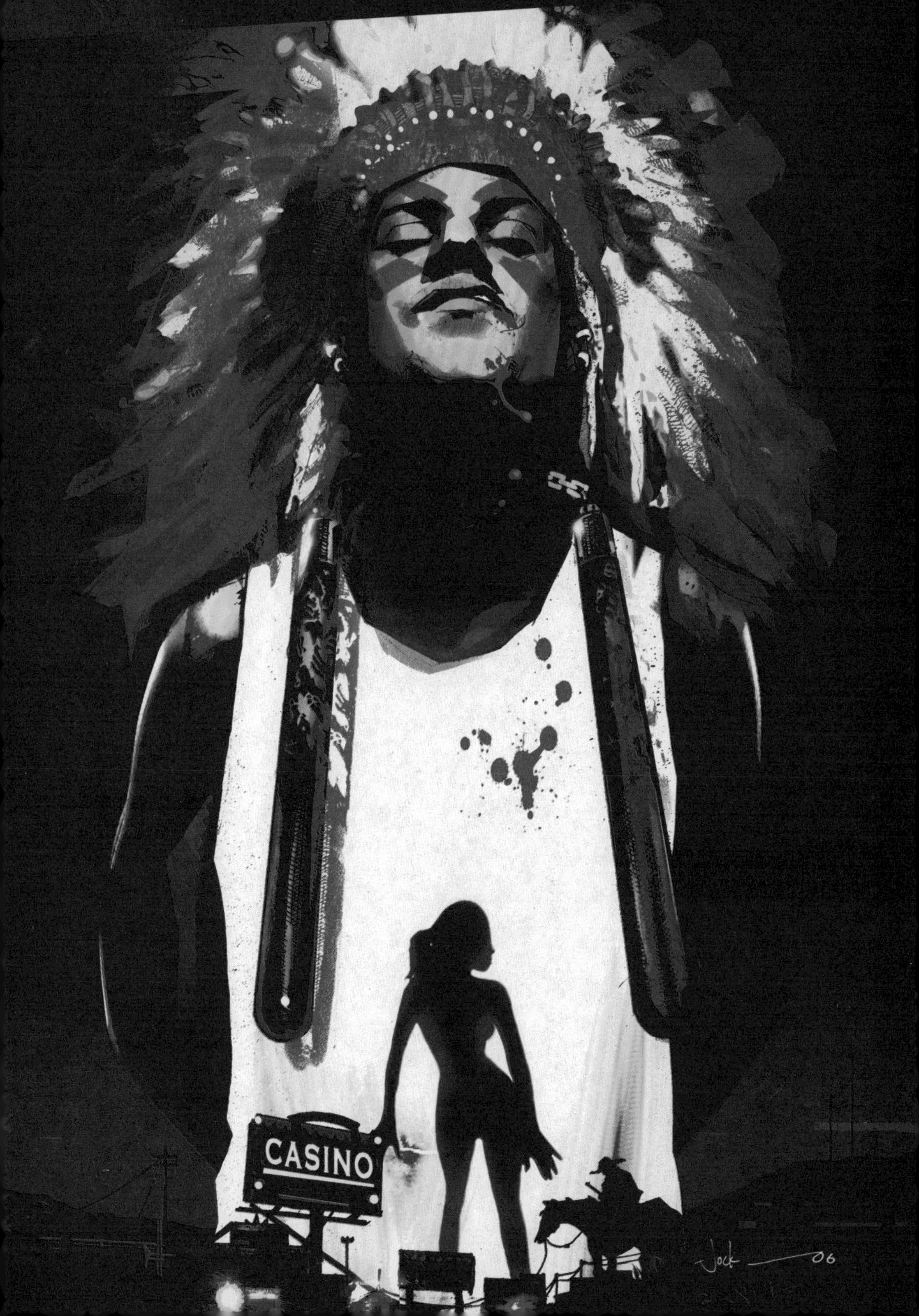
CASINO
Jock 06

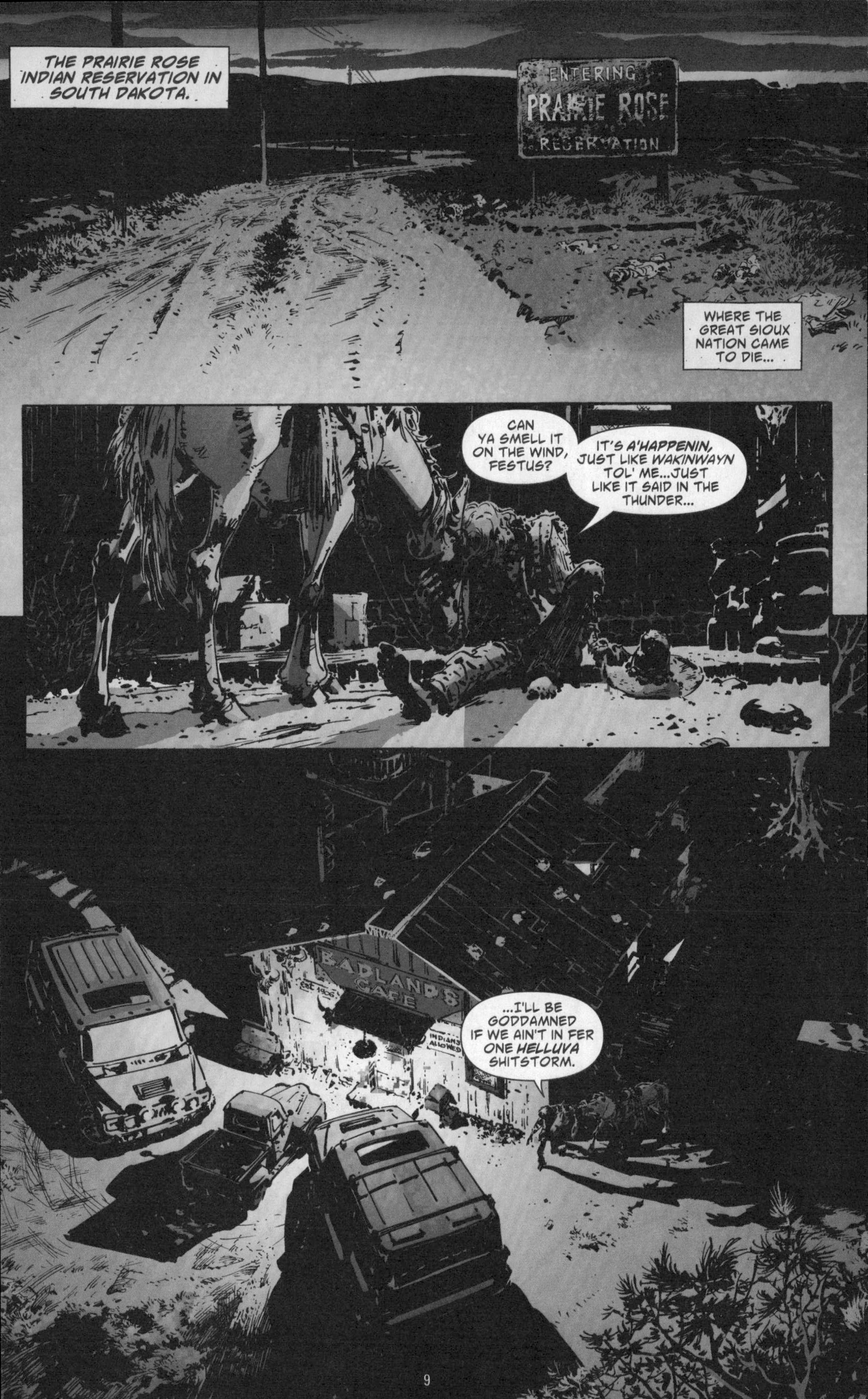
THE PRAIRIE ROSE INDIAN RESERVATION IN SOUTH DAKOTA.
ENTERING PRAIRIE ROSE RESERVATION
WHERE THE GREAT SIOUX NATION CAME TO DIE...
CAN YA SMELL IT ON THE WIND, FESTUS?
IT'S *A'HAPPENIN,* JUST LIKE *WAKINWAYN* TOL' ME...JUST LIKE IT SAID IN THE THUNDER...
BADLANDS CAFE
...I'LL BE GODDAMNED IF WE AIN'T IN FER ONE *HELLUVA* SHITSTORM.

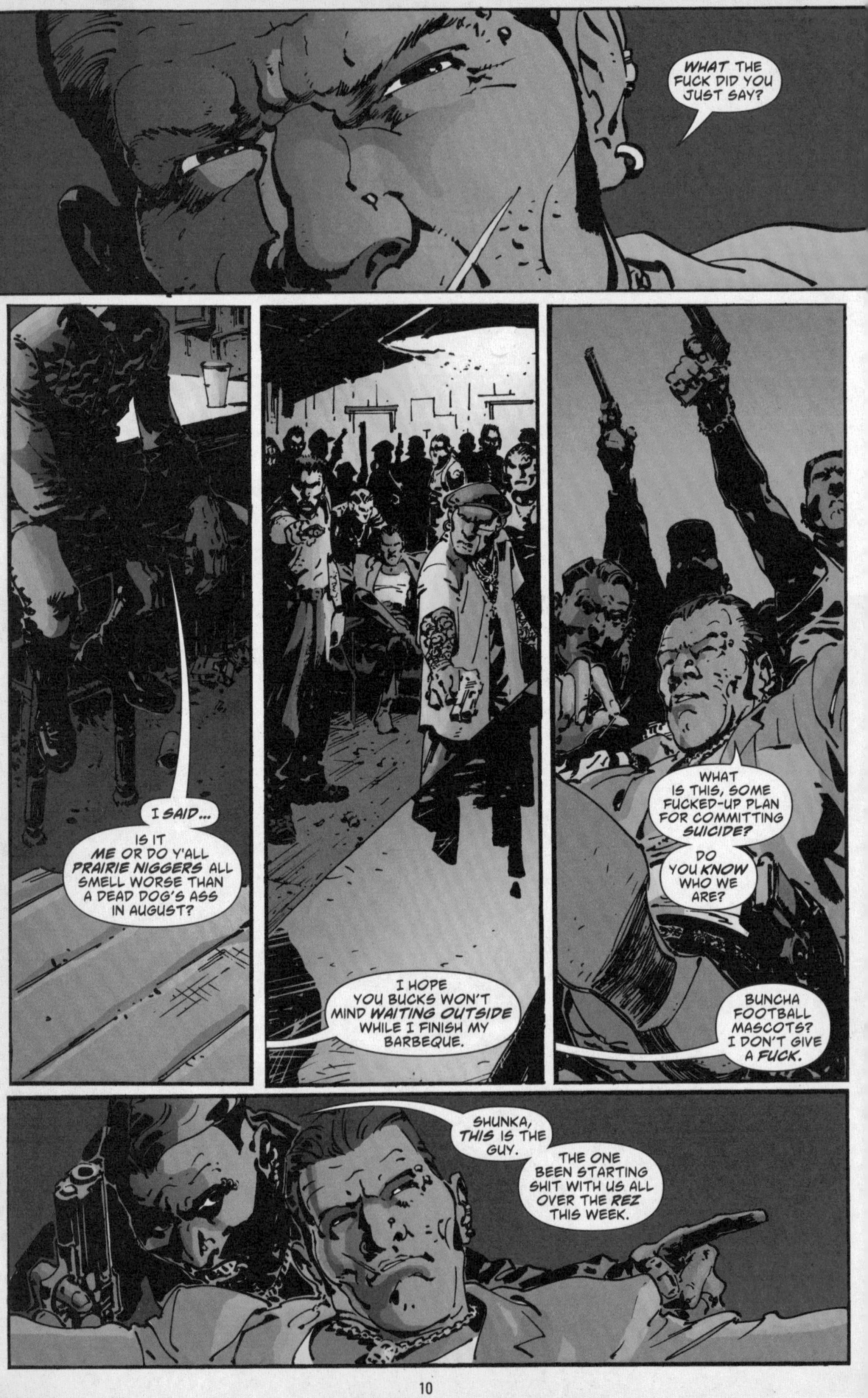
WHAT THE FUCK DID YOU JUST SAY?
I SAID...
IS IT ME OR DO Y'ALL PRAIRIE NIGGERS ALL SMELL WORSE THAN A DEAD DOG'S ASS IN AUGUST?
I HOPE YOU BUCKS WON'T MIND WAITING OUTSIDE WHILE I FINISH MY BARBEQUE.
WHAT IS THIS, SOME FUCKED-UP PLAN FOR COMMITTING SUICIDE?
DO YOU KNOW WHO WE ARE?
BUNCHA FOOTBALL MASCOTS? I DON'T GIVE A FUCK.
SHUNKA, THIS IS THE GUY.
THE ONE BEEN STARTING SHIT WITH US ALL OVER THE REZ THIS WEEK.

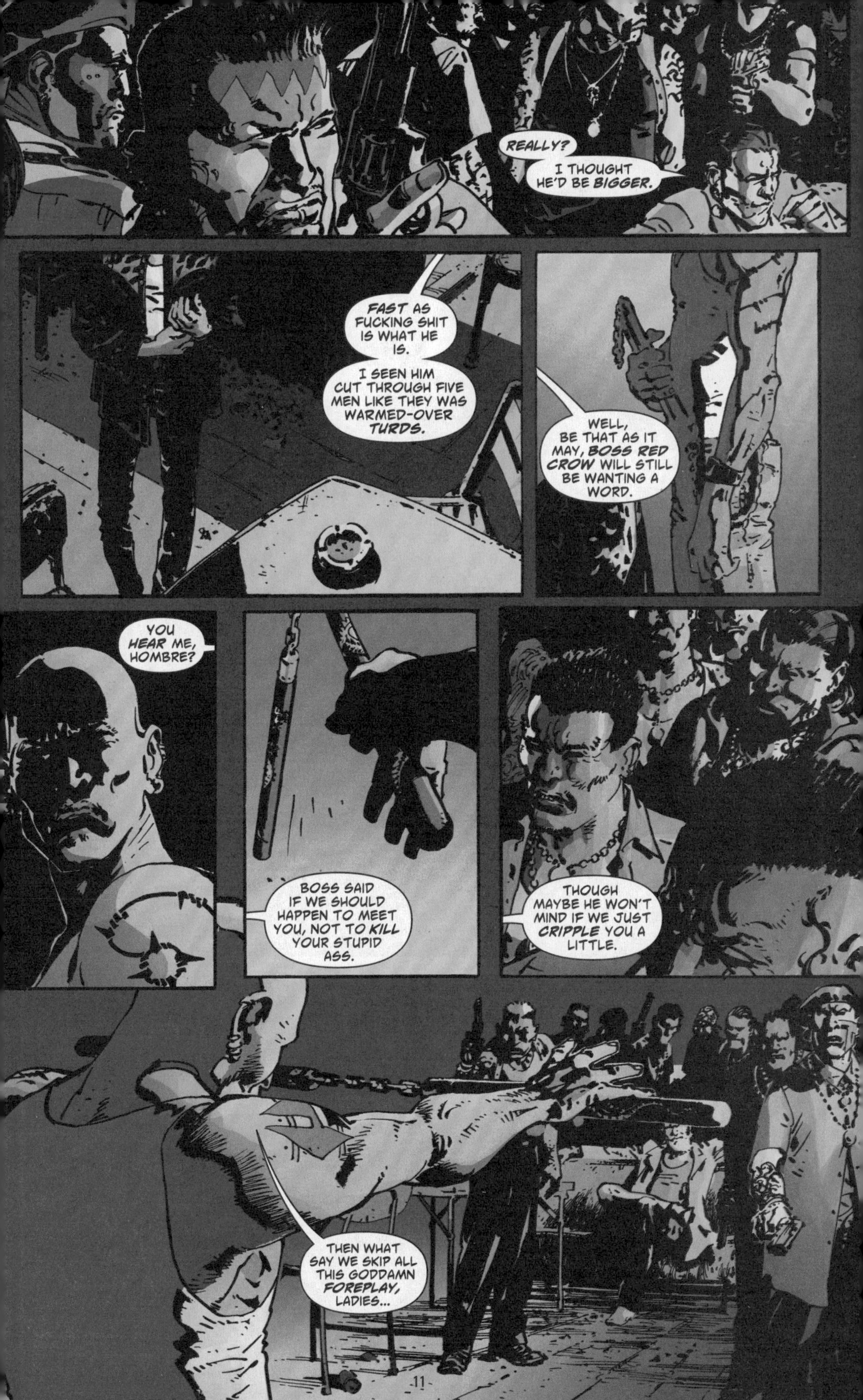
REALLY?
I THOUGHT HE'D BE BIGGER.
FAST AS FUCKING SHIT IS WHAT HE IS.
I SEEN HIM CUT THROUGH FIVE MEN LIKE THEY WAS WARMED-OVER TURDS.
WELL, BE THAT AS IT MAY, BOSS RED CROW WILL STILL BE WANTING A WORD.
YOU HEAR ME, HOMBRE?
BOSS SAID IF WE SHOULD HAPPEN TO MEET YOU, NOT TO KILL YOUR STUPID ASS.
THOUGH MAYBE HE WON'T MIND IF WE JUST CRIPPLE YOU A LITTLE.
THEN WHAT SAY WE SKIP ALL THIS GODDAMN FOREPLAY, LADIES...

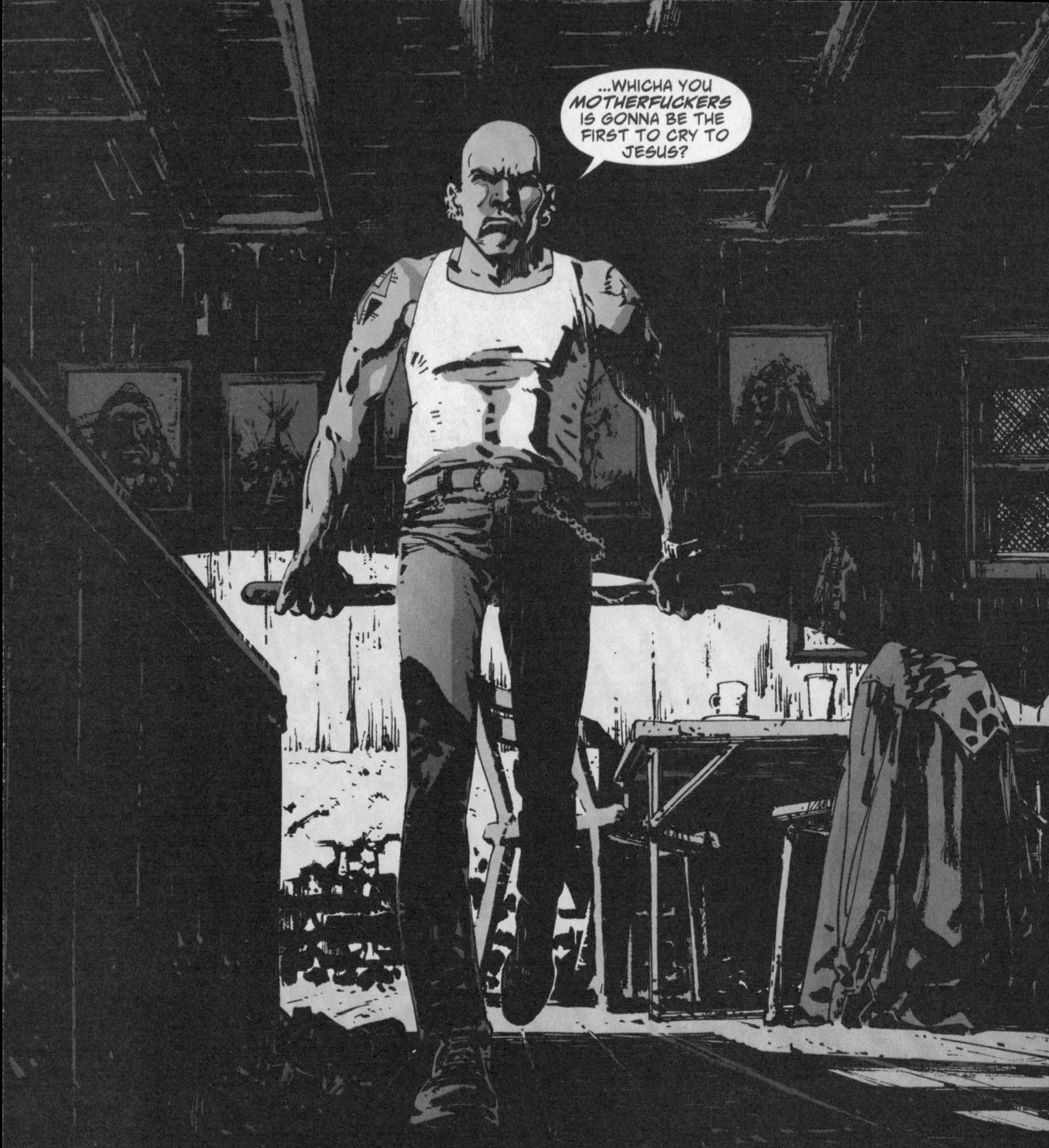
...WHICHA YOU MOTHERFUCKERS IS GONNA BE THE FIRST TO CRY TO JESUS?

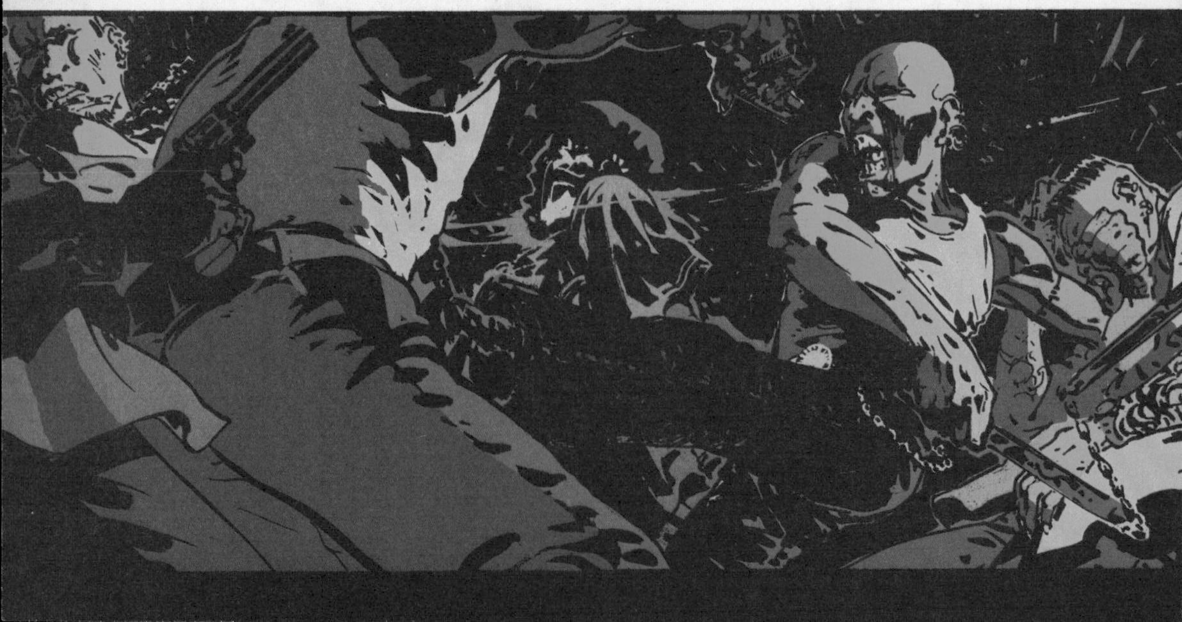

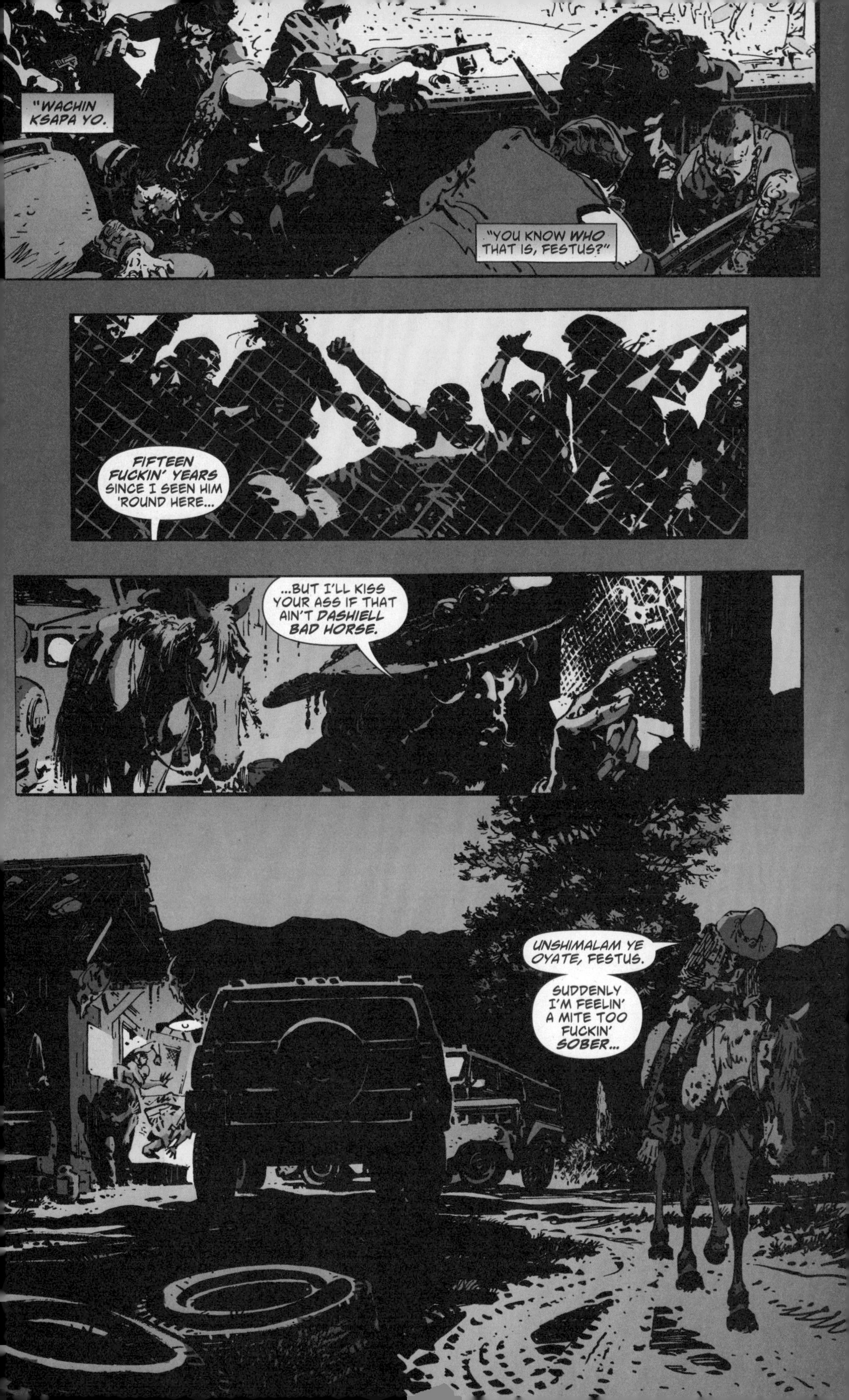
"WACHIN KSAPA YO.
"YOU KNOW WHO THAT IS, FESTUS?"
FIFTEEN FUCKIN' YEARS SINCE I SEEN HIM 'ROUND HERE...
...BUT I'LL KISS YOUR ASS IF THAT AIN'T DASHIELL BAD HORSE.
UNSHIMALAM YE OYATE, FESTUS.
SUDDENLY I'M FEELIN' A MITE TOO FUCKIN' SOBER...

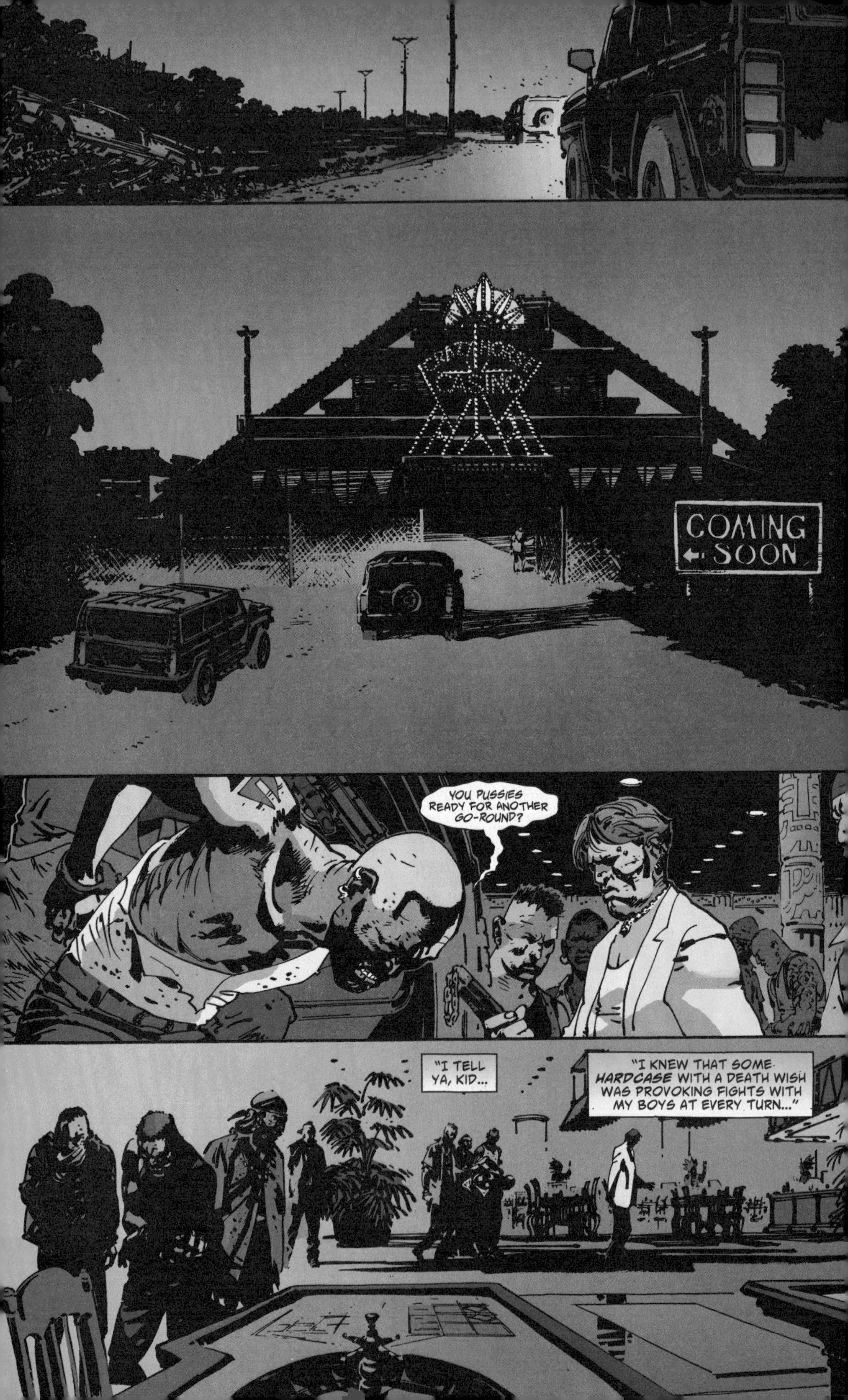
CRAZY HORSE CASINO
COMING
SOON
YOU PUSSIES READY FOR ANOTHER GO-ROUND?
"I TELL YA, KID...
"I KNEW THAT SOME HARDCASE WITH A DEATH WISH WAS PROVOKING FIGHTS WITH MY BOYS AT EVERY TURN..."

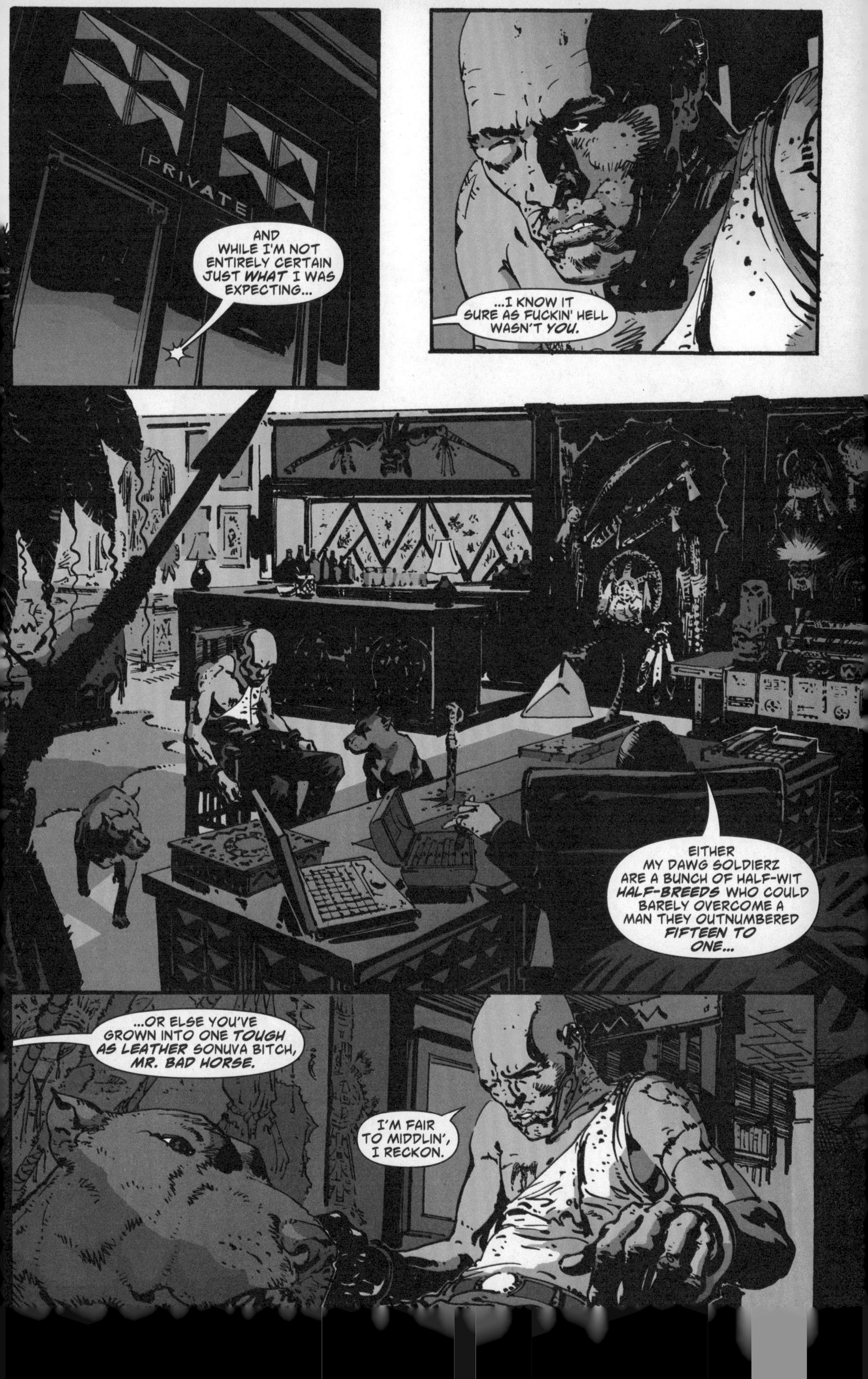
PRIVATE
AND WHILE I'M NOT ENTIRELY CERTAIN JUST WHAT I WAS EXPECTING...
...I KNOW IT SURE AS FUCKIN' HELL WASN'T YOU.
EITHER MY DAWG SOLDIERZ ARE A BUNCH OF HALF-WIT HALF-BREEDS WHO COULD BARELY OVERCOME A MAN THEY OUTNUMBERED FIFTEEN TO ONE...
...OR ELSE YOU'VE GROWN INTO ONE TOUGH AS LEATHER SONUVA BITCH, MR. BAD HORSE.
I'M FAIR TO MIDDLIN', I RECKON.

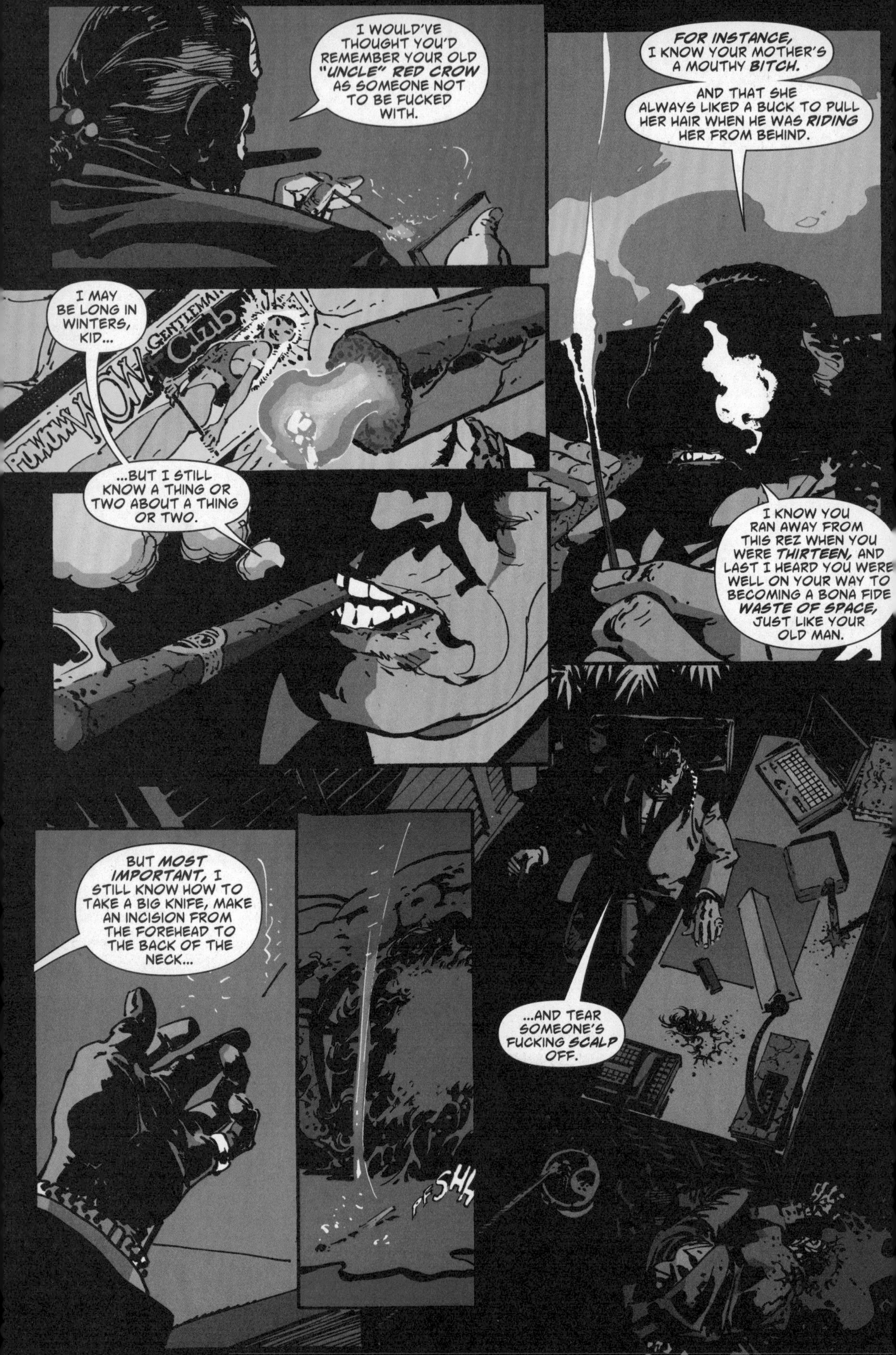
I WOULD'VE THOUGHT YOU'D REMEMBER YOUR OLD "UNCLE" RED CROW AS SOMEONE NOT TO BE FUCKED WITH.
FOR INSTANCE, I KNOW YOUR MOTHER'S A MOUTHY BITCH.
AND THAT SHE ALWAYS LIKED A BUCK TO PULL HER HAIR WHEN HE WAS RIDING HER FROM BEHIND.
I MAY BE LONG IN WINTERS, KID...
...BUT I STILL KNOW A THING OR TWO ABOUT A THING OR TWO.
I KNOW YOU RAN AWAY FROM THIS REZ WHEN YOU WERE THIRTEEN, AND LAST I HEARD YOU WERE WELL ON YOUR WAY TO BECOMING A BONA FIDE WASTE OF SPACE, JUST LIKE YOUR OLD MAN.
BUT MOST IMPORTANT, I STILL KNOW HOW TO TAKE A BIG KNIFE, MAKE AN INCISION FROM THE FOREHEAD TO THE BACK OF THE NECK...
...AND TEAR SOMEONE'S FUCKING SCALP OFF.

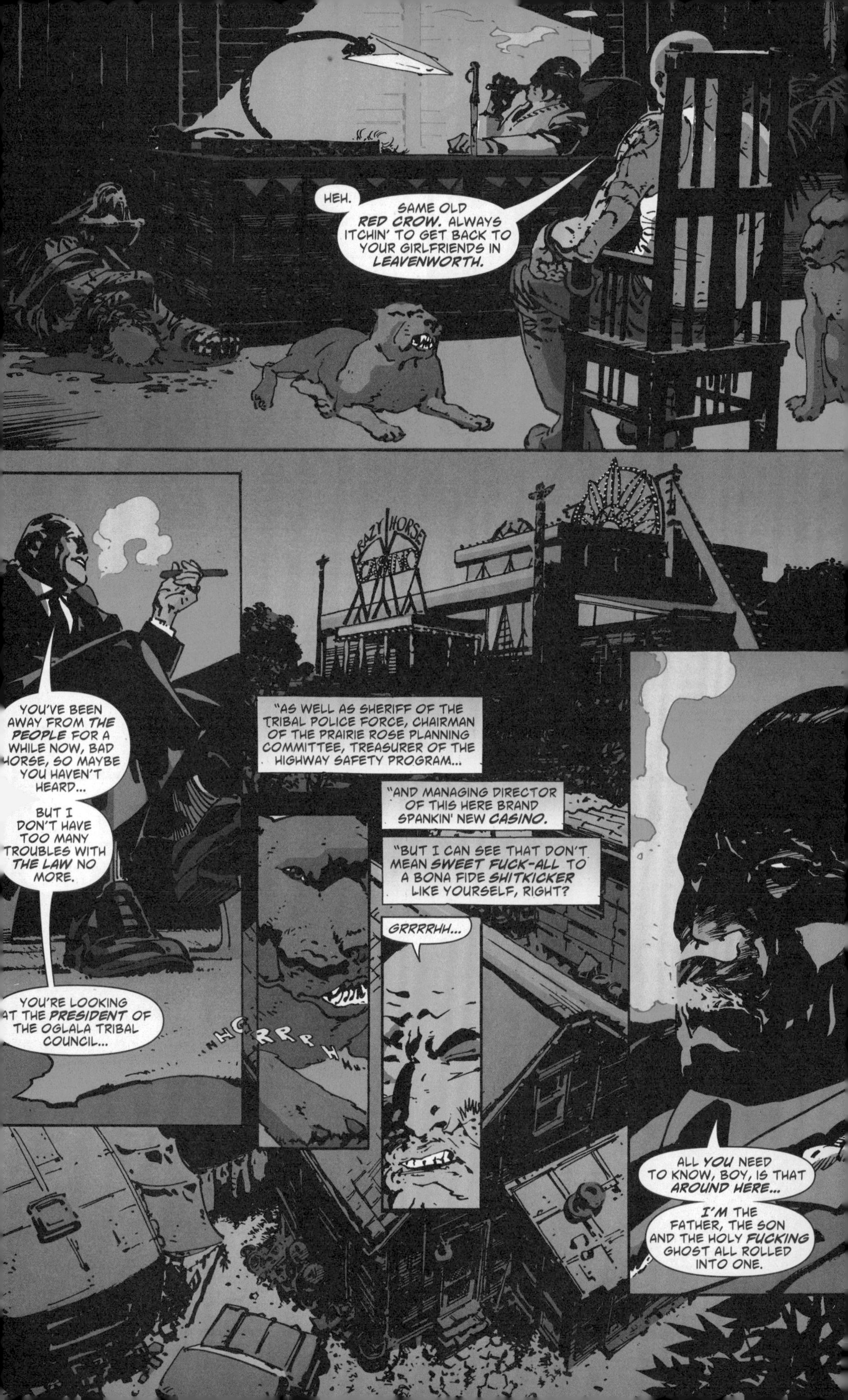
HEH.
SAME OLD RED CROW. ALWAYS ITCHIN' TO GET BACK TO YOUR GIRLFRIENDS IN LEAVENWORTH.
CRAZY HORSE CASINO
YOU'VE BEEN AWAY FROM THE PEOPLE FOR A WHILE NOW, BAD HORSE, SO MAYBE YOU HAVEN'T HEARD...
BUT I DON'T HAVE TOO MANY TROUBLES WITH THE LAW NO MORE.
YOU'RE LOOKING AT THE PRESIDENT OF THE OGLALA TRIBAL COUNCIL...
"AS WELL AS SHERIFF OF THE TRIBAL POLICE FORCE, CHAIRMAN OF THE PRAIRIE ROSE PLANNING COMMITTEE, TREASURER OF THE HIGHWAY SAFETY PROGRAM...
"AND MANAGING DIRECTOR OF THIS HERE BRAND SPANKIN' NEW CASINO.
"BUT I CAN SEE THAT DON'T MEAN SWEET FUCK-ALL TO A BONA FIDE SHITKICKER LIKE YOURSELF, RIGHT?
HGRRRPH
GRRRRHH...
ALL YOU NEED TO KNOW, BOY, IS THAT AROUND HERE...
I'M THE FATHER, THE SON AND THE HOLY FUCKING GHOST ALL ROLLED INTO ONE.

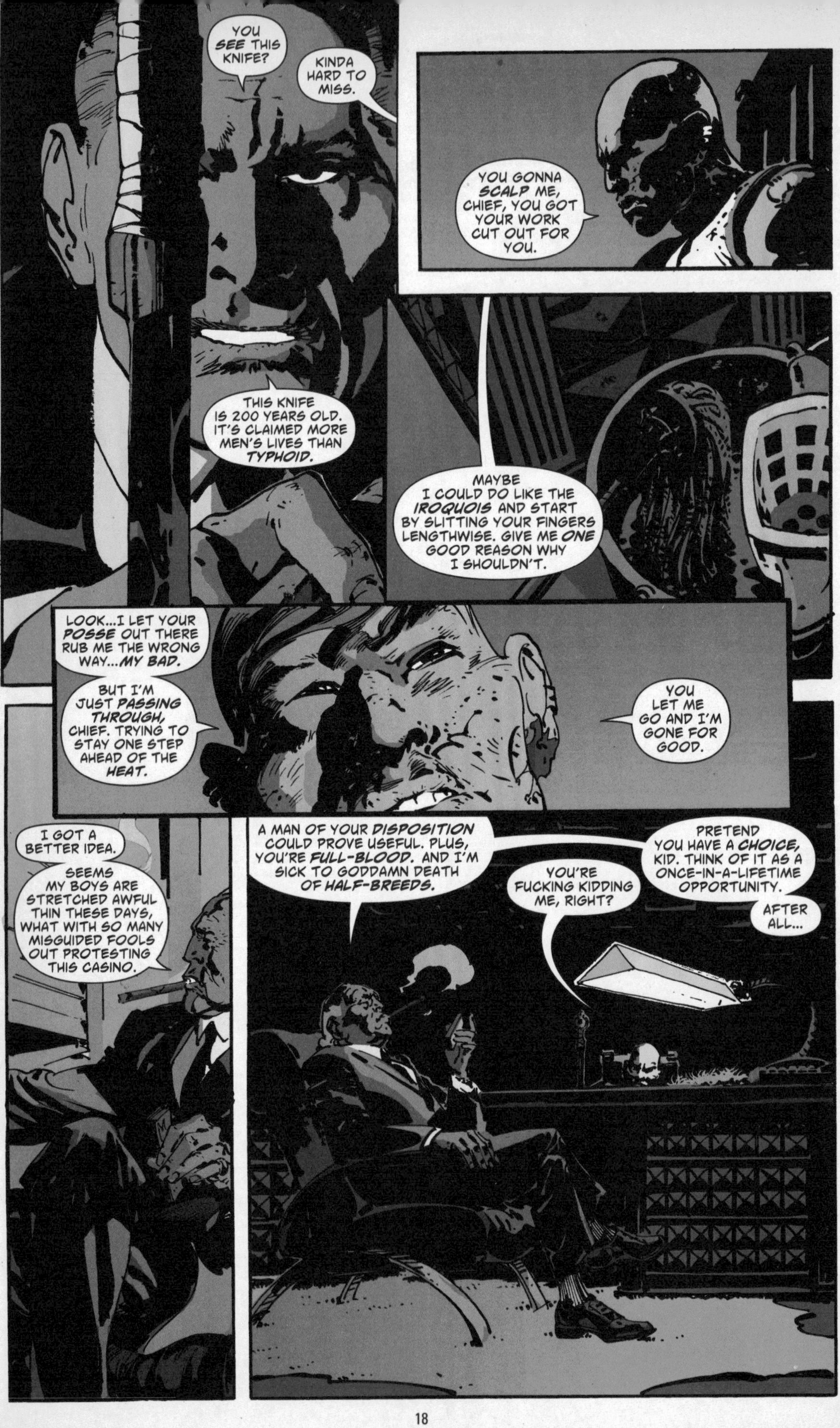
YOU SEE THIS KNIFE?
KINDA HARD TO MISS.
YOU GONNA SCALP ME, CHIEF, YOU GOT YOUR WORK CUT OUT FOR YOU.
THIS KNIFE IS 200 YEARS OLD. IT'S CLAIMED MORE MEN'S LIVES THAN TYPHOID.
MAYBE I COULD DO LIKE THE IROQUOIS AND START BY SLITTING YOUR FINGERS LENGTHWISE. GIVE ME ONE GOOD REASON WHY I SHOULDN'T.
LOOK...I LET YOUR POSSE OUT THERE RUB ME THE WRONG WAY...MY BAD.
BUT I'M JUST PASSING THROUGH, CHIEF. TRYING TO STAY ONE STEP AHEAD OF THE HEAT.
YOU LET ME GO AND I'M GONE FOR GOOD.
I GOT A BETTER IDEA.
SEEMS MY BOYS ARE STRETCHED AWFUL THIN THESE DAYS, WHAT WITH SO MANY MISGUIDED FOOLS OUT PROTESTING THIS CASINO.
A MAN OF YOUR DISPOSITION COULD PROVE USEFUL. PLUS, YOU'RE FULL-BLOOD. AND I'M SICK TO GODDAMN DEATH OF HALF-BREEDS.
YOU'RE FUCKING KIDDING ME, RIGHT?
PRETEND YOU HAVE A CHOICE, KID. THINK OF IT AS A ONCE-IN-A-LIFETIME OPPORTUNITY.
AFTER ALL...

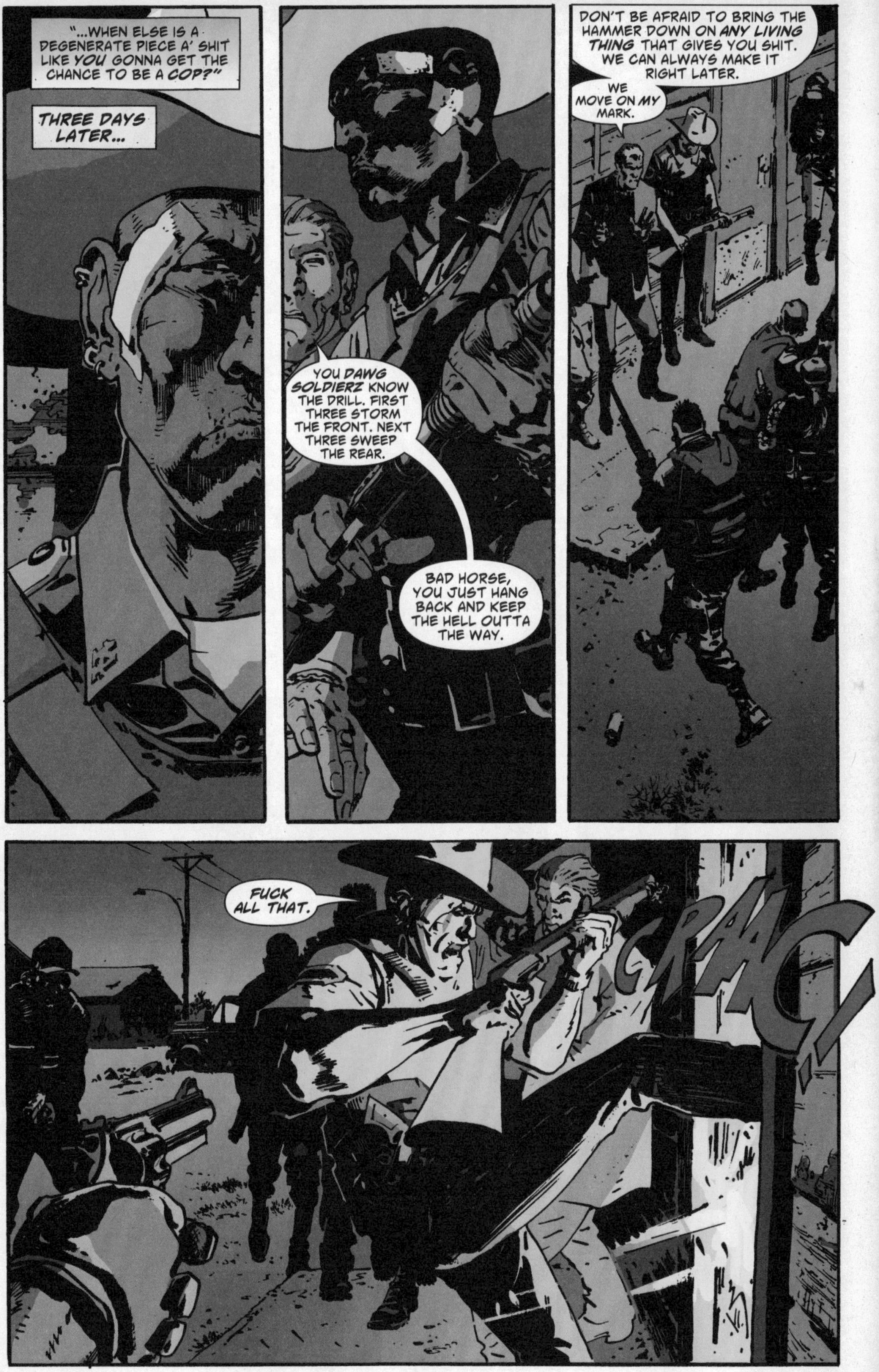
"...WHEN ELSE IS A DEGENERATE PIECE A' SHIT LIKE YOU GONNA GET THE CHANCE TO BE A COP?"
THREE DAYS LATER...
YOU DAWG SOLDIERZ KNOW THE DRILL. FIRST THREE STORM THE FRONT. NEXT THREE SWEEP THE REAR.
BAD HORSE, YOU JUST HANG BACK AND KEEP THE HELL OUTTA THE WAY.
DON'T BE AFRAID TO BRING THE HAMMER DOWN ON ANY LIVING THING THAT GIVES YOU SHIT. WE CAN ALWAYS MAKE IT RIGHT LATER.
WE MOVE ON MY MARK.
FUCK ALL THAT.
CRAAC!

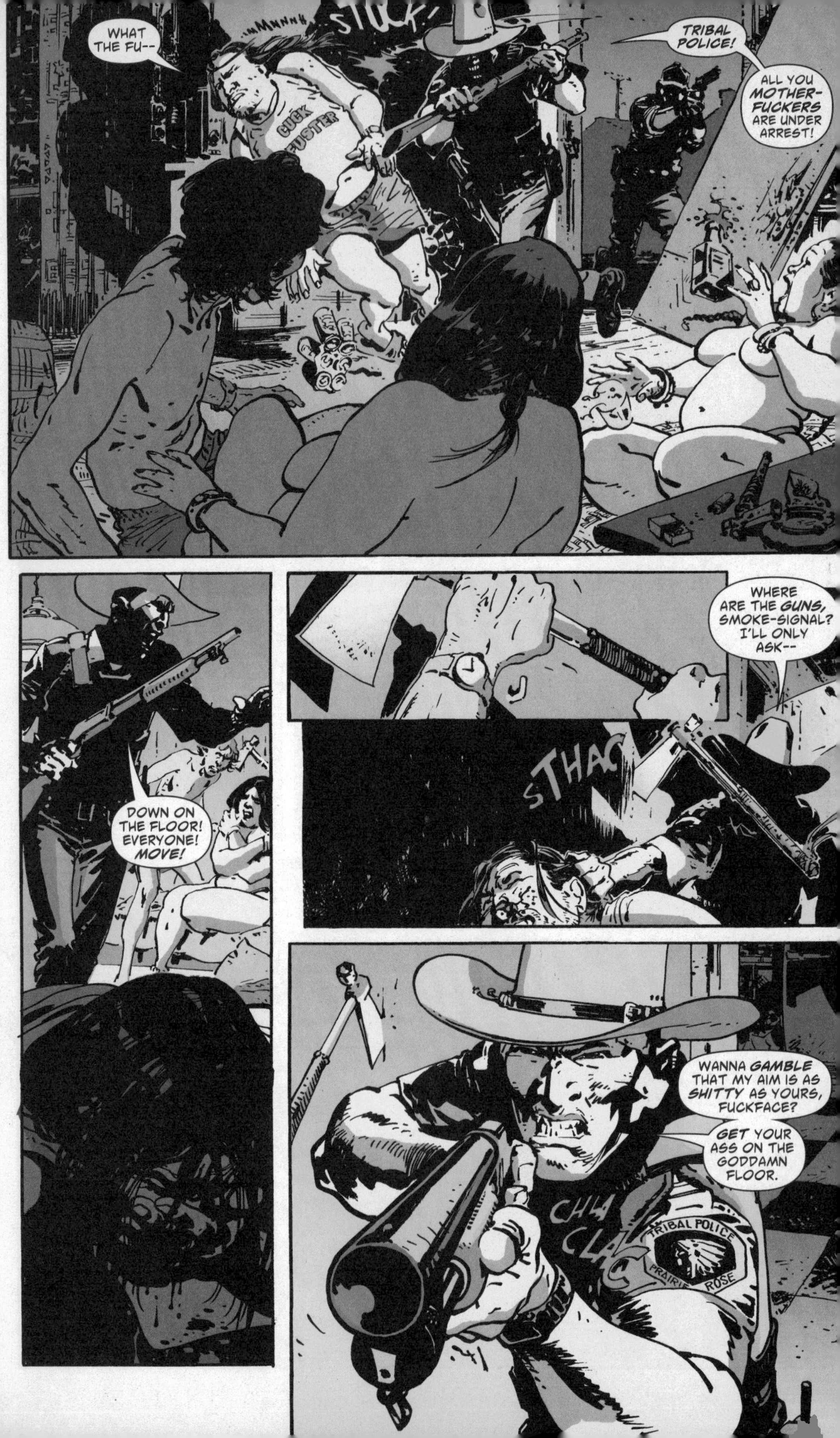
WHAT THE FU--
STUCK!
TRIBAL POLICE!
ALL YOU MOTHER-FUCKERS ARE UNDER ARREST!
DOWN ON THE FLOOR! EVERYONE! MOVE!
WHERE ARE THE GUNS, SMOKE-SIGNAL? I'LL ONLY ASK--
sTHAC
WANNA GAMBLE THAT MY AIM IS AS SHITTY AS YOURS, FUCKFACE?
GET YOUR ASS ON THE GODDAMN FLOOR.
TRIBAL POLICE
PRAIRIE ROSE

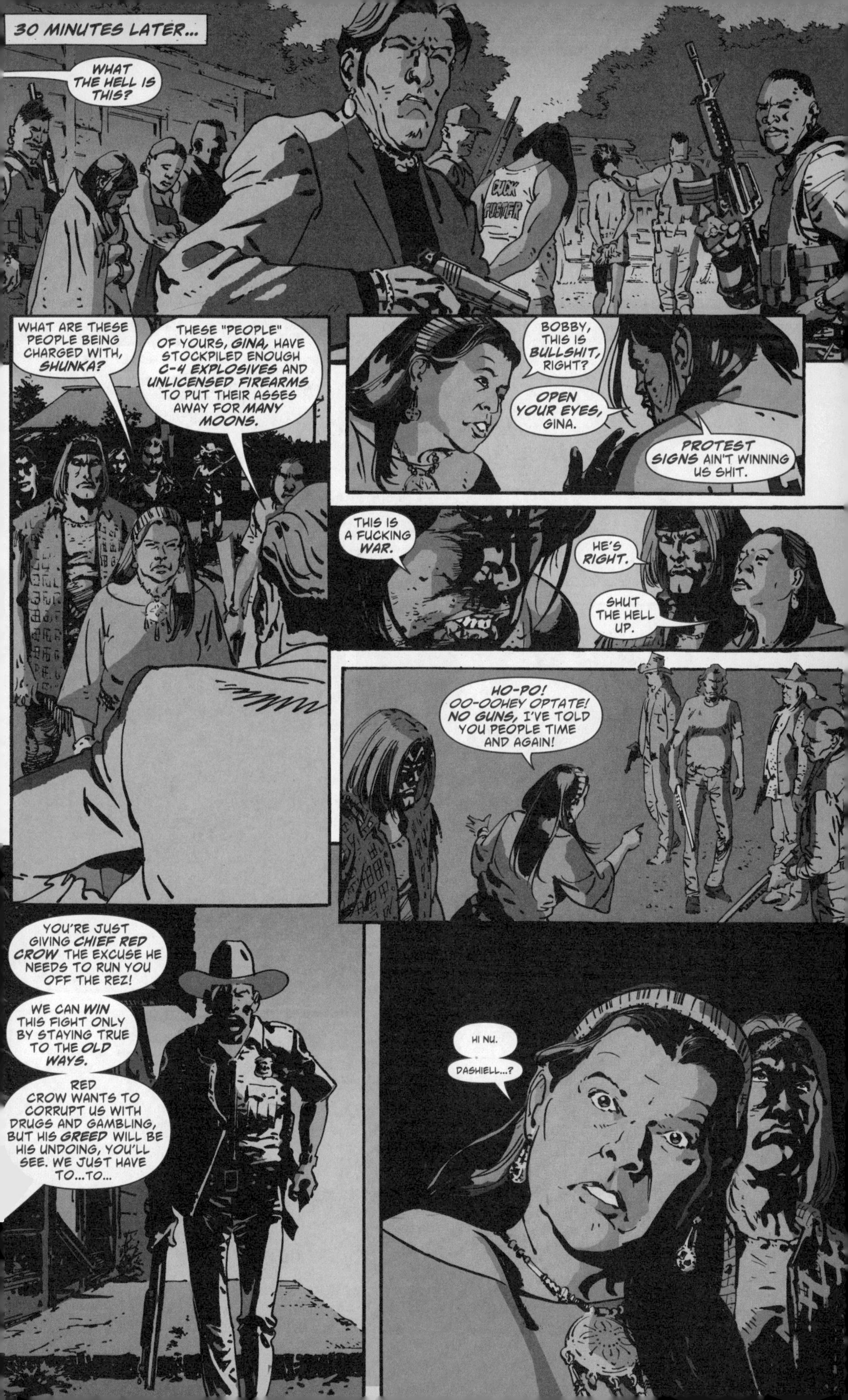
30 MINUTES LATER...
WHAT THE HELL IS THIS?
WHAT ARE THESE PEOPLE BEING CHARGED WITH, SHUNKA?
THESE "PEOPLE" OF YOURS, GINA, HAVE STOCKPILED ENOUGH C-4 EXPLOSIVES AND UNLICENSED FIREARMS TO PUT THEIR ASSES AWAY FOR MANY MOONS.
BOBBY, THIS IS BULLSHIT, RIGHT?
OPEN YOUR EYES, GINA.
PROTEST SIGNS AIN'T WINNING US SHIT.
THIS IS A FUCKING WAR.
HE'S RIGHT.
SHUT THE HELL UP.
HO-PO! OO-OOHEY OPTATE! NO GUNS, I'VE TOLD YOU PEOPLE TIME AND AGAIN!
YOU'RE JUST GIVING CHIEF RED CROW THE EXCUSE HE NEEDS TO RUN YOU OFF THE REZ!
WE CAN WIN THIS FIGHT ONLY BY STAYING TRUE TO THE OLD WAYS.
RED CROW WANTS TO CORRUPT US WITH DRUGS AND GAMBLING, BUT HIS GREED WILL BE HIS UNDOING, YOU'LL SEE. WE JUST HAVE TO...TO...
HI NU.
DASHIELL...?

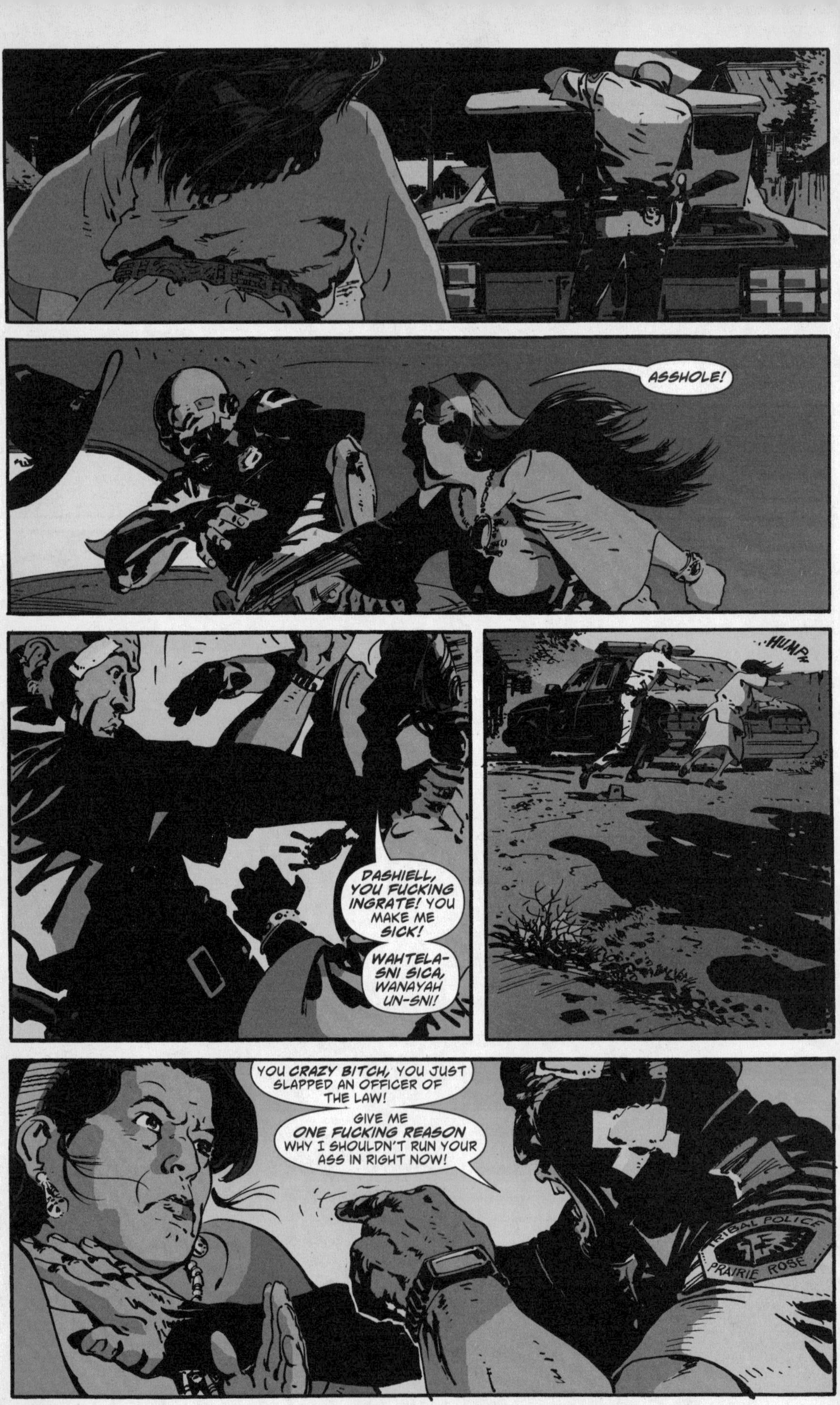
ASSHOLE!
DASHIELL, YOU FUCKING INGRATE! YOU MAKE ME SICK!
WAHTELA-SNI SICA, WANAYAH UN-SNI!
HUMPH
YOU CRAZY BITCH, YOU JUST SLAPPED AN OFFICER OF THE LAW!
GIVE ME ONE FUCKING REASON WHY I SHOULDN'T RUN YOUR ASS IN RIGHT NOW!
TRIBAL POLICE
PRAIRIE ROSE

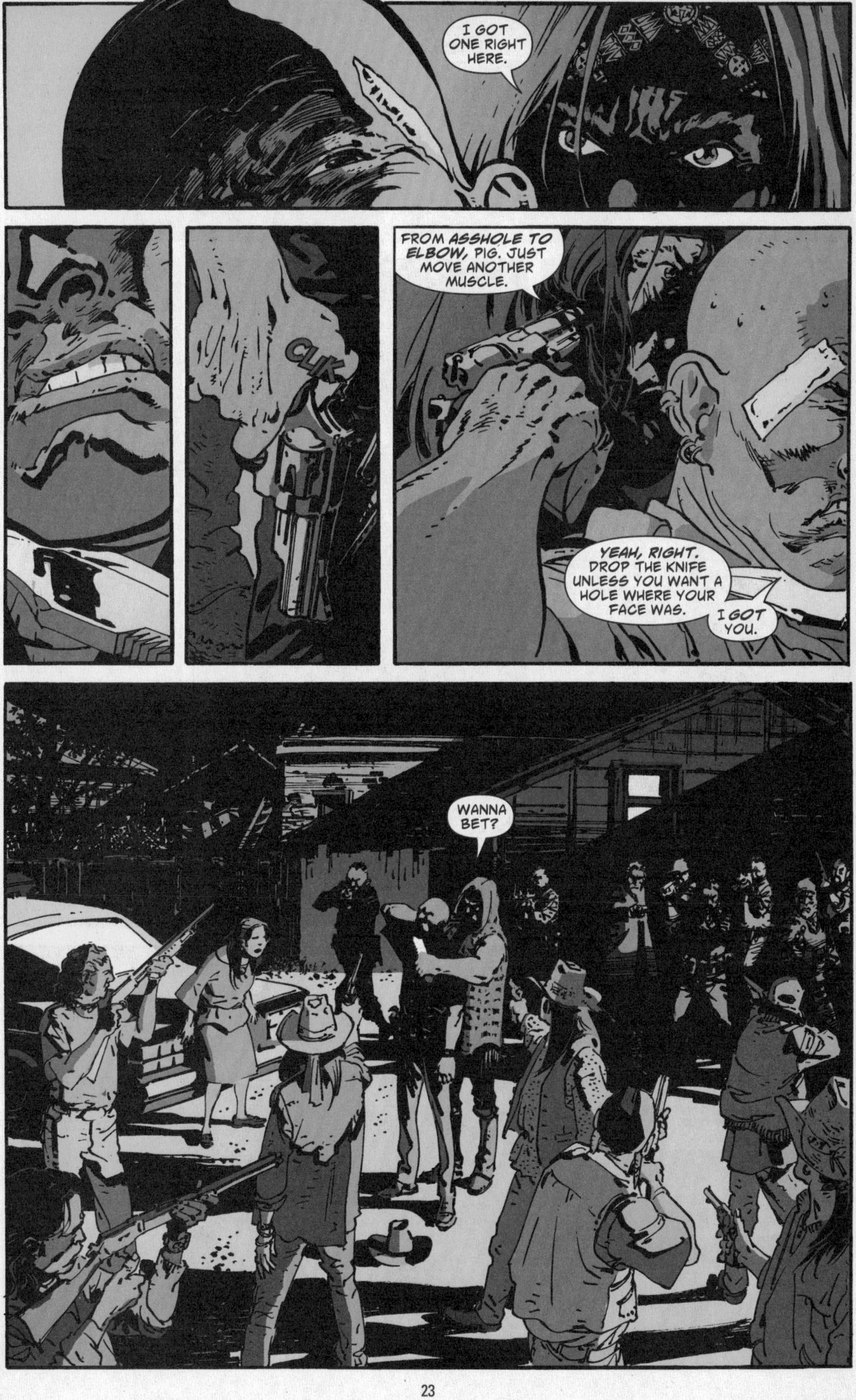
I GOT ONE RIGHT HERE.
CLIK
FROM ASSHOLE TO ELBOW, PIG. JUST MOVE ANOTHER MUSCLE.
YEAH, RIGHT. DROP THE KNIFE UNLESS YOU WANT A HOLE WHERE YOUR FACE WAS.
I GOT YOU.
WANNA BET?

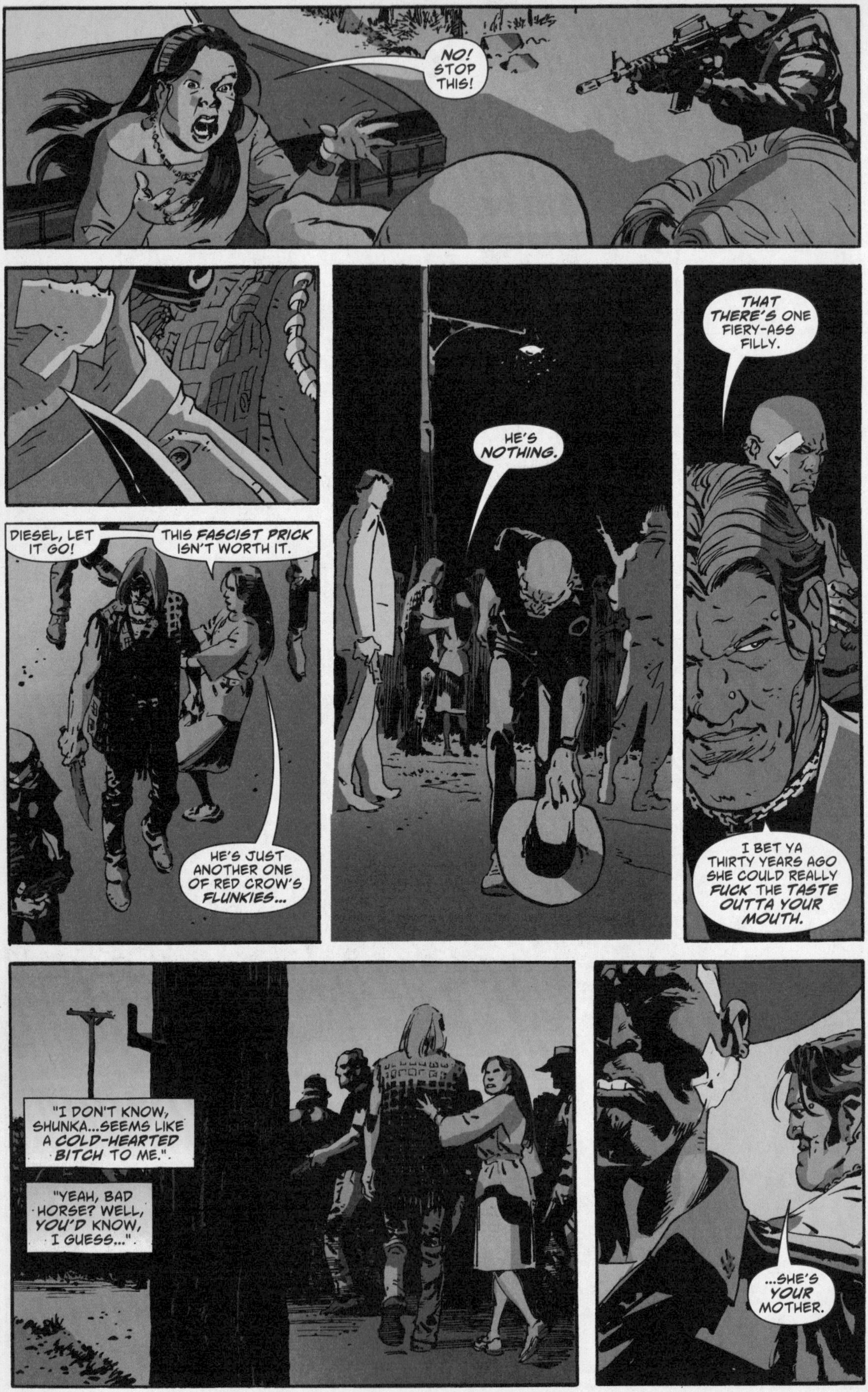
NO! STOP THIS!
HE'S NOTHING.
THAT THERE'S ONE FIERY-ASS FILLY.
DIESEL, LET IT GO!
THIS FASCIST PRICK ISN'T WORTH IT.
HE'S JUST ANOTHER ONE OF RED CROW'S FLUNKIES...
I BET YA THIRTY YEARS AGO SHE COULD REALLY FUCK THE TASTE OUTTA YOUR MOUTH.
"I DON'T KNOW, SHUNKA...SEEMS LIKE A COLD-HEARTED BITCH TO ME."
"YEAH, BAD HORSE? WELL, YOU'D KNOW, I GUESS..."
...SHE'S YOUR MOTHER.

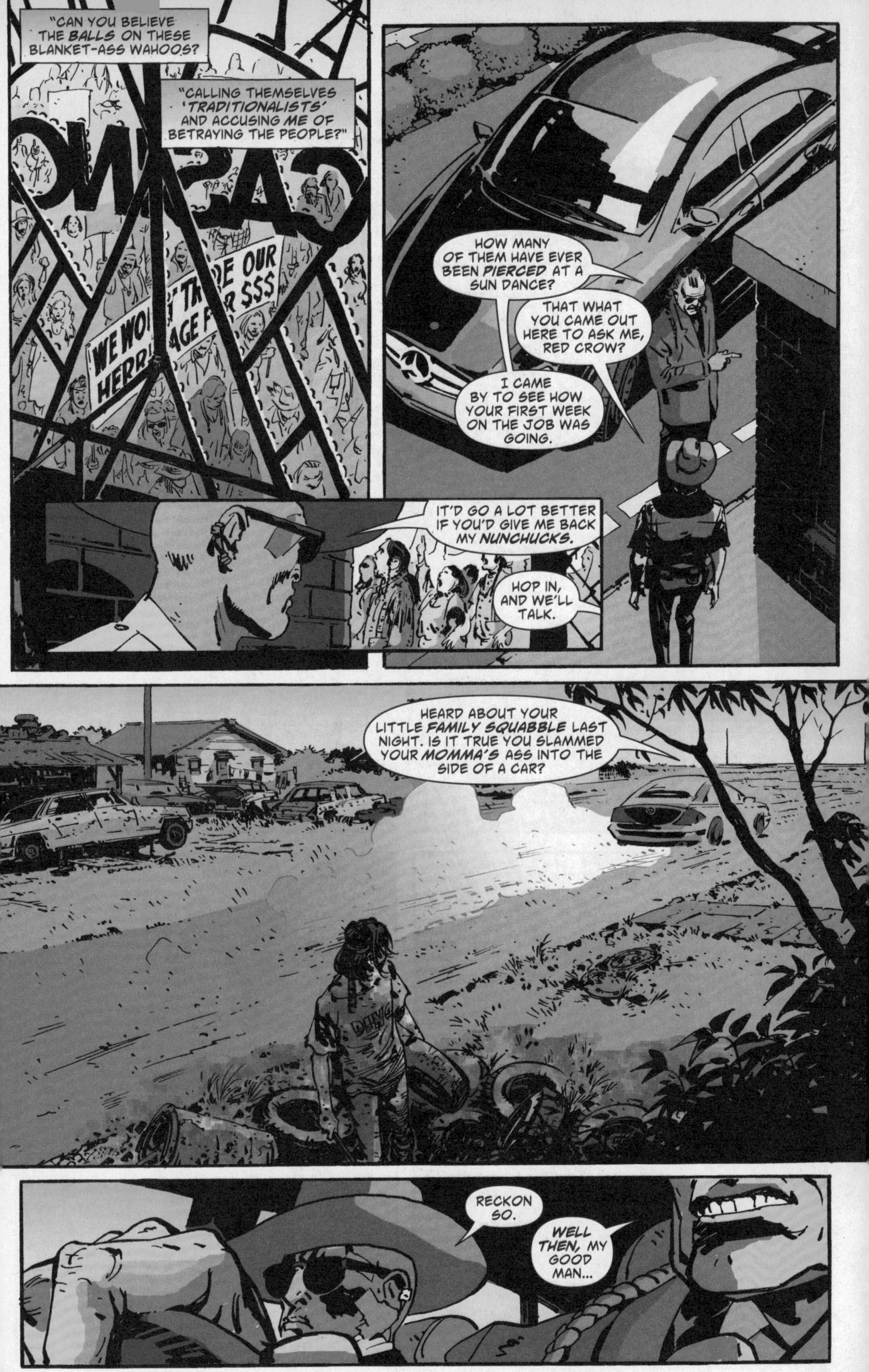
"CAN YOU BELIEVE THE BALLS ON THESE BLANKET-ASS WAHOOS?
"CALLING THEMSELVES 'TRADITIONALISTS' AND ACCUSING ME OF BETRAYING THE PEOPLE?"
HOW MANY OF THEM HAVE EVER BEEN PIERCED AT A SUN DANCE?
THAT WHAT YOU CAME OUT HERE TO ASK ME, RED CROW?
I CAME BY TO SEE HOW YOUR FIRST WEEK ON THE JOB WAS GOING.
IT'D GO A LOT BETTER IF YOU'D GIVE ME BACK MY NUNCHUCKS.
HOP IN, AND WE'LL TALK.
HEARD ABOUT YOUR LITTLE FAMILY SQUABBLE LAST NIGHT. IS IT TRUE YOU SLAMMED YOUR MOMMA'S ASS INTO THE SIDE OF A CAR?
RECKON SO.
WELL THEN, MY GOOD MAN...

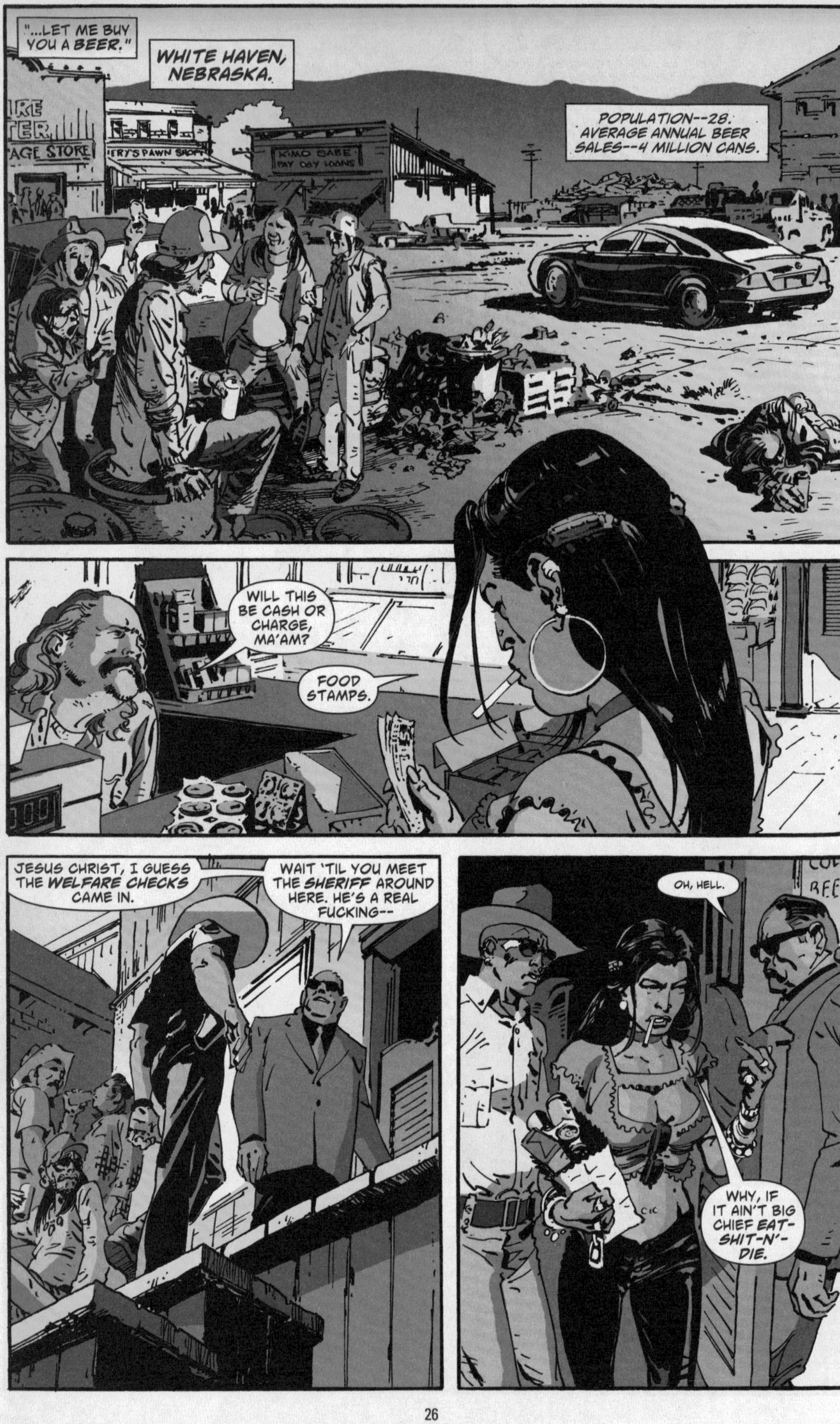
"...LET ME BUY YOU A BEER."
WHITE HAVEN, NEBRASKA.
POPULATION--28. AVERAGE ANNUAL BEER SALES--4 MILLION CANS.
KIMO SABE PAY DAY LOANS
WILL THIS BE CASH OR CHARGE, MA'AM?
FOOD STAMPS.
JESUS CHRIST, I GUESS THE WELFARE CHECKS CAME IN.
WAIT 'TIL YOU MEET THE SHERIFF AROUND HERE. HE'S A REAL FUCKING--
OH, HELL.
WHY, IF IT AIN'T BIG CHIEF EAT-SHIT-N'-DIE.

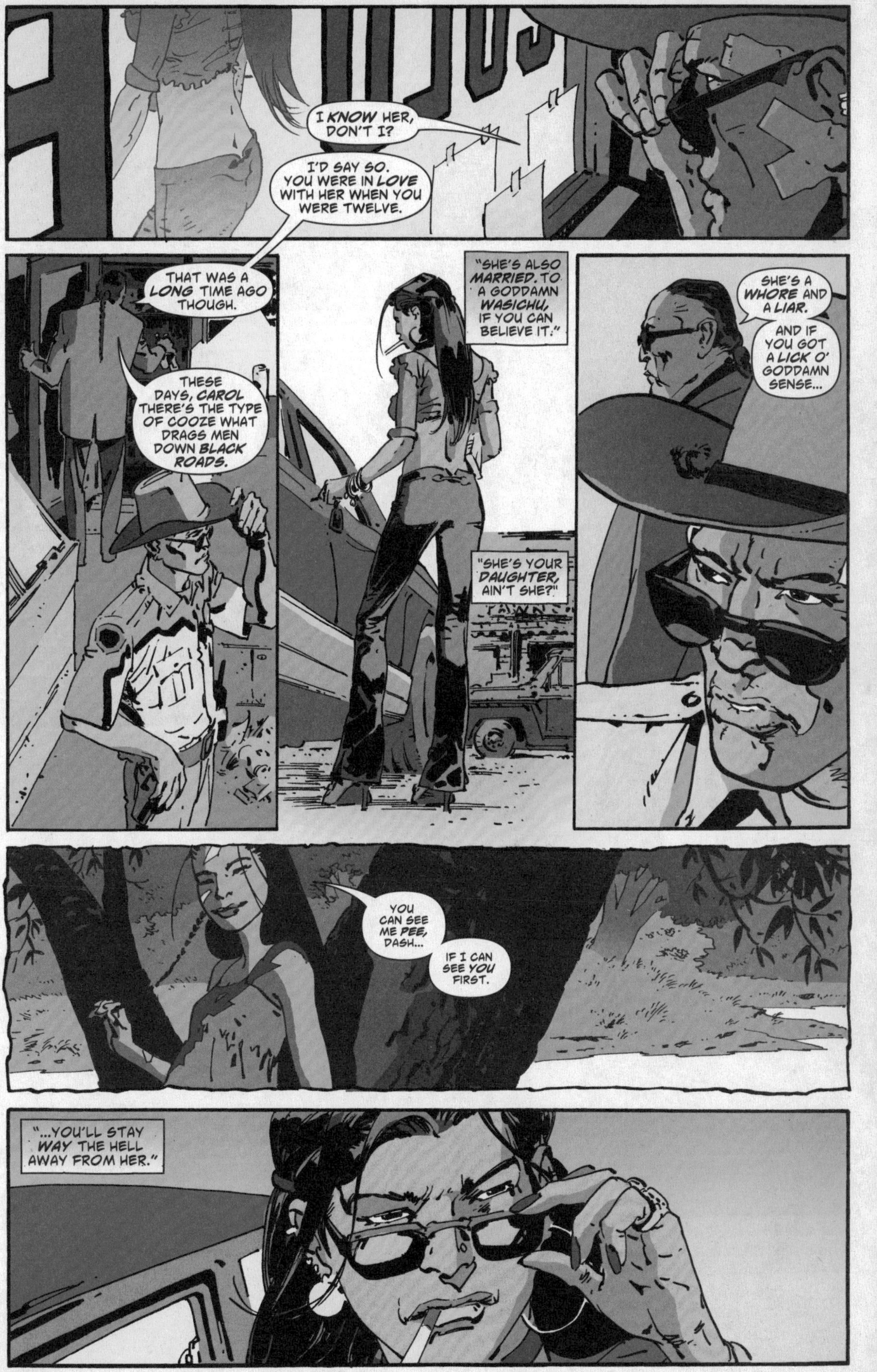
I KNOW HER, DON'T I?
I'D SAY SO. YOU WERE IN LOVE WITH HER WHEN YOU WERE TWELVE.
THAT WAS A LONG TIME AGO THOUGH.
THESE DAYS, CAROL THERE'S THE TYPE OF COOZE WHAT DRAGS MEN DOWN BLACK ROADS.
"SHE'S ALSO MARRIED. TO A GODDAMN WASICHU, IF YOU CAN BELIEVE IT."
"SHE'S YOUR DAUGHTER, AIN'T SHE?"
SHE'S A WHORE AND A LIAR.
AND IF YOU GOT A LICK O' GODDAMN SENSE...
YOU CAN SEE ME PEE, DASH...
IF I CAN SEE YOU FIRST.
"...YOU'LL STAY WAY THE HELL AWAY FROM HER."

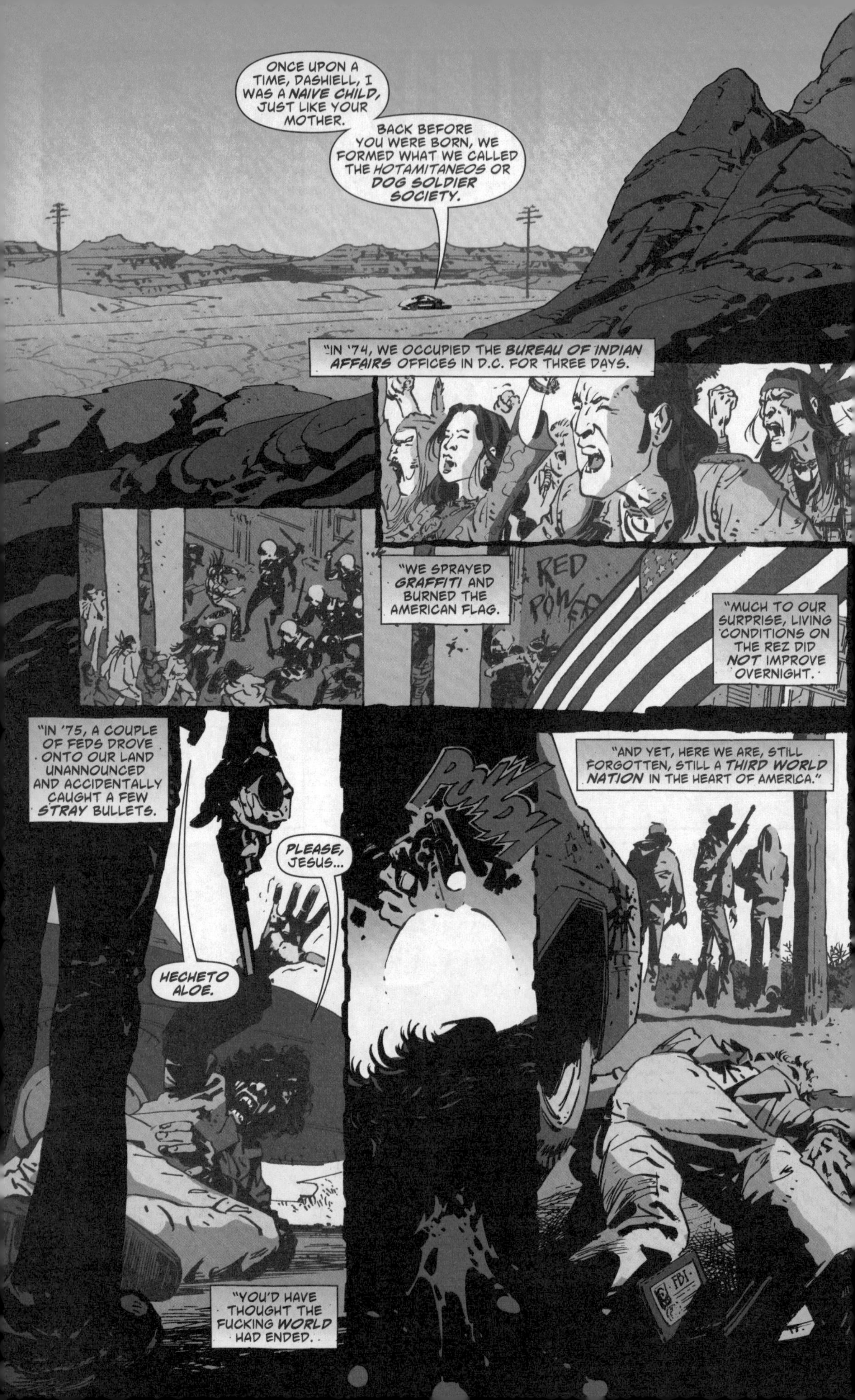
ONCE UPON A TIME, DASHIELL, I WAS A *NAIVE CHILD*, JUST LIKE YOUR MOTHER.
BACK BEFORE YOU WERE BORN, WE FORMED WHAT WE CALLED THE *HOTAMITANEOS* OR ***DOG SOLDIER SOCIETY***.
"IN '74, WE OCCUPIED THE *BUREAU OF INDIAN AFFAIRS* OFFICES IN D.C. FOR THREE DAYS.
"WE SPRAYED *GRAFFITI* AND BURNED THE AMERICAN FLAG.
"MUCH TO OUR SURPRISE, LIVING CONDITIONS ON THE REZ DID *NOT* IMPROVE OVERNIGHT.
"IN '75, A COUPLE OF FEDS DROVE ONTO OUR LAND UNANNOUNCED AND ACCIDENTALLY CAUGHT A FEW *STRAY* BULLETS.
PLEASE, JESUS...
HECHETO ALOE.
"AND YET, HERE WE ARE, STILL FORGOTTEN, STILL A *THIRD WORLD NATION* IN THE HEART OF AMERICA."
"YOU'D HAVE THOUGHT THE FUCKING *WORLD* HAD ENDED.
FBI

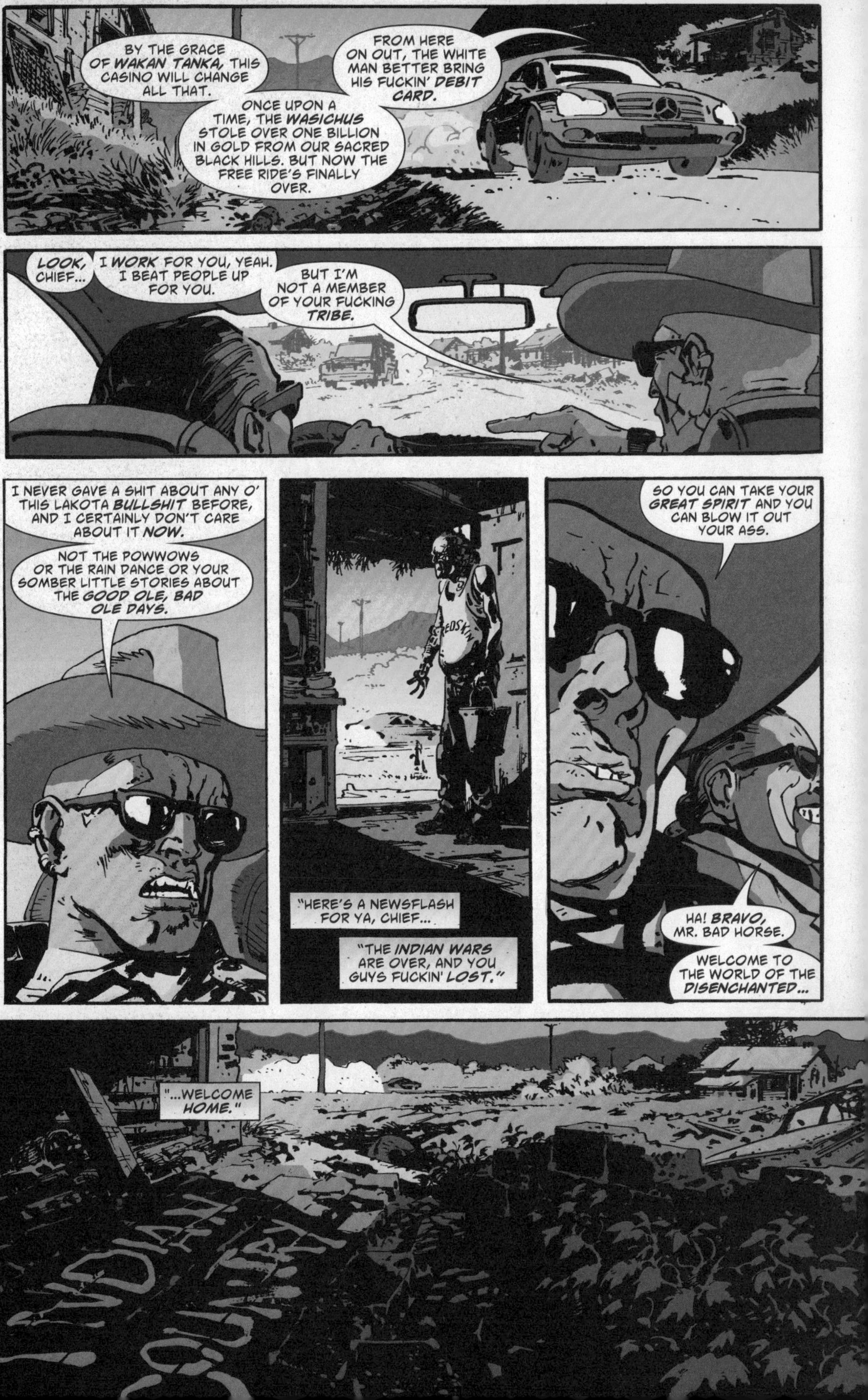
BY THE GRACE OF WAKAN TANKA, THIS CASINO WILL CHANGE ALL THAT.
ONCE UPON A TIME, THE WASICHUS STOLE OVER ONE BILLION IN GOLD FROM OUR SACRED BLACK HILLS. BUT NOW THE FREE RIDE'S FINALLY OVER.
FROM HERE ON OUT, THE WHITE MAN BETTER BRING HIS FUCKIN' DEBIT CARD.
LOOK, CHIEF...
I WORK FOR YOU, YEAH. I BEAT PEOPLE UP FOR YOU.
BUT I'M NOT A MEMBER OF YOUR FUCKING TRIBE.
I NEVER GAVE A SHIT ABOUT ANY O' THIS LAKOTA BULLSHIT BEFORE, AND I CERTAINLY DON'T CARE ABOUT IT NOW.
NOT THE POWWOWS OR THE RAIN DANCE OR YOUR SOMBER LITTLE STORIES ABOUT THE GOOD OLE, BAD OLE DAYS.
"HERE'S A NEWSFLASH FOR YA, CHIEF...
"THE INDIAN WARS ARE OVER, AND YOU GUYS FUCKIN' LOST."
SO YOU CAN TAKE YOUR GREAT SPIRIT AND YOU CAN BLOW IT OUT YOUR ASS.
HA! BRAVO, MR. BAD HORSE.
WELCOME TO THE WORLD OF THE DISENCHANTED...
"...WELCOME HOME."

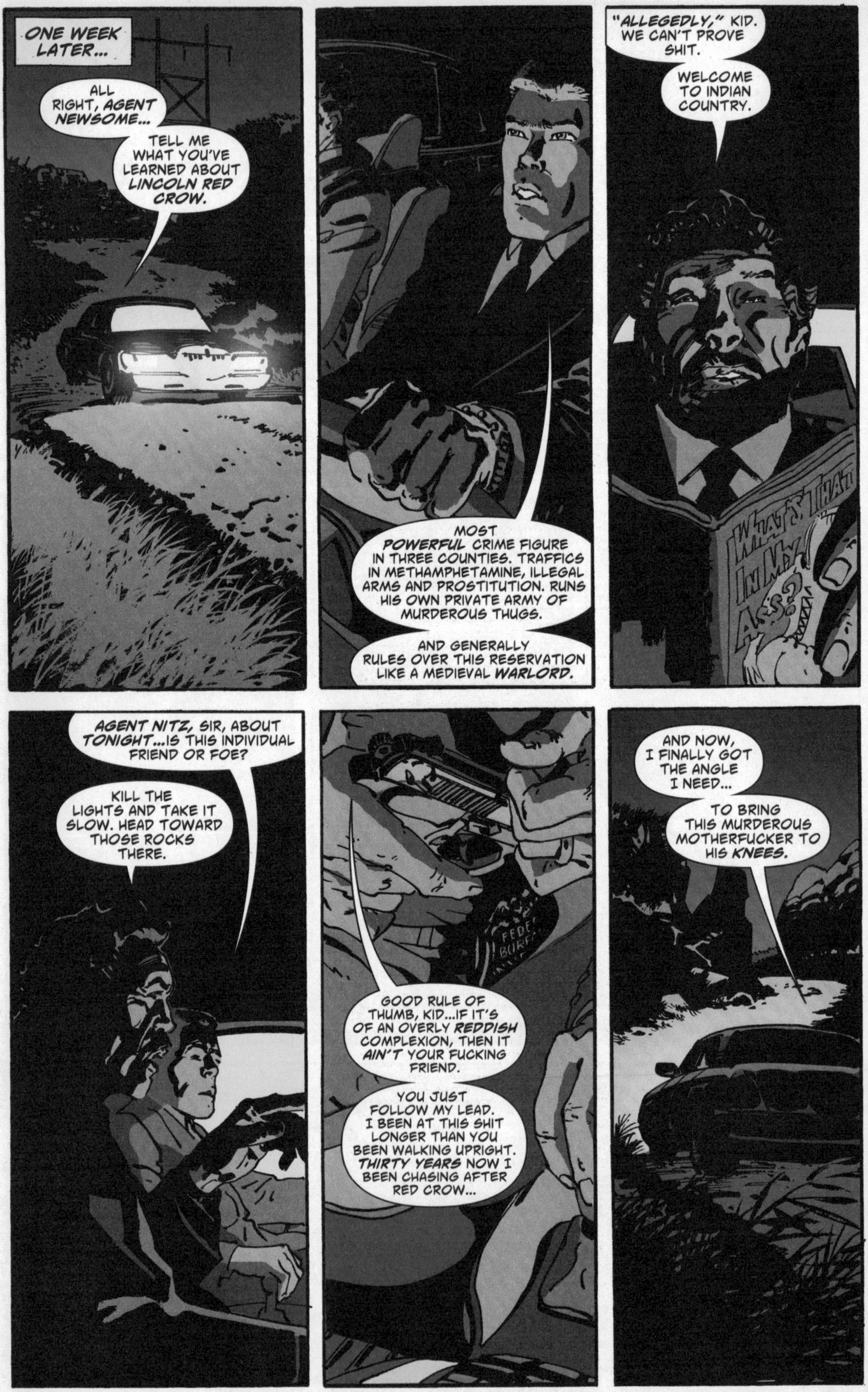
ONE WEEK LATER...
ALL RIGHT, AGENT NEWSOME...
TELL ME WHAT YOU'VE LEARNED ABOUT LINCOLN RED CROW.
MOST POWERFUL CRIME FIGURE IN THREE COUNTIES. TRAFFICS IN METHAMPHETAMINE, ILLEGAL ARMS AND PROSTITUTION. RUNS HIS OWN PRIVATE ARMY OF MURDEROUS THUGS.
AND GENERALLY RULES OVER THIS RESERVATION LIKE A MEDIEVAL WARLORD.
"ALLEGEDLY," KID. WE CAN'T PROVE SHIT.
WELCOME TO INDIAN COUNTRY.
WHAT'S THAT IN MY ASS?
AGENT NITZ, SIR, ABOUT TONIGHT...IS THIS INDIVIDUAL FRIEND OR FOE?
KILL THE LIGHTS AND TAKE IT SLOW. HEAD TOWARD THOSE ROCKS THERE.
GOOD RULE OF THUMB, KID...IF IT'S OF AN OVERLY REDDISH COMPLEXION, THEN IT AIN'T YOUR FUCKING FRIEND.
YOU JUST FOLLOW MY LEAD. I BEEN AT THIS SHIT LONGER THAN YOU BEEN WALKING UPRIGHT. THIRTY YEARS NOW I BEEN CHASING AFTER RED CROW...
AND NOW, I FINALLY GOT THE ANGLE I NEED...
TO BRING THIS MURDEROUS MOTHERFUCKER TO HIS KNEES.

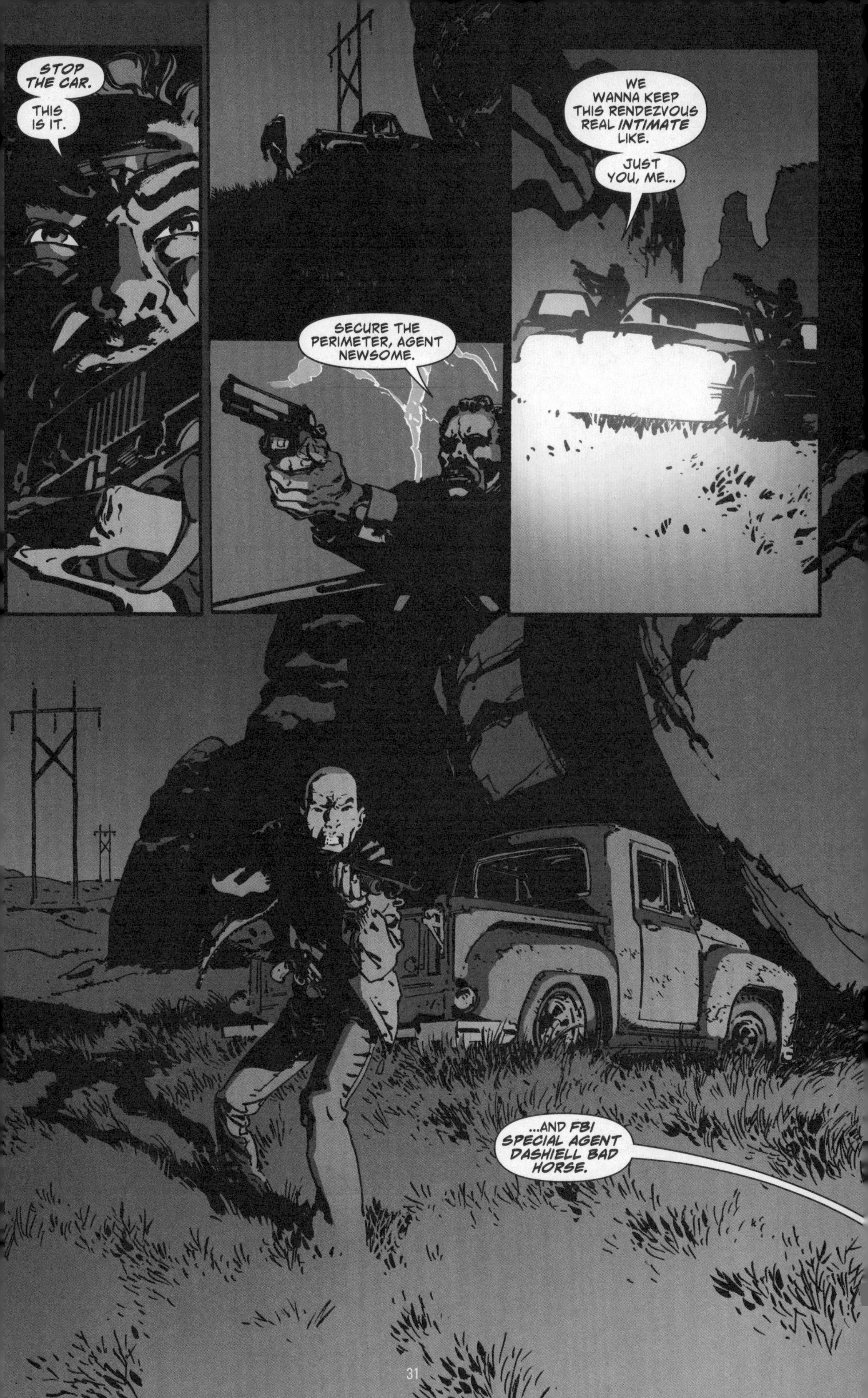
STOP THE CAR.
THIS IS IT.
SECURE THE PERIMETER, AGENT NEWSOME.
WE WANNA KEEP THIS RENDEZVOUS REAL *INTIMATE* LIKE.
JUST YOU, ME...
...AND FBI SPECIAL AGENT DASHIELL BAD HORSE.

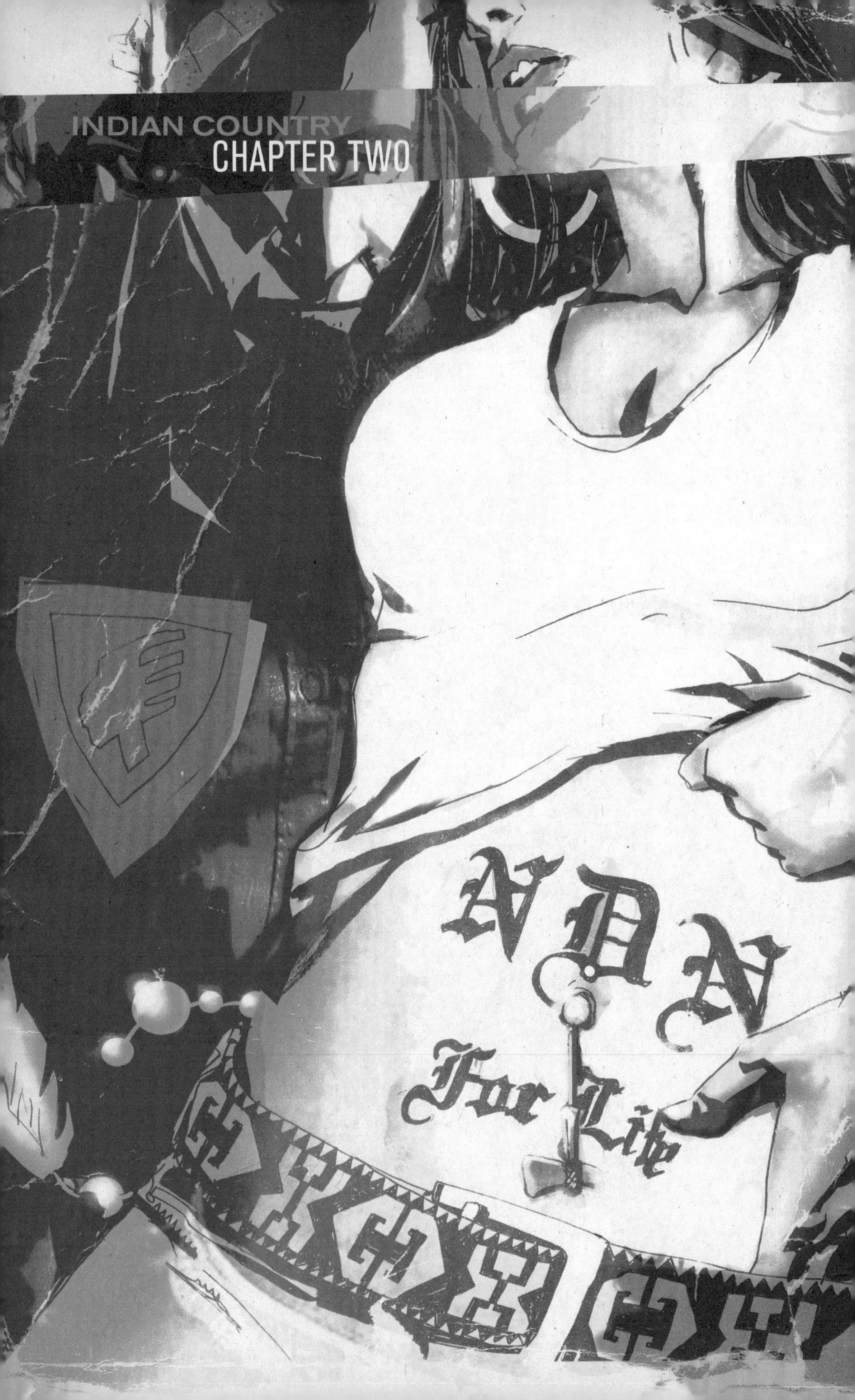
INDIAN COUNTRY
CHAPTER TWO
NDN
For Life

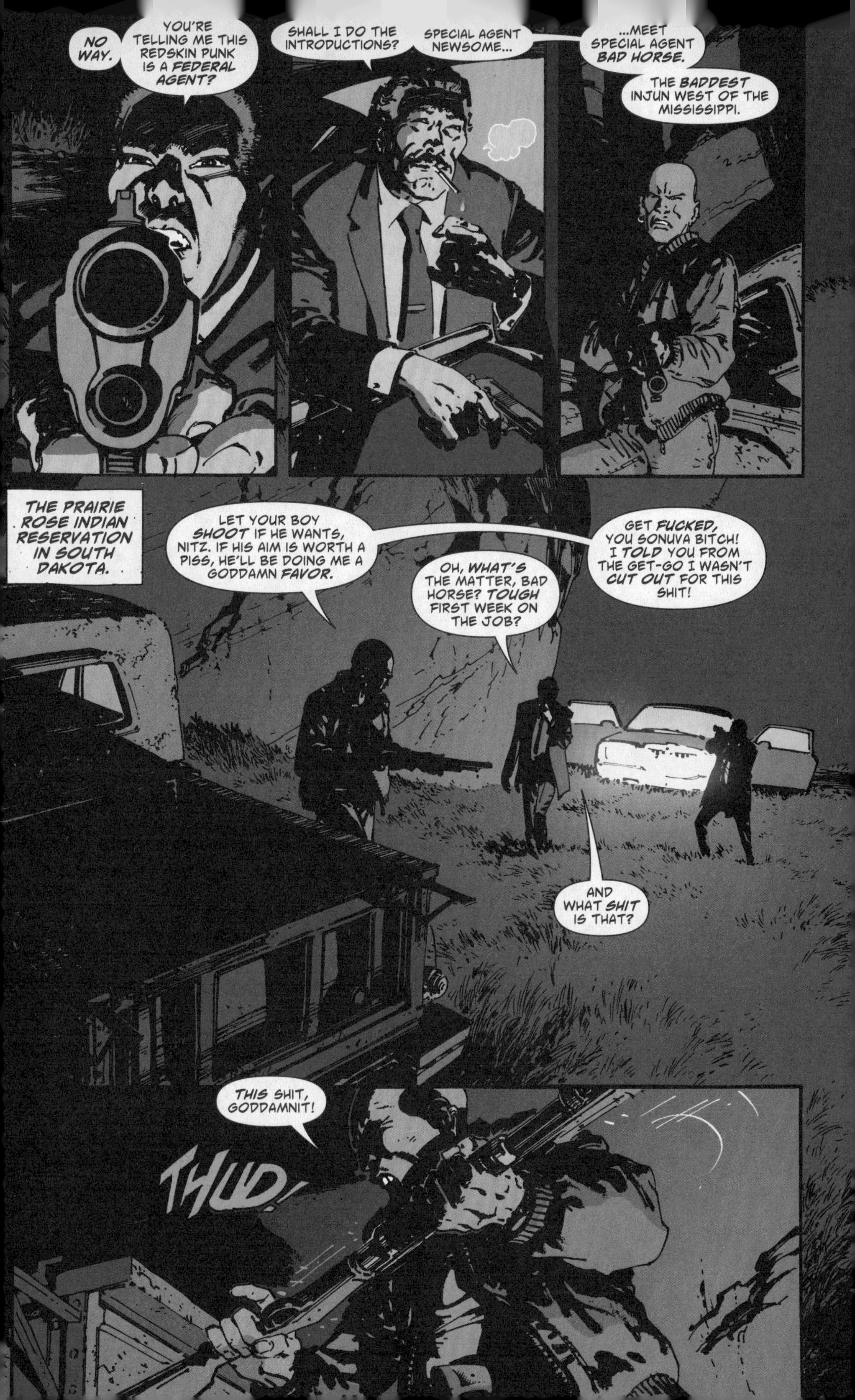
NO WAY.
YOU'RE TELLING ME THIS REDSKIN PUNK IS A FEDERAL AGENT?
SHALL I DO THE INTRODUCTIONS?
SPECIAL AGENT NEWSOME...
...MEET SPECIAL AGENT BAD HORSE.
THE BADDEST INJUN WEST OF THE MISSISSIPPI.
THE PRAIRIE ROSE INDIAN RESERVATION IN SOUTH DAKOTA.
LET YOUR BOY SHOOT IF HE WANTS, NITZ. IF HIS AIM IS WORTH A PISS, HE'LL BE DOING ME A GODDAMN FAVOR.
GET FUCKED, YOU SONUVA BITCH! I TOLD YOU FROM THE GET-GO I WASN'T CUT OUT FOR THIS SHIT!
OH, WHAT'S THE MATTER, BAD HORSE? TOUGH FIRST WEEK ON THE JOB?
AND WHAT SHIT IS THAT?
THIS SHIT, GODDAMNIT!
THUD!

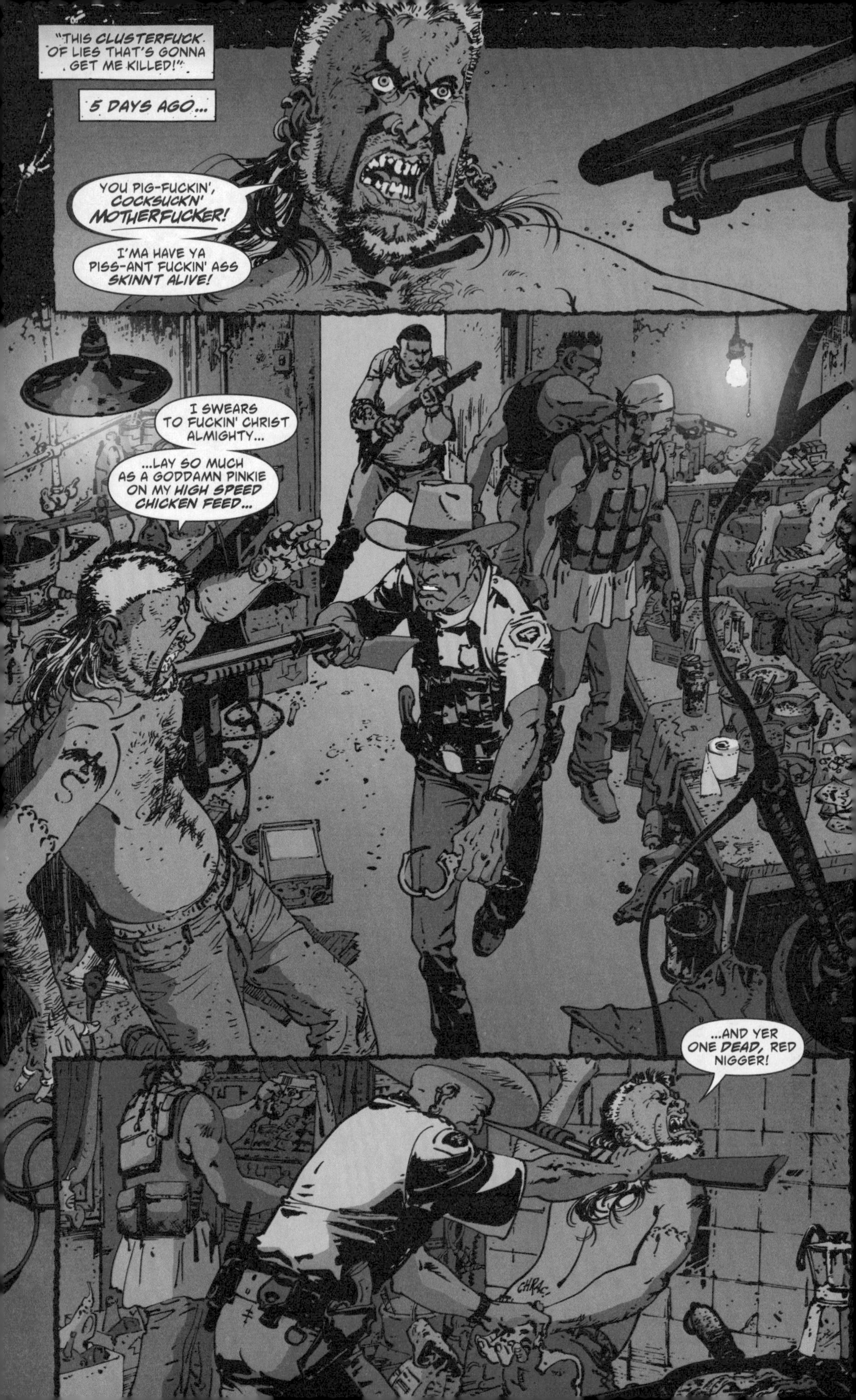
"THIS CLUSTERFUCK OF LIES THAT'S GONNA GET ME KILLED!"
5 DAYS AGO...
YOU PIG-FUCKIN', COCKSUCKN' MOTHERFUCKER!
I'MA HAVE YA PISS-ANT FUCKIN' ASS SKINNT ALIVE!
I SWEARS TO FUCKIN' CHRIST ALMIGHTY...
...LAY SO MUCH AS A GODDAMN PINKIE ON MY HIGH SPEED CHICKEN FEED...
...AND YER ONE DEAD, RED NIGGER!

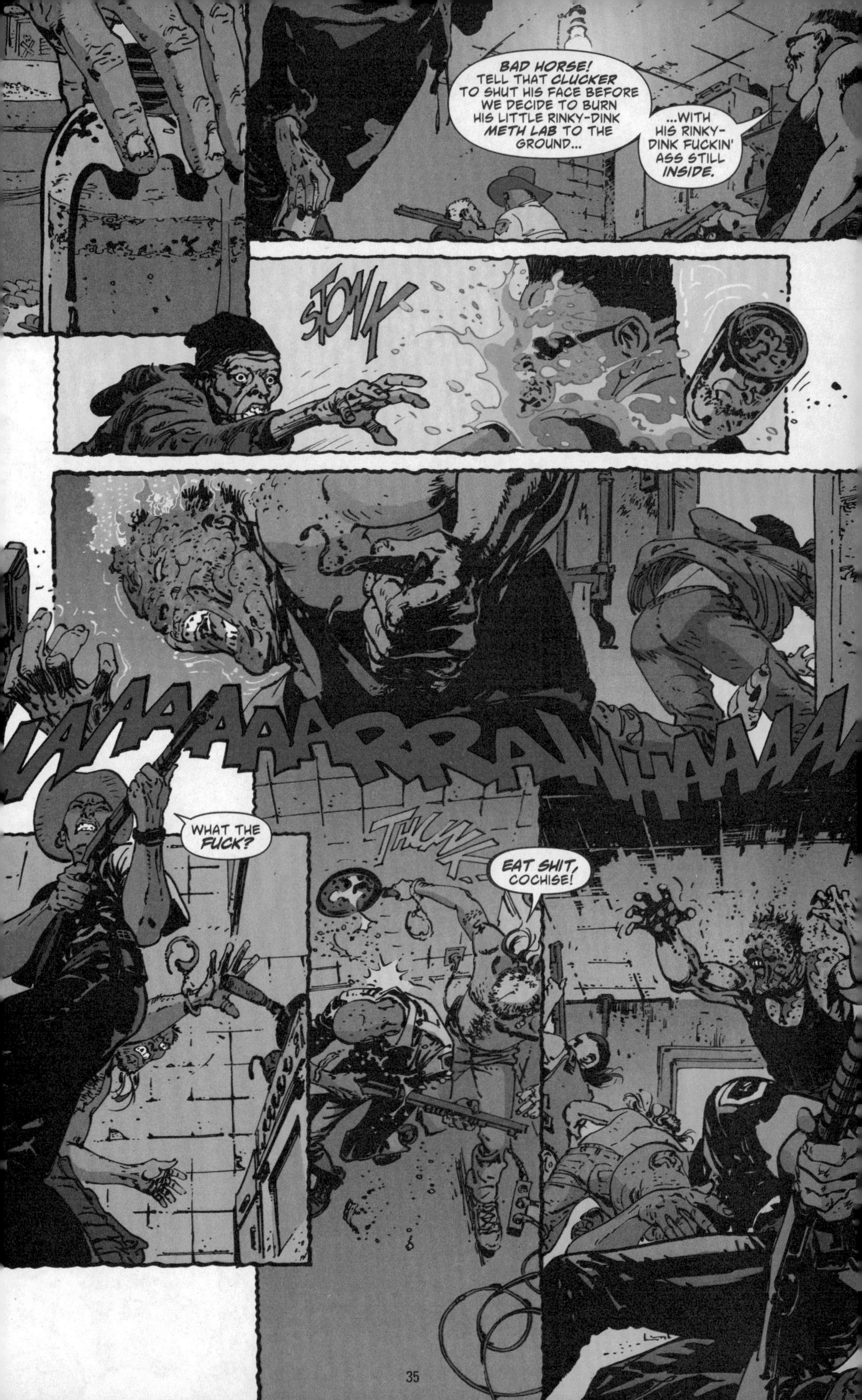
BAD HORSE! TELL THAT CLUCKER TO SHUT HIS FACE BEFORE WE DECIDE TO BURN HIS LITTLE RINKY-DINK METH LAB TO THE GROUND...
...WITH HIS RINKY-DINK FUCKIN' ASS STILL INSIDE.
STONK
WAAAARRRAWHAAAA
WHAT THE FUCK?
THUNK
EAT SHIT, COCHISE!

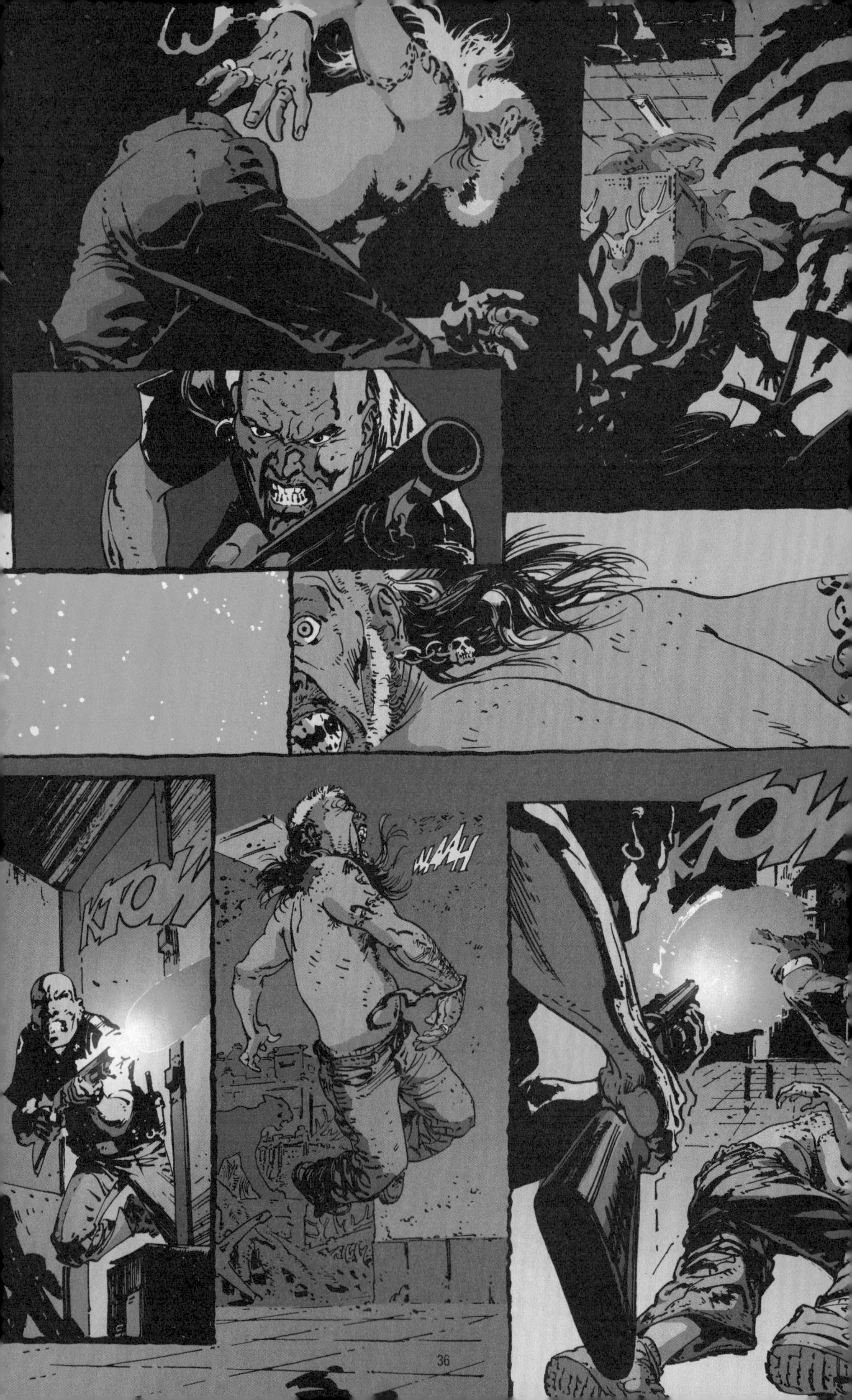
KTOW
WAAH
KTOW

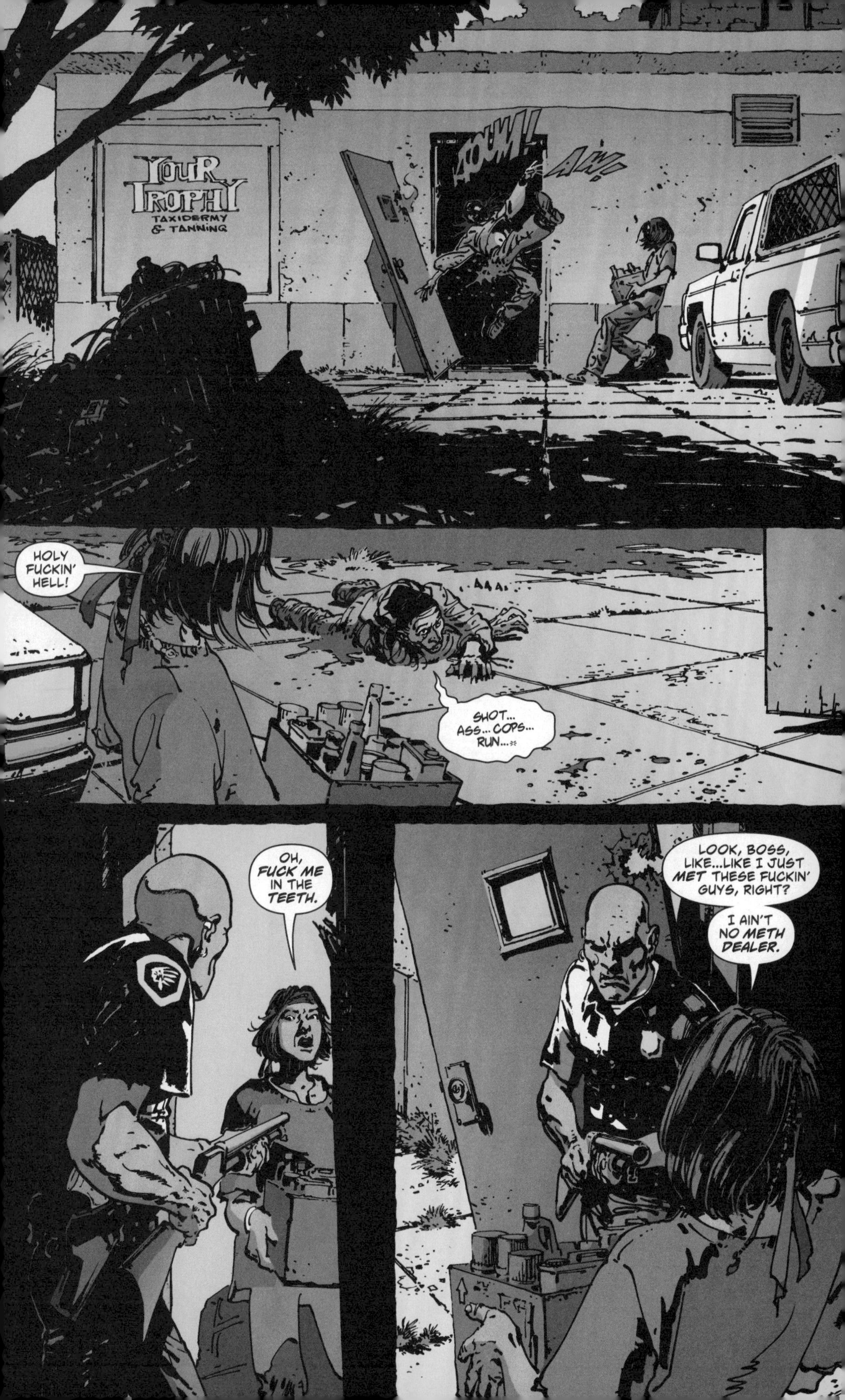
YOUR TROPHY
TAXIDERMY & TANNING
KOUM!!
AH!
HOLY FUCKIN' HELL!
AAA.
SHOT... ASS... COPS... RUN...
OH, FUCK ME IN THE TEETH.
LOOK, BOSS, LIKE...LIKE I JUST MET THESE FUCKIN' GUYS, RIGHT?
I AIN'T NO METH DEALER.

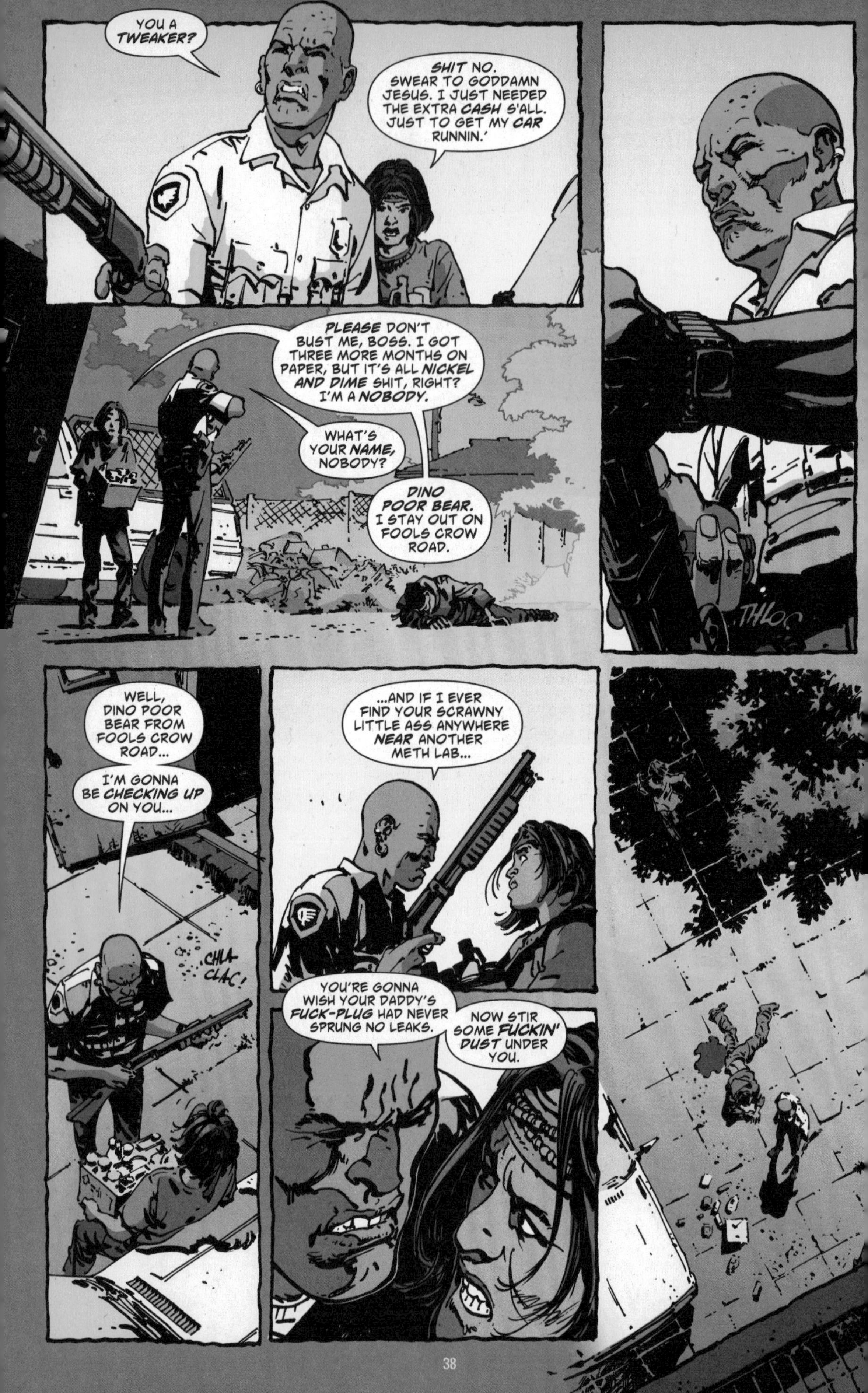

YOU A TWEAKER?
SHIT NO. SWEAR TO GODDAMN JESUS. I JUST NEEDED THE EXTRA CASH S'ALL. JUST TO GET MY CAR RUNNIN.'
PLEASE DON'T BUST ME, BOSS. I GOT THREE MORE MONTHS ON PAPER, BUT IT'S ALL NICKEL AND DIME SHIT, RIGHT? I'M A NOBODY.
WHAT'S YOUR NAME, NOBODY?
DINO POOR BEAR. I STAY OUT ON FOOLS CROW ROAD.
WELL, DINO POOR BEAR FROM FOOLS CROW ROAD...
I'M GONNA BE CHECKING UP ON YOU...
CHLA-CLAC!
...AND IF I EVER FIND YOUR SCRAWNY LITTLE ASS ANYWHERE NEAR ANOTHER METH LAB...
YOU'RE GONNA WISH YOUR DADDY'S FUCK-PLUG HAD NEVER SPRUNG NO LEAKS.
NOW STIR SOME FUCKIN' DUST UNDER YOU.

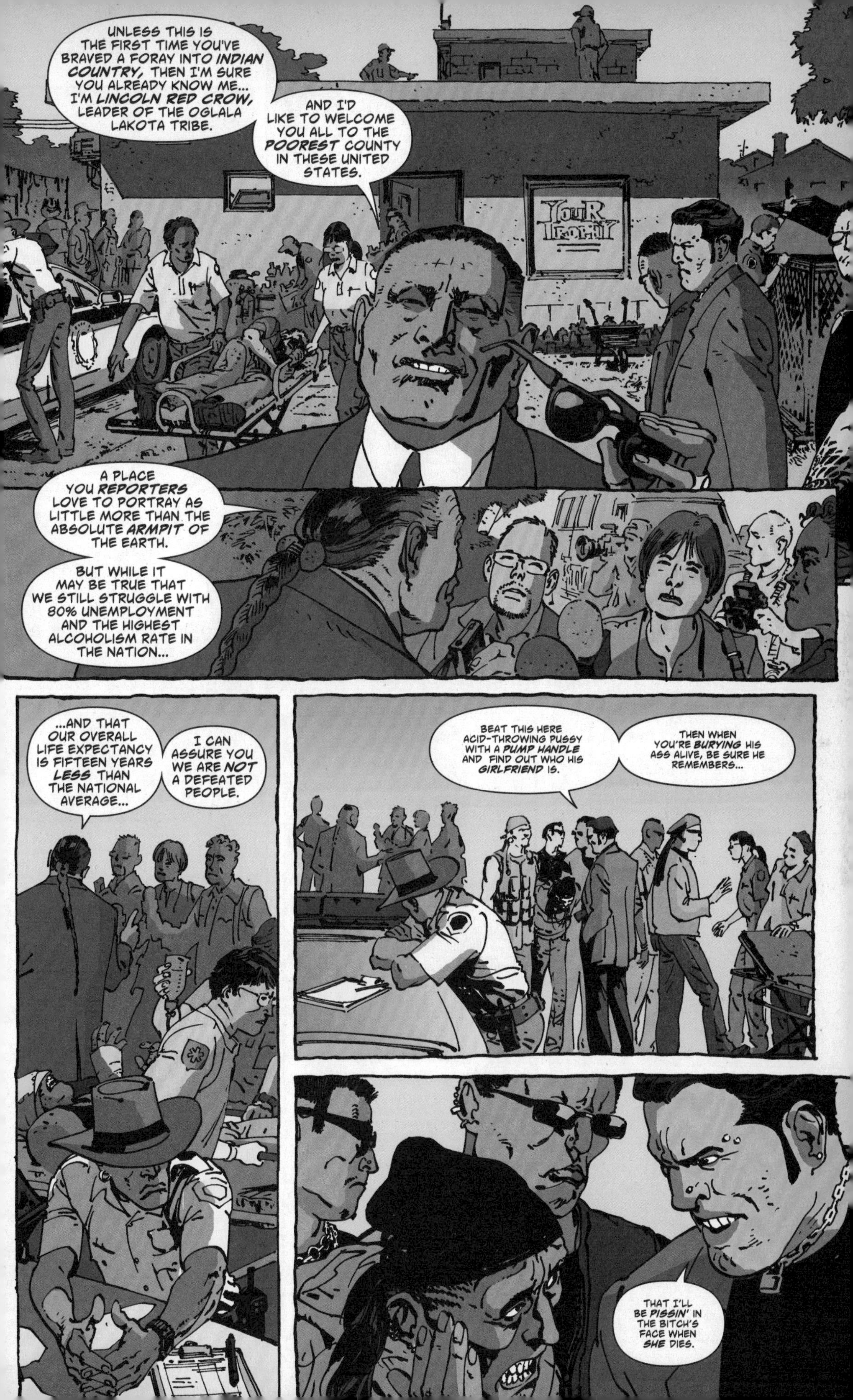
UNLESS THIS IS THE FIRST TIME YOU'VE BRAVED A FORAY INTO INDIAN COUNTRY, THEN I'M SURE YOU ALREADY KNOW ME... I'M LINCOLN RED CROW, LEADER OF THE OGLALA LAKOTA TRIBE.
AND I'D LIKE TO WELCOME YOU ALL TO THE POOREST COUNTY IN THESE UNITED STATES.
YOUR TROPHY
A PLACE YOU REPORTERS LOVE TO PORTRAY AS LITTLE MORE THAN THE ABSOLUTE ARMPIT OF THE EARTH.
BUT WHILE IT MAY BE TRUE THAT WE STILL STRUGGLE WITH 80% UNEMPLOYMENT AND THE HIGHEST ALCOHOLISM RATE IN THE NATION...
...AND THAT OUR OVERALL LIFE EXPECTANCY IS FIFTEEN YEARS LESS THAN THE NATIONAL AVERAGE...
I CAN ASSURE YOU WE ARE NOT A DEFEATED PEOPLE.
BEAT THIS HERE ACID-THROWING PUSSY WITH A PUMP HANDLE AND FIND OUT WHO HIS GIRLFRIEND IS.
THEN WHEN YOU'RE BURYING HIS ASS ALIVE, BE SURE HE REMEMBERS...
THAT I'LL BE PISSIN' IN THE BITCH'S FACE WHEN SHE DIES.

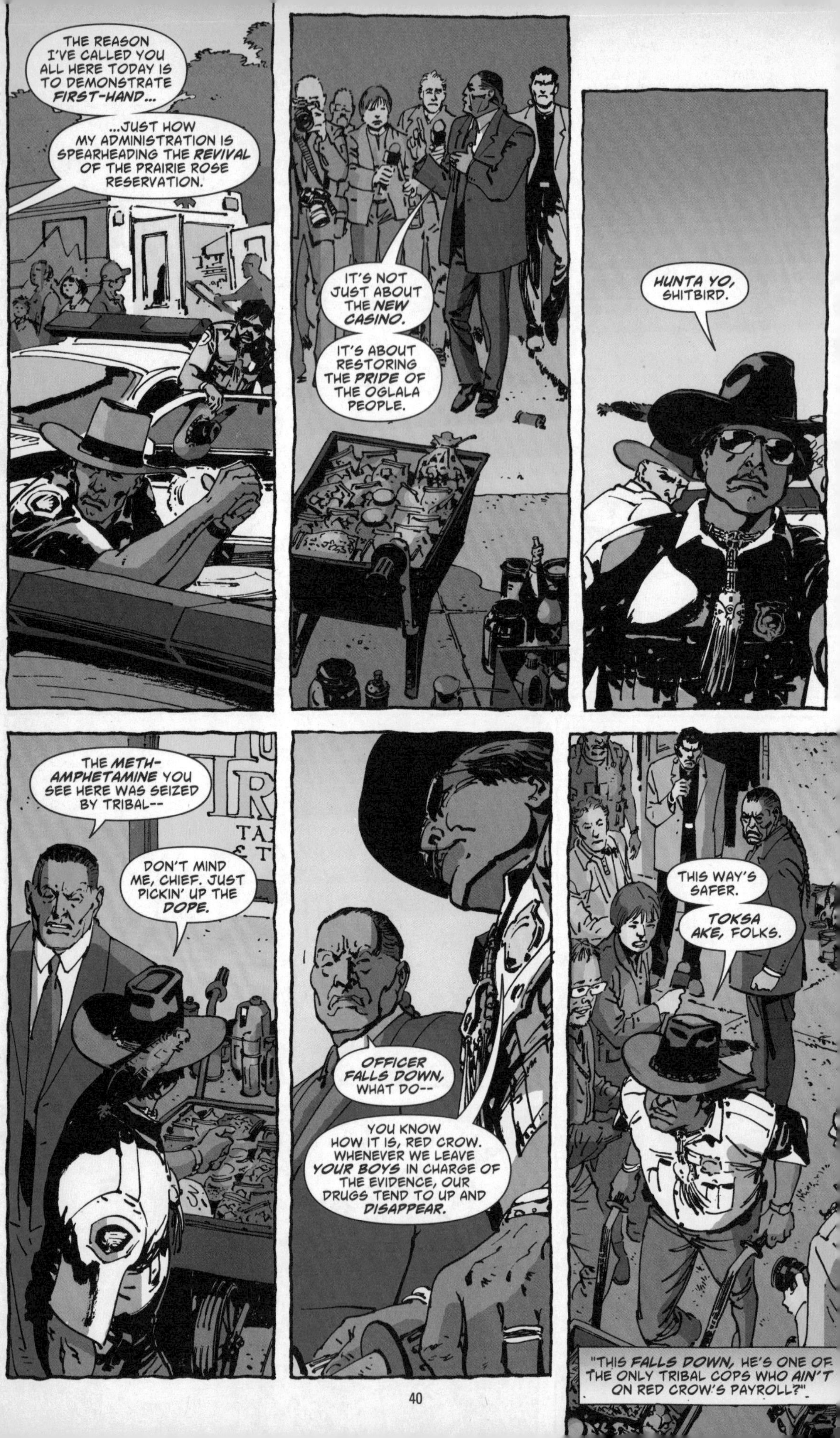
THE REASON I'VE CALLED YOU ALL HERE TODAY IS TO DEMONSTRATE FIRST-HAND...
...JUST HOW MY ADMINISTRATION IS SPEARHEADING THE REVIVAL OF THE PRAIRIE ROSE RESERVATION.
IT'S NOT JUST ABOUT THE NEW CASINO.
IT'S ABOUT RESTORING THE PRIDE OF THE OGLALA PEOPLE.
HUNTA YO, SHITBIRD.
THE METH-AMPHETAMINE YOU SEE HERE WAS SEIZED BY TRIBAL--
DON'T MIND ME, CHIEF. JUST PICKIN' UP THE DOPE.
OFFICER FALLS DOWN, WHAT DO--
YOU KNOW HOW IT IS, RED CROW. WHENEVER WE LEAVE YOUR BOYS IN CHARGE OF THE EVIDENCE, OUR DRUGS TEND TO UP AND DISAPPEAR.
THIS WAY'S SAFER.
TOKSA AKE, FOLKS.
"THIS FALLS DOWN, HE'S ONE OF THE ONLY TRIBAL COPS WHO AIN'T ON RED CROW'S PAYROLL?"

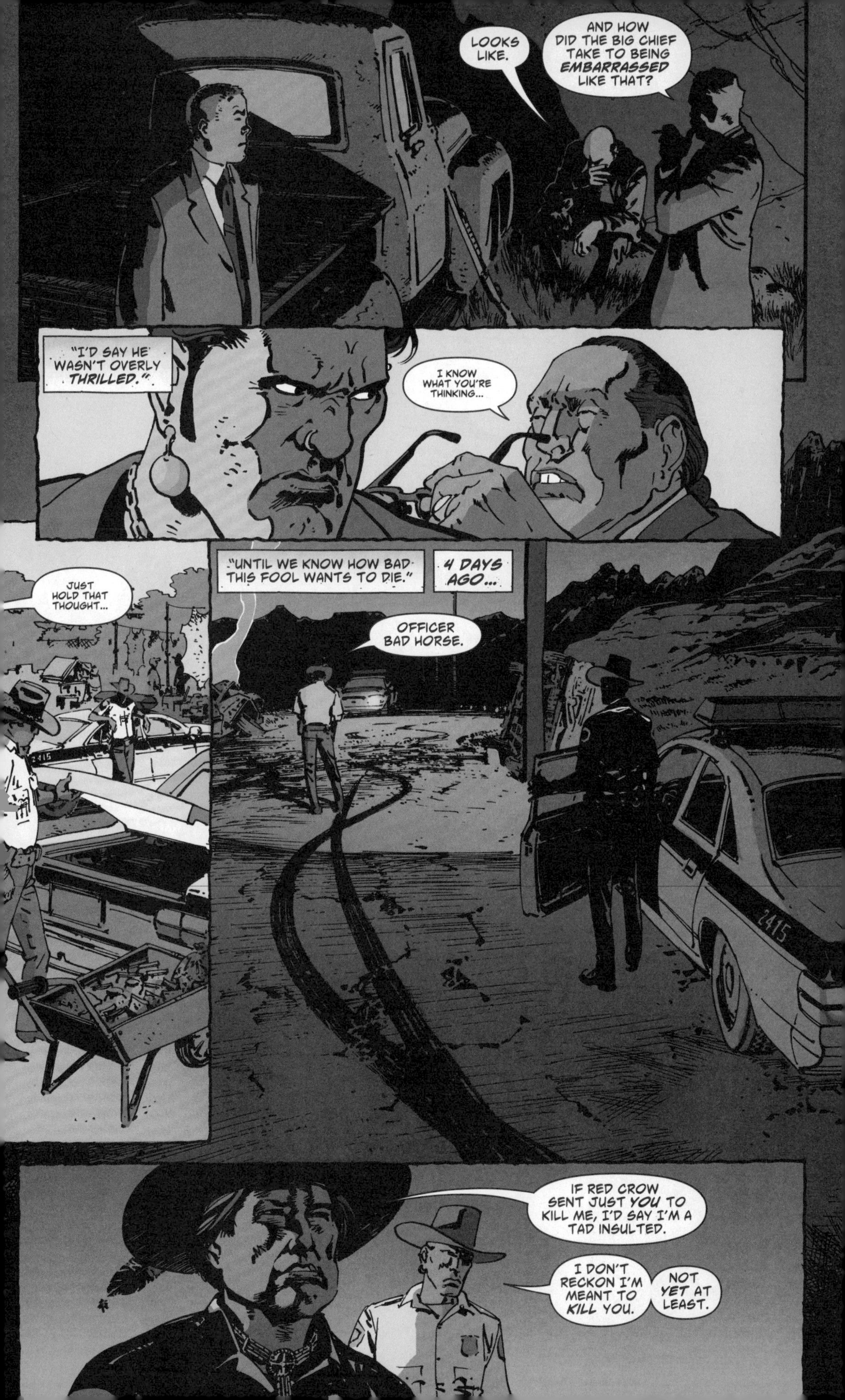
LOOKS LIKE.
AND HOW DID THE BIG CHIEF TAKE TO BEING EMBARRASSED LIKE THAT?
"I'D SAY HE WASN'T OVERLY THRILLED."
I KNOW WHAT YOU'RE THINKING...
JUST HOLD THAT THOUGHT...
"UNTIL WE KNOW HOW BAD THIS FOOL WANTS TO DIE."
4 DAYS AGO...
OFFICER BAD HORSE.
IF RED CROW SENT JUST YOU TO KILL ME, I'D SAY I'M A TAD INSULTED.
I DON'T RECKON I'M MEANT TO KILL YOU.
NOT YET AT LEAST.

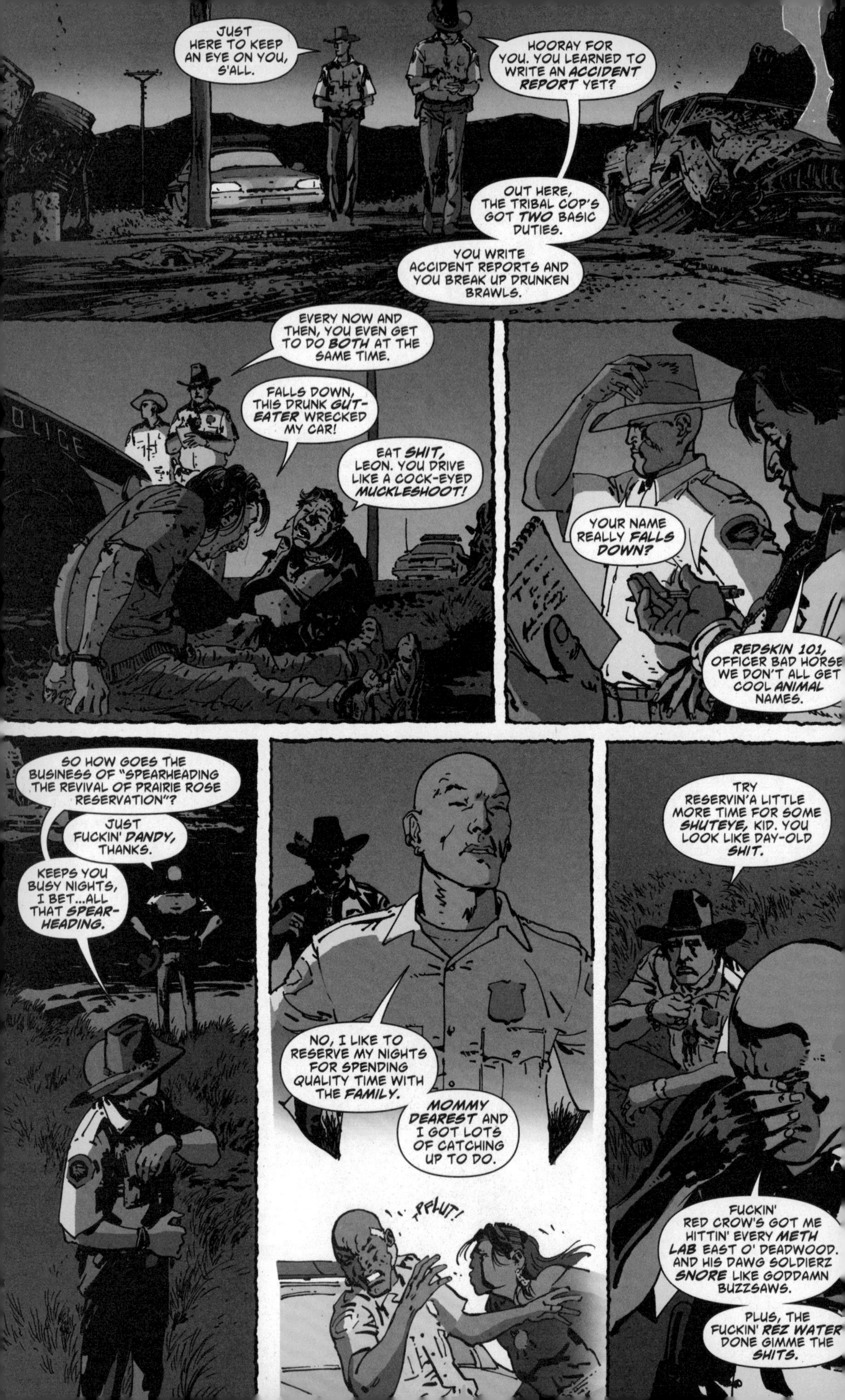
JUST HERE TO KEEP AN EYE ON YOU, S'ALL.
HOORAY FOR YOU. YOU LEARNED TO WRITE AN ACCIDENT REPORT YET?
OUT HERE, THE TRIBAL COP'S GOT TWO BASIC DUTIES.
YOU WRITE ACCIDENT REPORTS AND YOU BREAK UP DRUNKEN BRAWLS.
EVERY NOW AND THEN, YOU EVEN GET TO DO BOTH AT THE SAME TIME.
POLICE
FALLS DOWN, THIS DRUNK GUT-EATER WRECKED MY CAR!
EAT SHIT, LEON. YOU DRIVE LIKE A COCK-EYED MUCKLESHOOT!
YOUR NAME REALLY FALLS DOWN?
REDSKIN 101, OFFICER BAD HORSE WE DON'T ALL GET COOL ANIMAL NAMES.
SO HOW GOES THE BUSINESS OF "SPEARHEADING THE REVIVAL OF PRAIRIE ROSE RESERVATION"?
JUST FUCKIN' DANDY, THANKS.
KEEPS YOU BUSY NIGHTS, I BET...ALL THAT SPEAR-HEADING.
NO, I LIKE TO RESERVE MY NIGHTS FOR SPENDING QUALITY TIME WITH THE FAMILY.
MOMMY DEAREST AND I GOT LOTS OF CATCHING UP TO DO.
PPLUT!
TRY RESERVIN'A LITTLE MORE TIME FOR SOME SHUTEYE, KID. YOU LOOK LIKE DAY-OLD SHIT.
FUCKIN' RED CROW'S GOT ME HITTIN' EVERY METH LAB EAST O' DEADWOOD. AND HIS DAWG SOLDIERZ SNORE LIKE GODDAMN BUZZSAWS.
PLUS, THE FUCKIN' REZ WATER DONE GIMME THE SHITS.

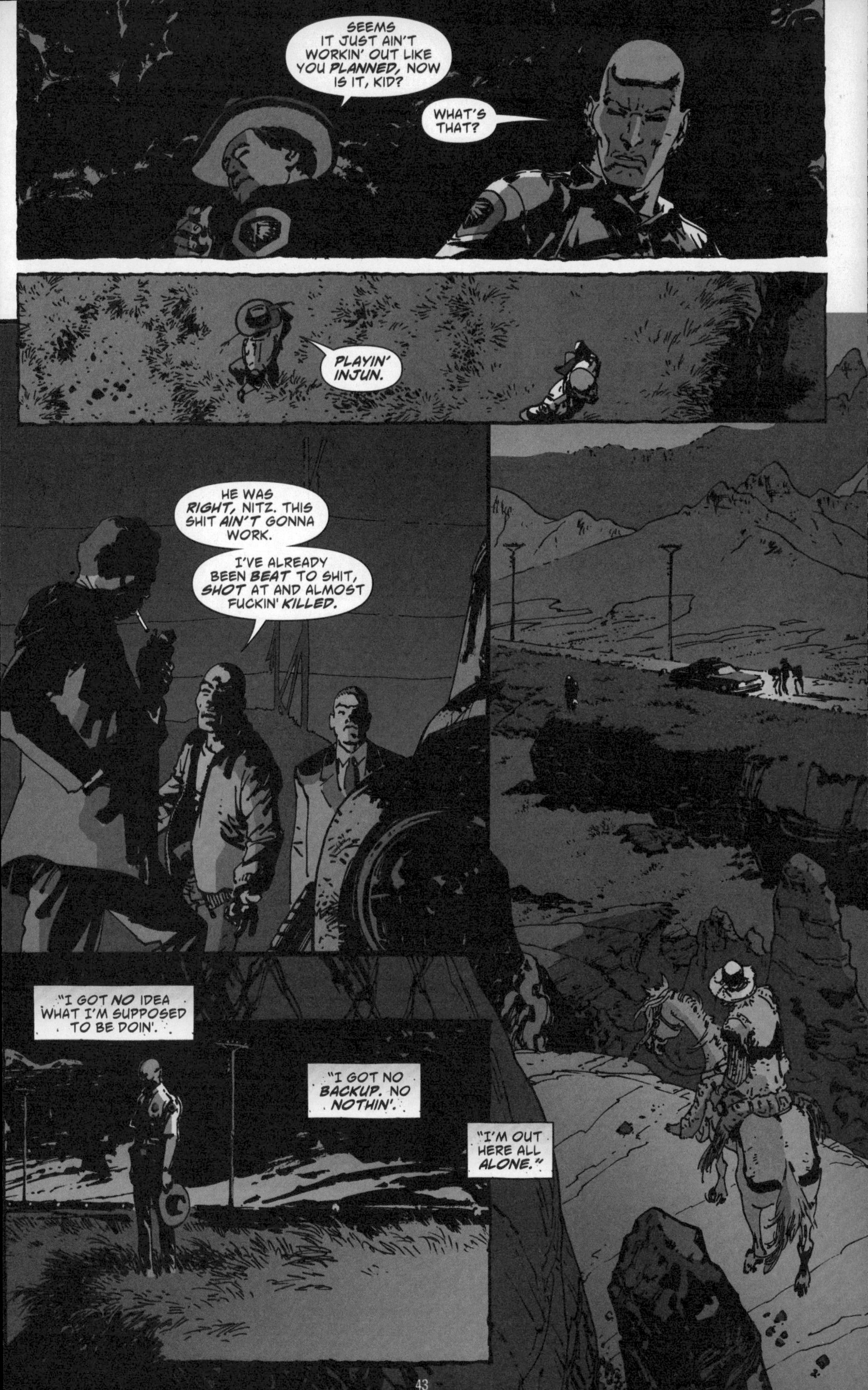
SEEMS IT JUST AIN'T WORKIN' OUT LIKE YOU PLANNED, NOW IS IT, KID?
WHAT'S THAT?
PLAYIN' INJUN.
HE WAS RIGHT, NITZ. THIS SHIT AIN'T GONNA WORK.
I'VE ALREADY BEEN BEAT TO SHIT, SHOT AT AND ALMOST FUCKIN' KILLED.
"I GOT NO IDEA WHAT I'M SUPPOSED TO BE DOIN'.
"I GOT NO BACKUP. NO NOTHIN'.
"I'M OUT HERE ALL ALONE."

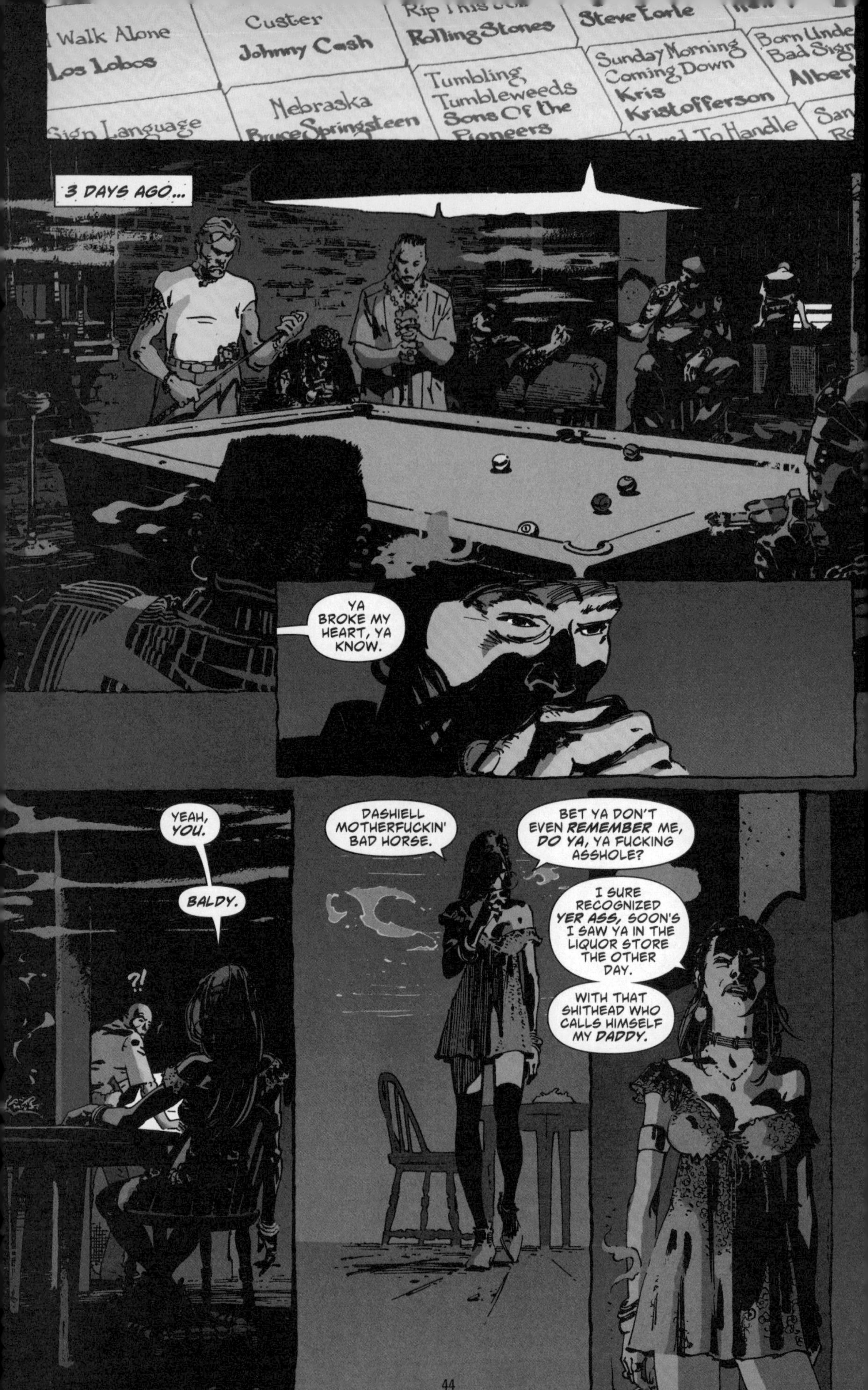

Walk Alone
Los Lobos
Custer
Johnny Cash
Rolling Stones
Steve Earle
Sunday Morning Coming Down
Kris Kristofferson
Tumbling Tumbleweeds
Sons Of the
Nebraska
Bruce Springsteen
Sign Language
3 DAYS AGO...
YA BROKE MY HEART, YA KNOW.
YEAH, YOU.
BALDY.
?!
DASHIELL MOTHERFUCKIN' BAD HORSE.
BET YA DON'T EVEN REMEMBER ME, DO YA, YA FUCKING ASSHOLE?
I SURE RECOGNIZED YER ASS, SOON'S I SAW YA IN THE LIQUOR STORE THE OTHER DAY.
WITH THAT SHITHEAD WHO CALLS HIMSELF MY DADDY.

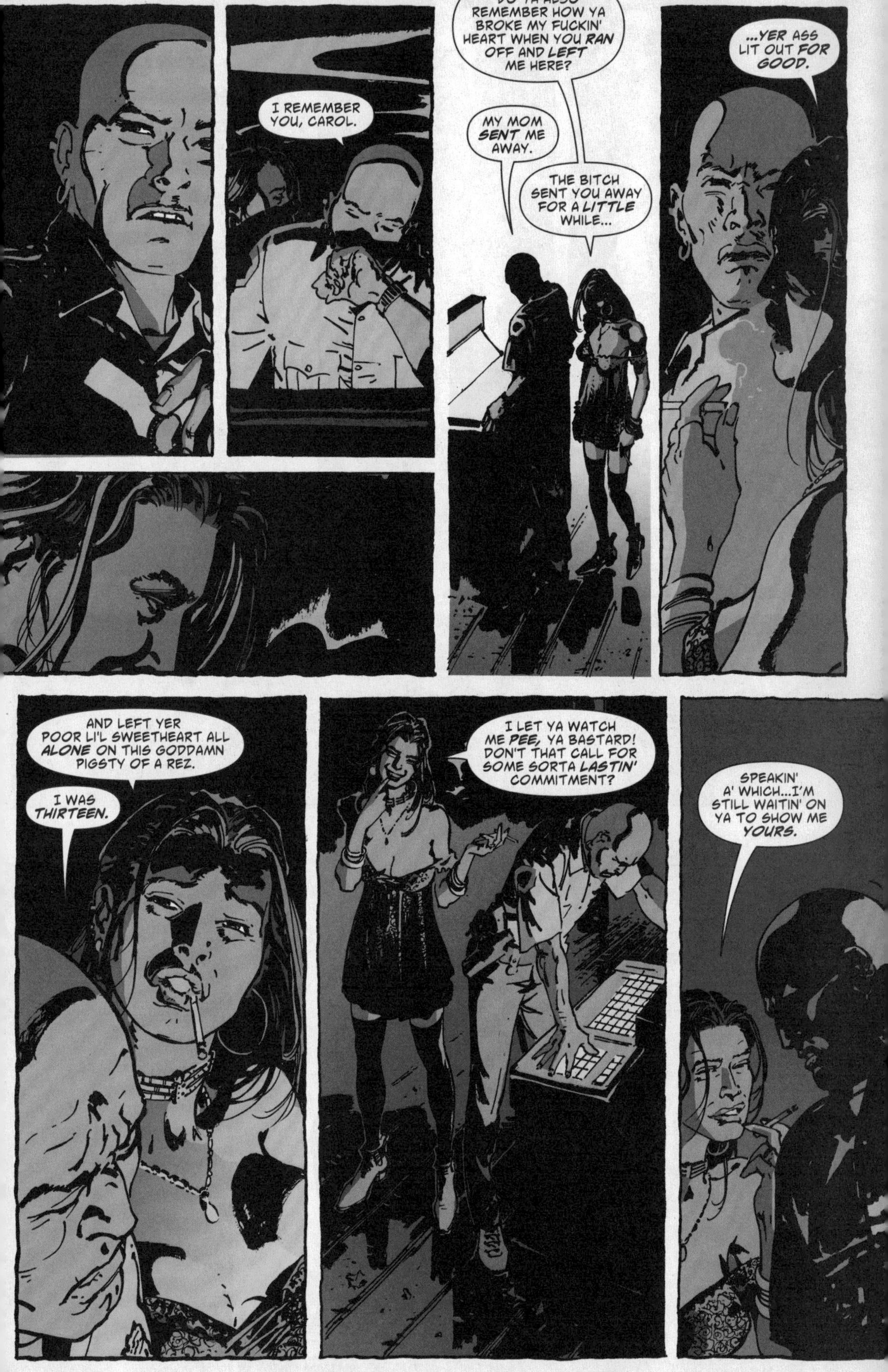
I REMEMBER YOU, CAROL.
YEAH? DO YA ALSO REMEMBER HOW YA BROKE MY FUCKIN' HEART WHEN YOU RAN OFF AND LEFT ME HERE?
MY MOM SENT ME AWAY.
THE BITCH SENT YOU AWAY FOR A LITTLE WHILE...
...YER ASS LIT OUT FOR GOOD.
AND LEFT YER POOR LI'L SWEETHEART ALL ALONE ON THIS GODDAMN PIGSTY OF A REZ.
I WAS THIRTEEN.
I LET YA WATCH ME PEE, YA BASTARD! DON'T THAT CALL FOR SOME SORTA LASTIN' COMMITMENT?
SPEAKIN' A' WHICH...I'M STILL WAITIN' ON YA TO SHOW ME YOURS.

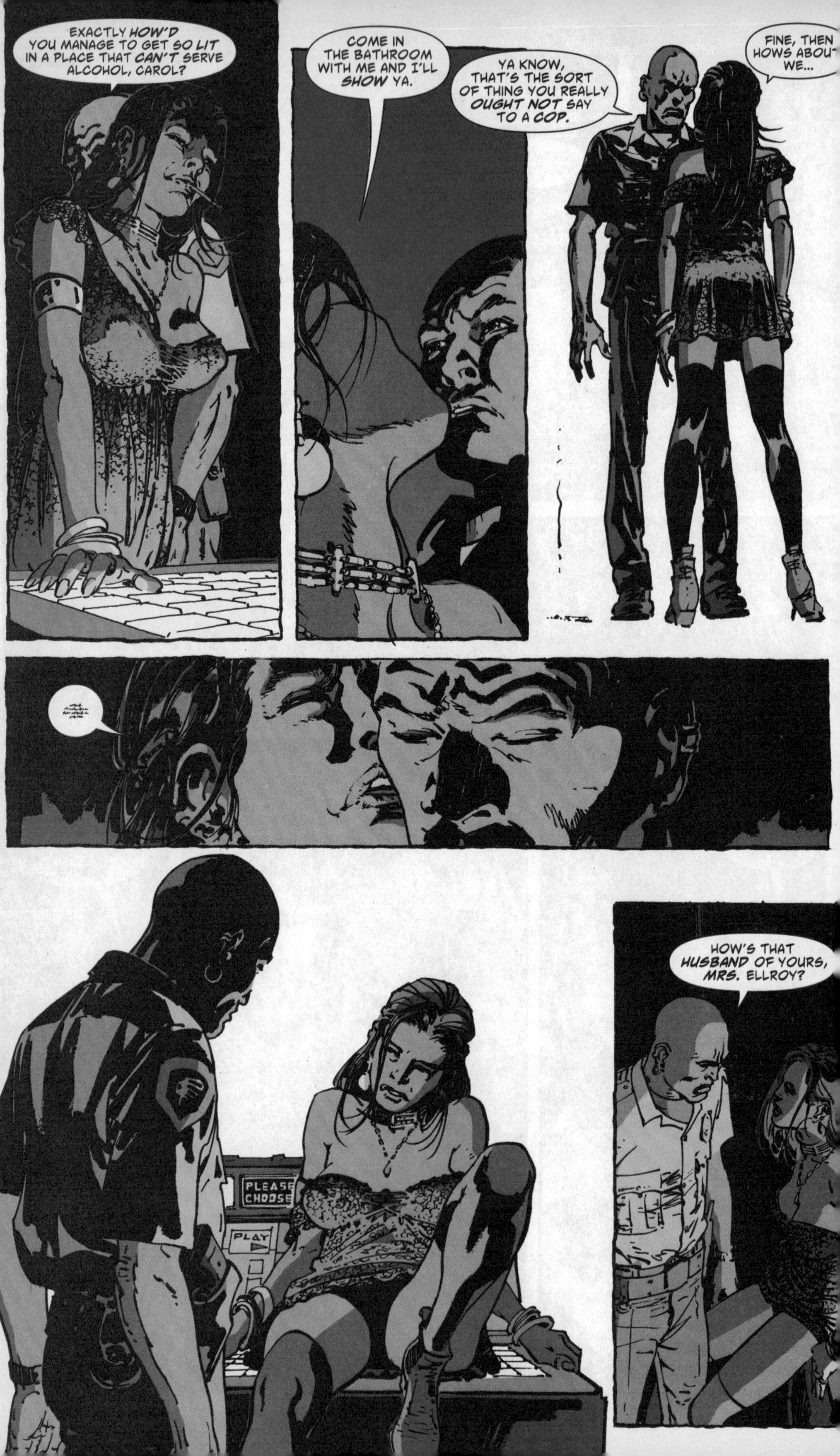
EXACTLY HOW'D YOU MANAGE TO GET SO LIT IN A PLACE THAT CAN'T SERVE ALCOHOL, CAROL?
COME IN THE BATHROOM WITH ME AND I'LL SHOW YA.
YA KNOW, THAT'S THE SORT OF THING YOU REALLY OUGHT NOT SAY TO A COP.
FINE, THEN HOWS ABOUT WE...
PLEASE CHOOSE
PLAY
HOW'S THAT HUSBAND OF YOURS, MRS. ELLROY?

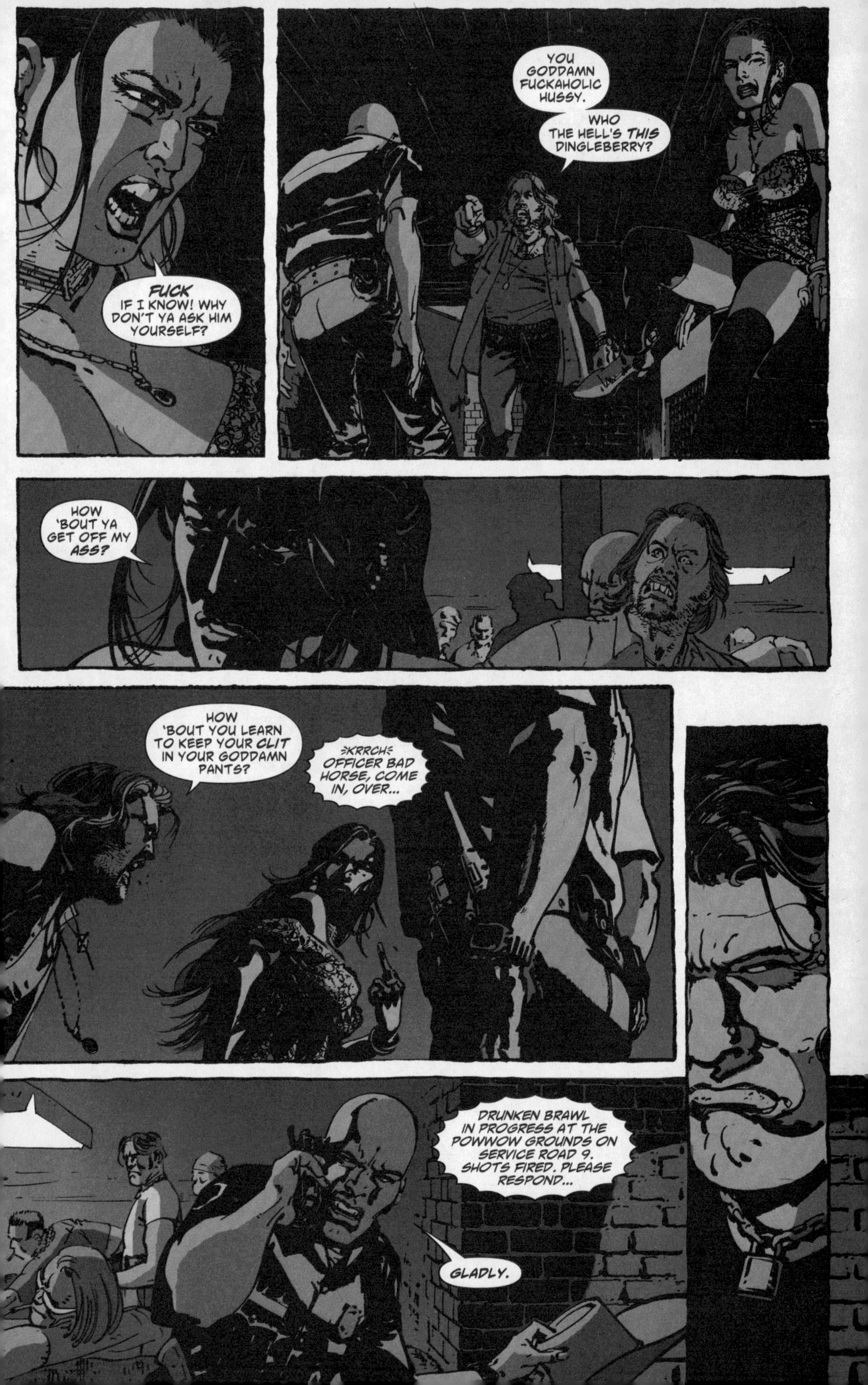
FUCK IF I KNOW! WHY DON'T YA ASK HIM YOURSELF?
YOU GODDAMN FUCKAHOLIC HUSSY.
WHO THE HELL'S THIS DINGLEBERRY?
HOW 'BOUT YA GET OFF MY ASS?
HOW 'BOUT YOU LEARN TO KEEP YOUR CLIT IN YOUR GODDAMN PANTS?
KRRCH OFFICER BAD HORSE, COME IN, OVER...
DRUNKEN BRAWL IN PROGRESS AT THE POWWOW GROUNDS ON SERVICE ROAD 9. SHOTS FIRED. PLEASE RESPOND...
GLADLY.

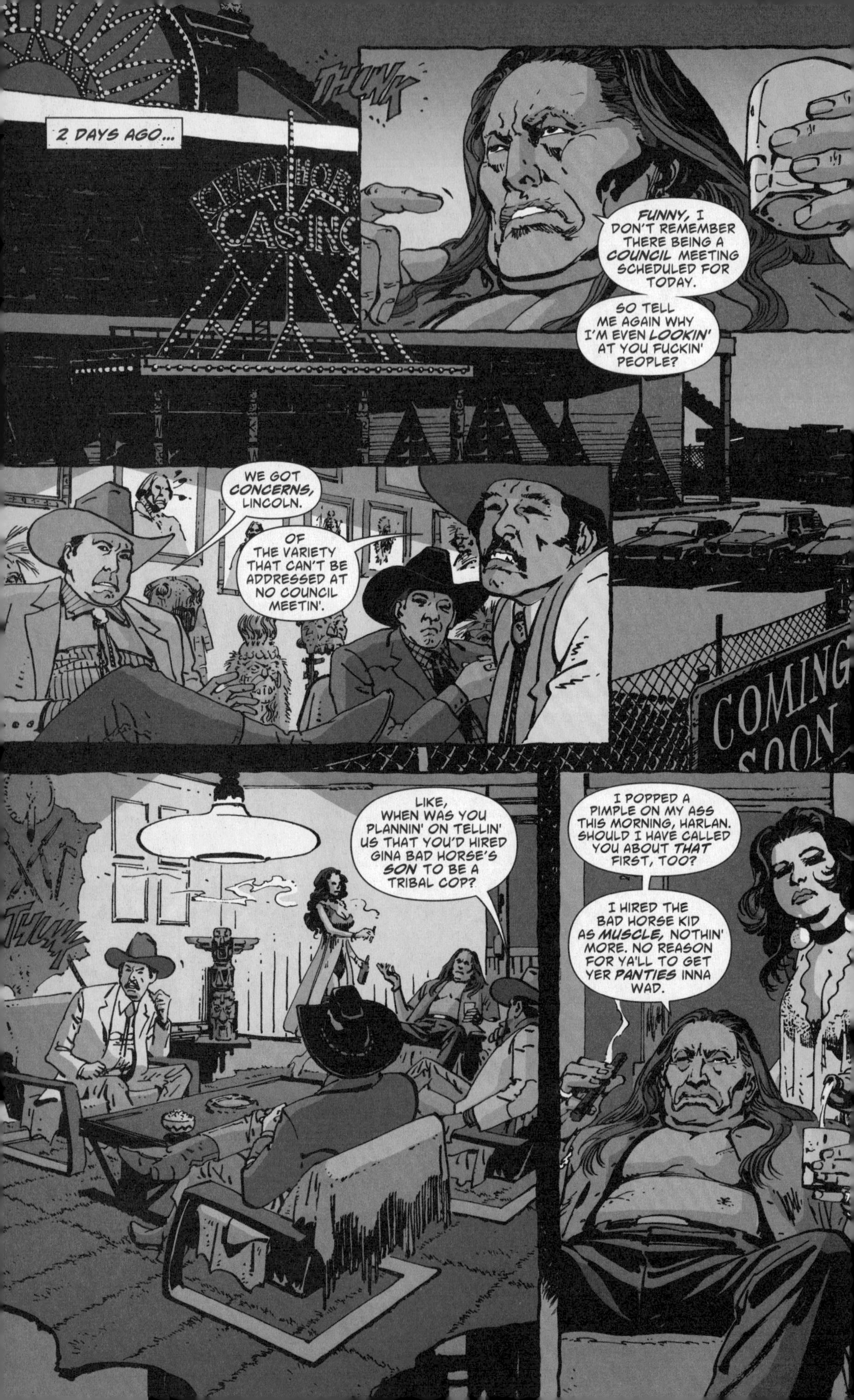
2 DAYS AGO...
THUNK
FUNNY, I DON'T REMEMBER THERE BEING A COUNCIL MEETING SCHEDULED FOR TODAY.
SO TELL ME AGAIN WHY I'M EVEN LOOKIN' AT YOU FUCKIN' PEOPLE?
WE GOT CONCERNS, LINCOLN.
OF THE VARIETY THAT CAN'T BE ADDRESSED AT NO COUNCIL MEETIN'.
COMING SOON
THUNK
LIKE, WHEN WAS YOU PLANNIN' ON TELLIN' US THAT YOU'D HIRED GINA BAD HORSE'S SON TO BE A TRIBAL COP?
I POPPED A PIMPLE ON MY ASS THIS MORNING, HARLAN. SHOULD I HAVE CALLED YOU ABOUT THAT FIRST, TOO?
I HIRED THE BAD HORSE KID AS MUSCLE, NOTHIN' MORE. NO REASON FOR YA'LL TO GET YER PANTIES INNA WAD.

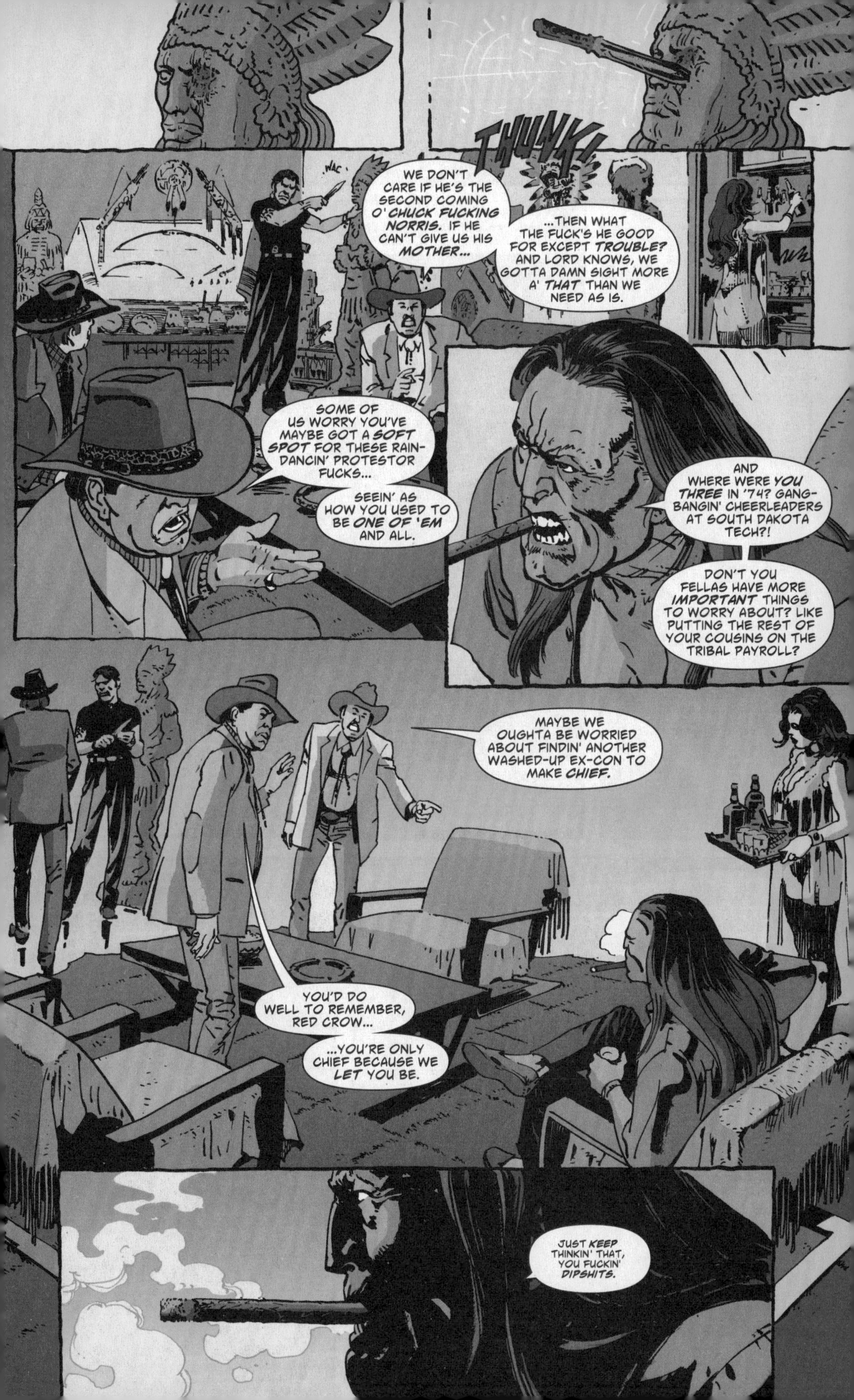
THUNK!
WE DON'T CARE IF HE'S THE SECOND COMING O' CHUCK FUCKING NORRIS. IF HE CAN'T GIVE US HIS MOTHER...
...THEN WHAT THE FUCK'S HE GOOD FOR EXCEPT TROUBLE? AND LORD KNOWS, WE GOTTA DAMN SIGHT MORE A' THAT THAN WE NEED AS IS.
SOME OF US WORRY YOU'VE MAYBE GOT A SOFT SPOT FOR THESE RAIN-DANCIN' PROTESTOR FUCKS...
SEEIN' AS HOW YOU USED TO BE ONE OF 'EM AND ALL.
AND WHERE WERE YOU THREE IN '74? GANG-BANGIN' CHEERLEADERS AT SOUTH DAKOTA TECH?!
DON'T YOU FELLAS HAVE MORE IMPORTANT THINGS TO WORRY ABOUT? LIKE PUTTING THE REST OF YOUR COUSINS ON THE TRIBAL PAYROLL?
MAYBE WE OUGHTA BE WORRIED ABOUT FINDIN' ANOTHER WASHED-UP EX-CON TO MAKE CHIEF.
YOU'D DO WELL TO REMEMBER, RED CROW...
...YOU'RE ONLY CHIEF BECAUSE WE LET YOU BE.
JUST KEEP THINKIN' THAT, YOU FUCKIN' DIPSHITS.

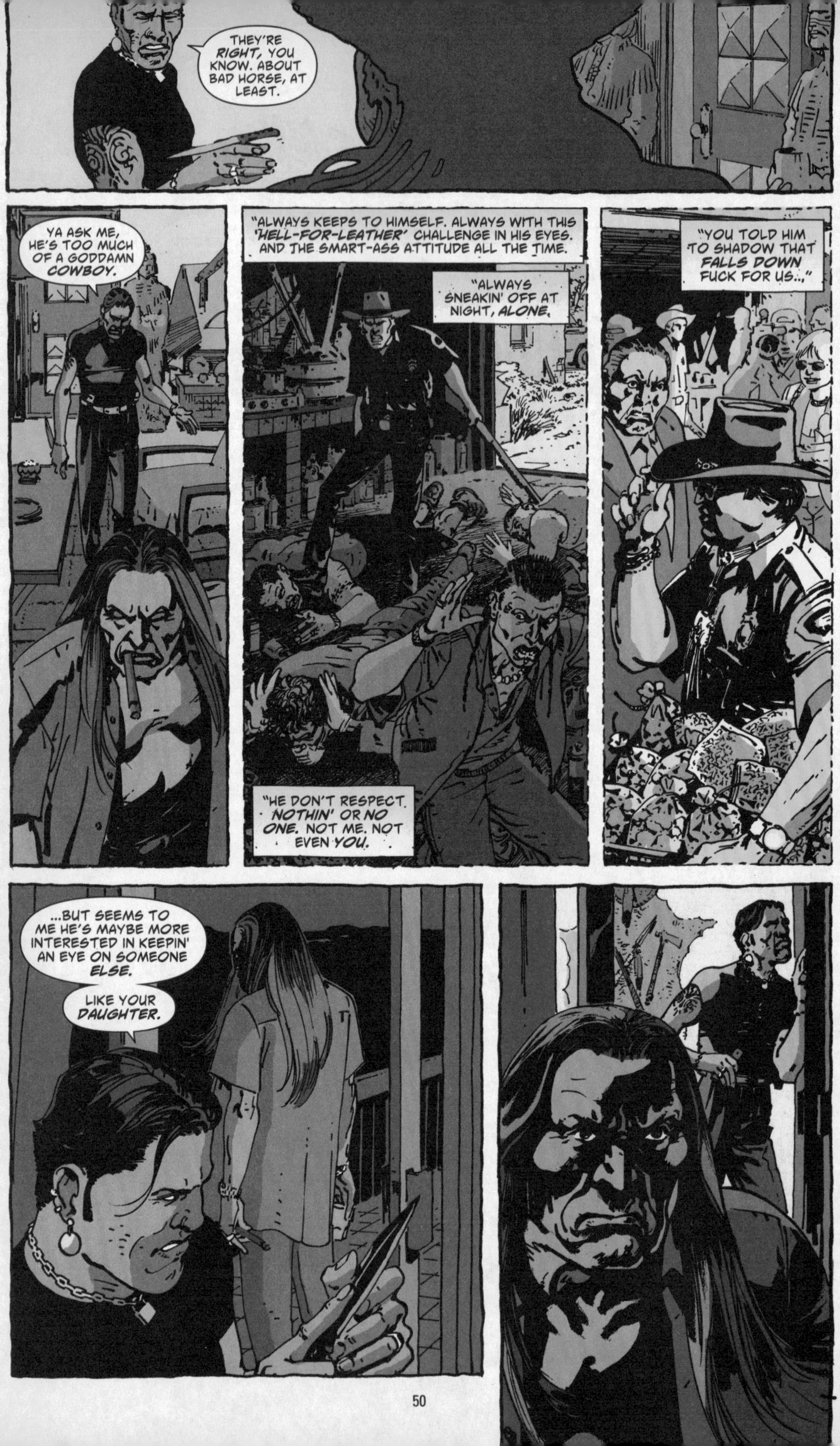
THEY'RE RIGHT, YOU KNOW. ABOUT BAD HORSE, AT LEAST.
YA ASK ME, HE'S TOO MUCH OF A GODDAMN COWBOY.
"ALWAYS KEEPS TO HIMSELF. ALWAYS WITH THIS 'HELL-FOR-LEATHER' CHALLENGE IN HIS EYES. AND THE SMART-ASS ATTITUDE ALL THE TIME.
"ALWAYS SNEAKIN' OFF AT NIGHT, ALONE.
"HE DON'T RESPECT NOTHIN' OR NO ONE. NOT ME. NOT EVEN YOU.
"YOU TOLD HIM TO SHADOW THAT FALLS DOWN FUCK FOR US..."
...BUT SEEMS TO ME HE'S MAYBE MORE INTERESTED IN KEEPIN' AN EYE ON SOMEONE ELSE.
LIKE YOUR DAUGHTER.

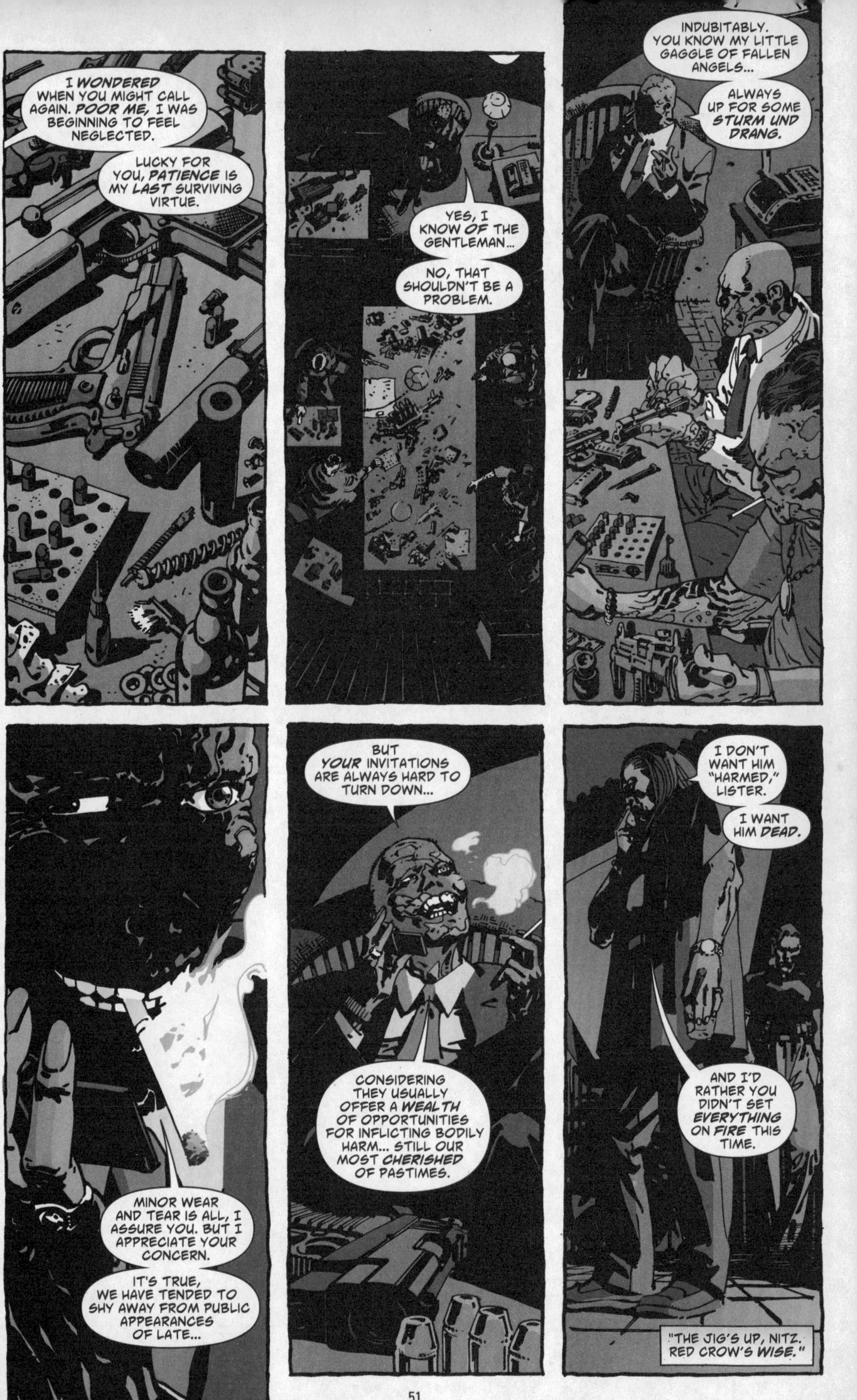

I WONDERED WHEN YOU MIGHT CALL AGAIN. POOR ME, I WAS BEGINNING TO FEEL NEGLECTED.
LUCKY FOR YOU, PATIENCE IS MY LAST SURVIVING VIRTUE.
YES, I KNOW OF THE GENTLEMAN...
NO, THAT SHOULDN'T BE A PROBLEM.
INDUBITABLY. YOU KNOW MY LITTLE GAGGLE OF FALLEN ANGELS...
ALWAYS UP FOR SOME STURM UND DRANG.
MINOR WEAR AND TEAR IS ALL, I ASSURE YOU. BUT I APPRECIATE YOUR CONCERN.
IT'S TRUE, WE HAVE TENDED TO SHY AWAY FROM PUBLIC APPEARANCES OF LATE...
BUT YOUR INVITATIONS ARE ALWAYS HARD TO TURN DOWN...
CONSIDERING THEY USUALLY OFFER A WEALTH OF OPPORTUNITIES FOR INFLICTING BODILY HARM... STILL OUR MOST CHERISHED OF PASTIMES.
I DON'T WANT HIM "HARMED," LISTER.
I WANT HIM DEAD.
AND I'D RATHER YOU DIDN'T SET EVERYTHING ON FIRE THIS TIME.
"THE JIG'S UP, NITZ. RED CROW'S WISE."

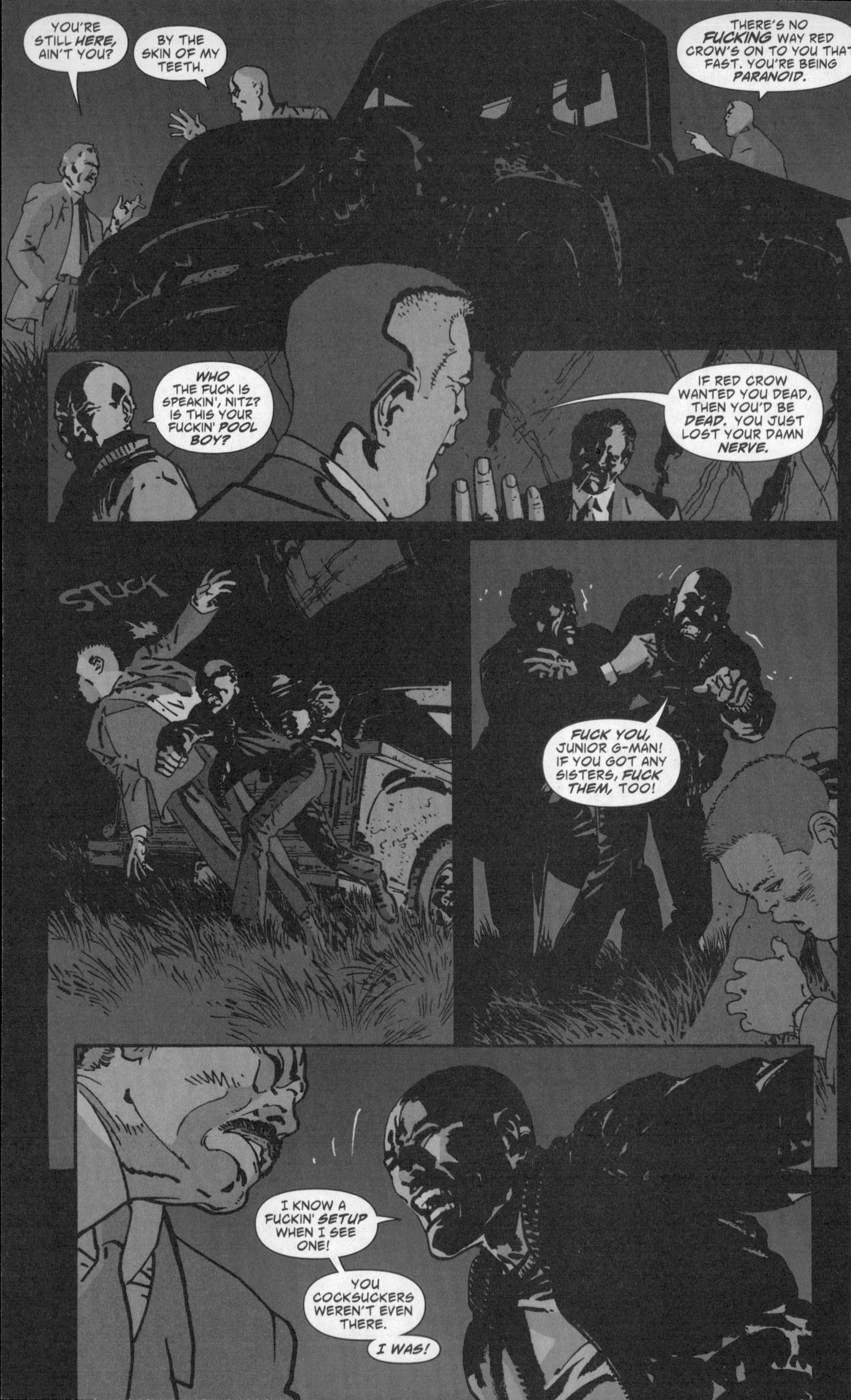
YOU'RE STILL HERE, AIN'T YOU?
BY THE SKIN OF MY TEETH.
THERE'S NO FUCKING WAY RED CROW'S ON TO YOU THAT FAST. YOU'RE BEING PARANOID.
WHO THE FUCK IS SPEAKIN', NITZ? IS THIS YOUR FUCKIN' POOL BOY?
IF RED CROW WANTED YOU DEAD, THEN YOU'D BE DEAD. YOU JUST LOST YOUR DAMN NERVE.
STUCK
FUCK YOU, JUNIOR G-MAN! IF YOU GOT ANY SISTERS, FUCK THEM, TOO!
I KNOW A FUCKIN' SETUP WHEN I SEE ONE!
YOU COCKSUCKERS WEREN'T EVEN THERE.
I WAS!

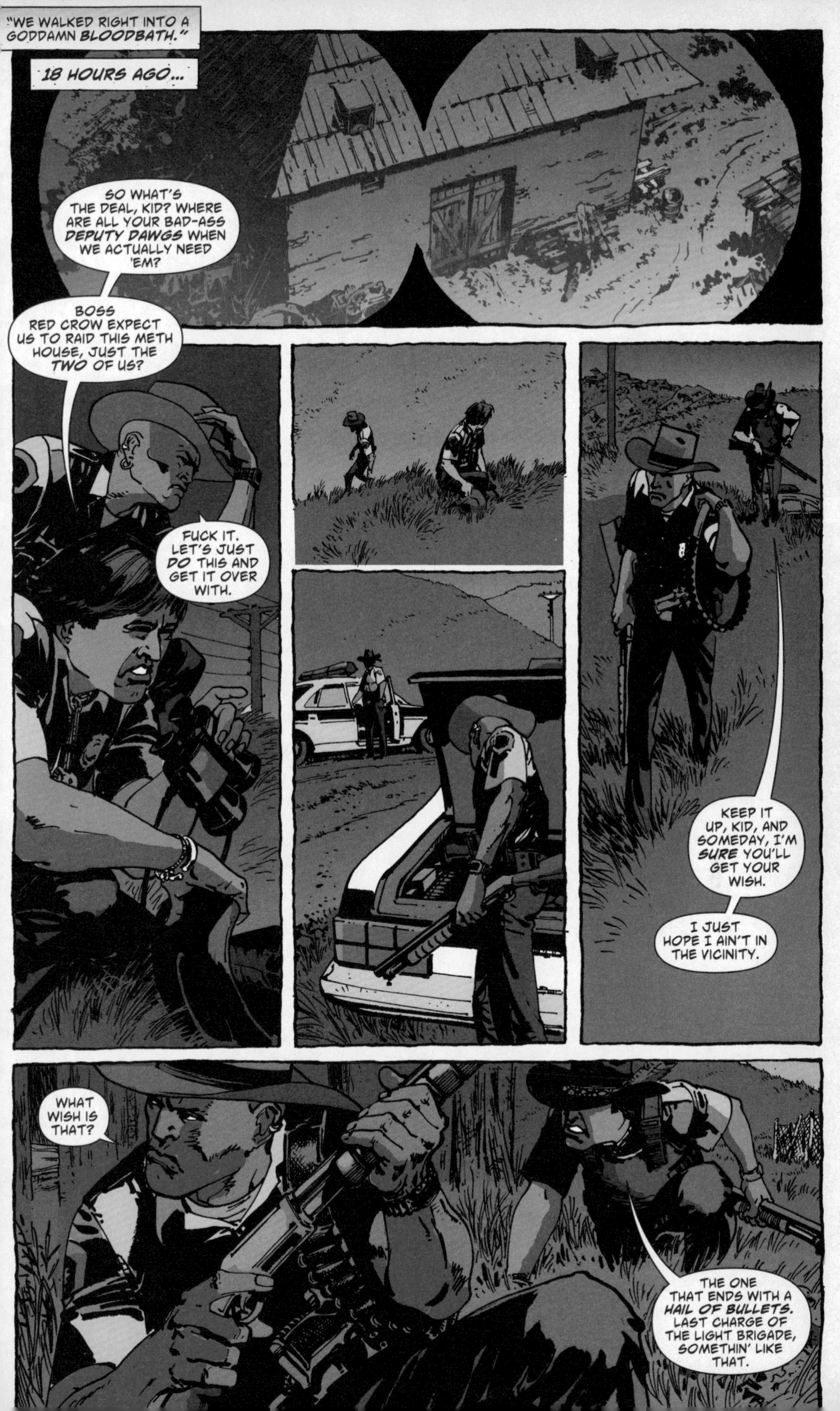
"WE WALKED RIGHT INTO A GODDAMN BLOODBATH."
18 HOURS AGO...
SO WHAT'S THE DEAL, KID? WHERE ARE ALL YOUR BAD-ASS DEPUTY DAWGS WHEN WE ACTUALLY NEED 'EM?
BOSS RED CROW EXPECT US TO RAID THIS METH HOUSE, JUST THE TWO OF US?
FUCK IT. LET'S JUST DO THIS AND GET IT OVER WITH.
KEEP IT UP, KID, AND SOMEDAY, I'M SURE YOU'LL GET YOUR WISH.
I JUST HOPE I AIN'T IN THE VICINITY.
WHAT WISH IS THAT?
THE ONE THAT ENDS WITH A HAIL OF BULLETS. LAST CHARGE OF THE LIGHT BRIGADE, SOMETHIN' LIKE THAT.

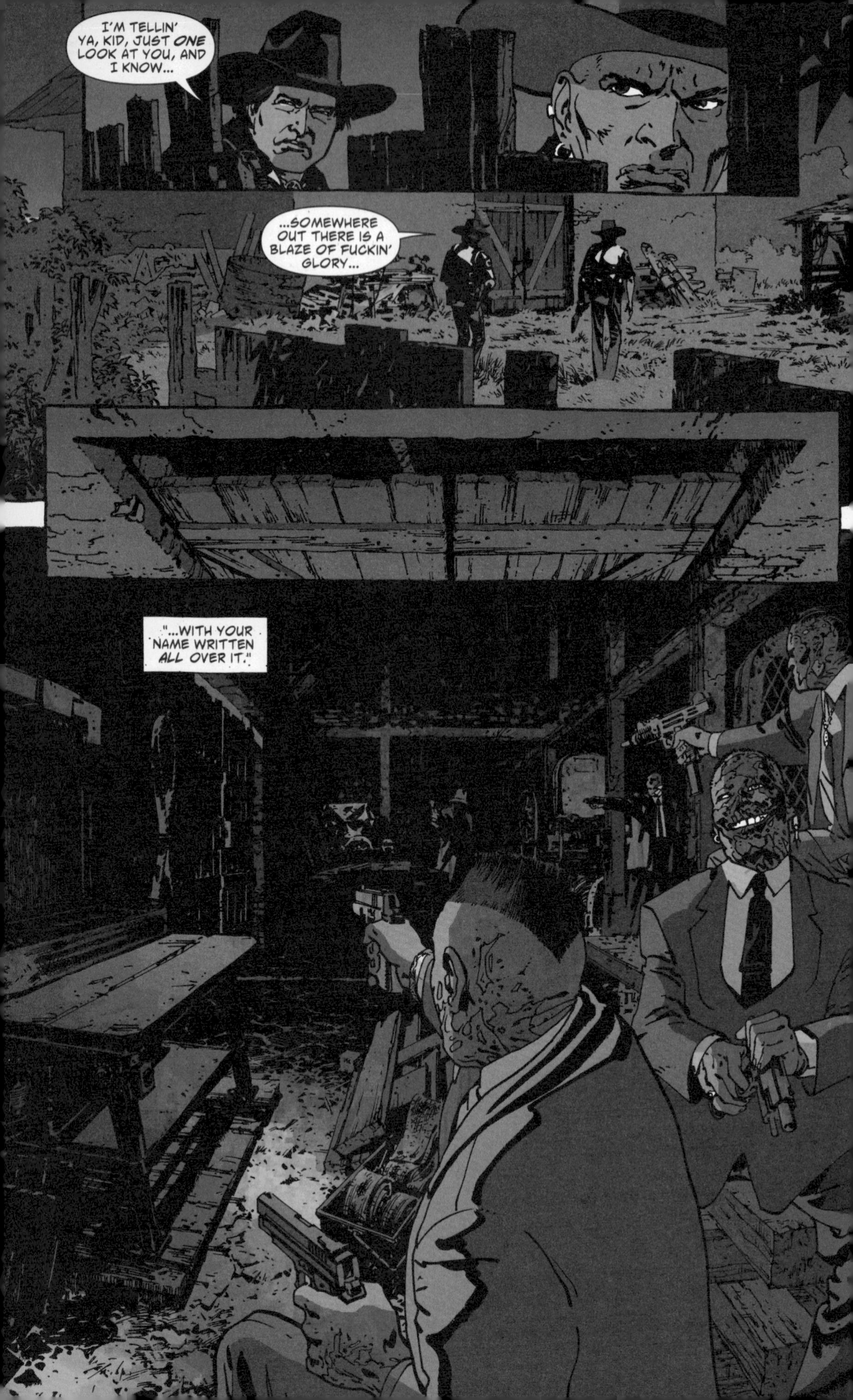
I'M TELLIN' YA, KID, JUST ONE LOOK AT YOU, AND I KNOW...
...SOMEWHERE OUT THERE IS A BLAZE OF FUCKIN' GLORY...
"...WITH YOUR NAME WRITTEN ALL OVER IT."

INDIAN COUNTRY
CHAPTER THREE

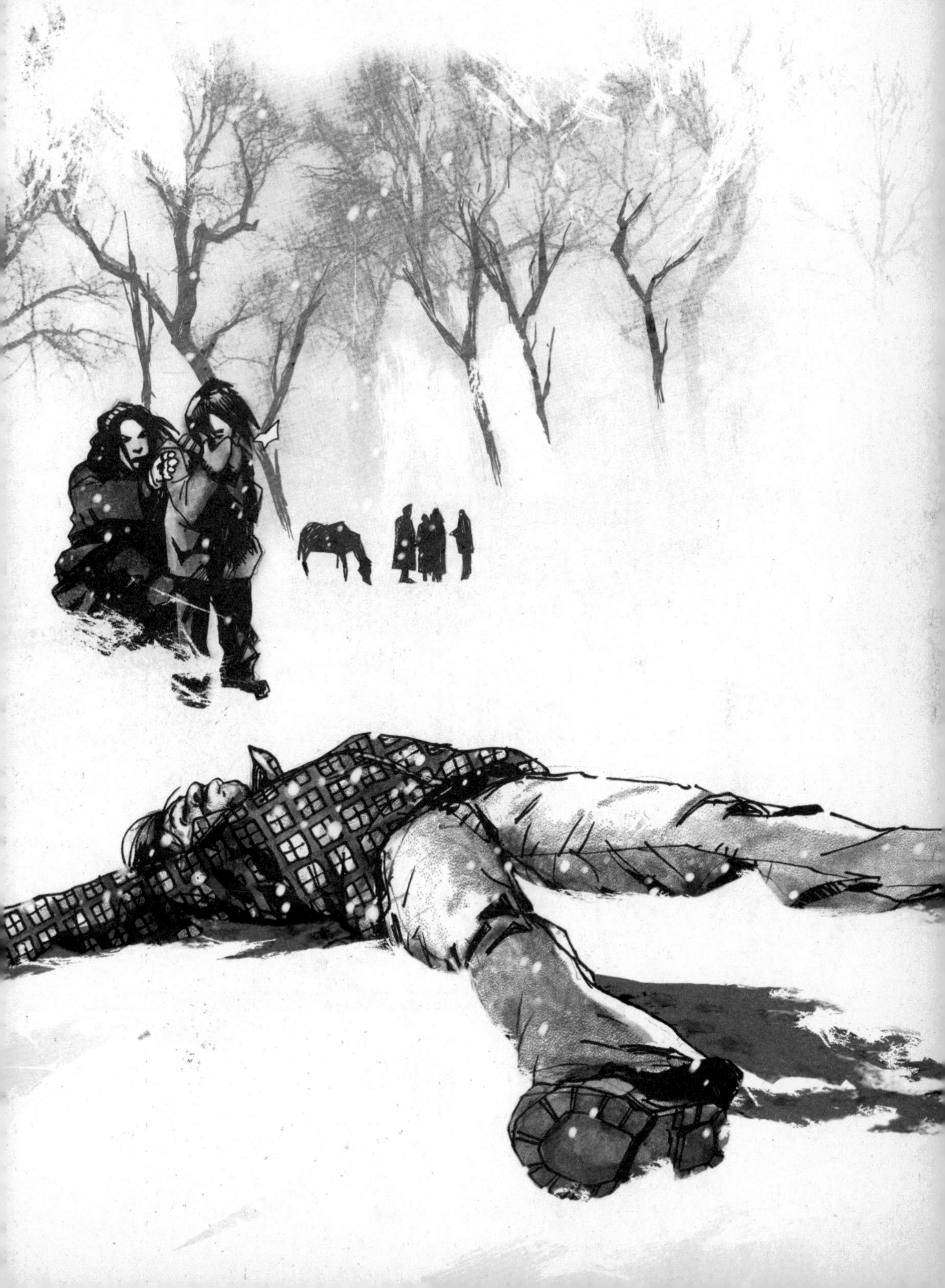

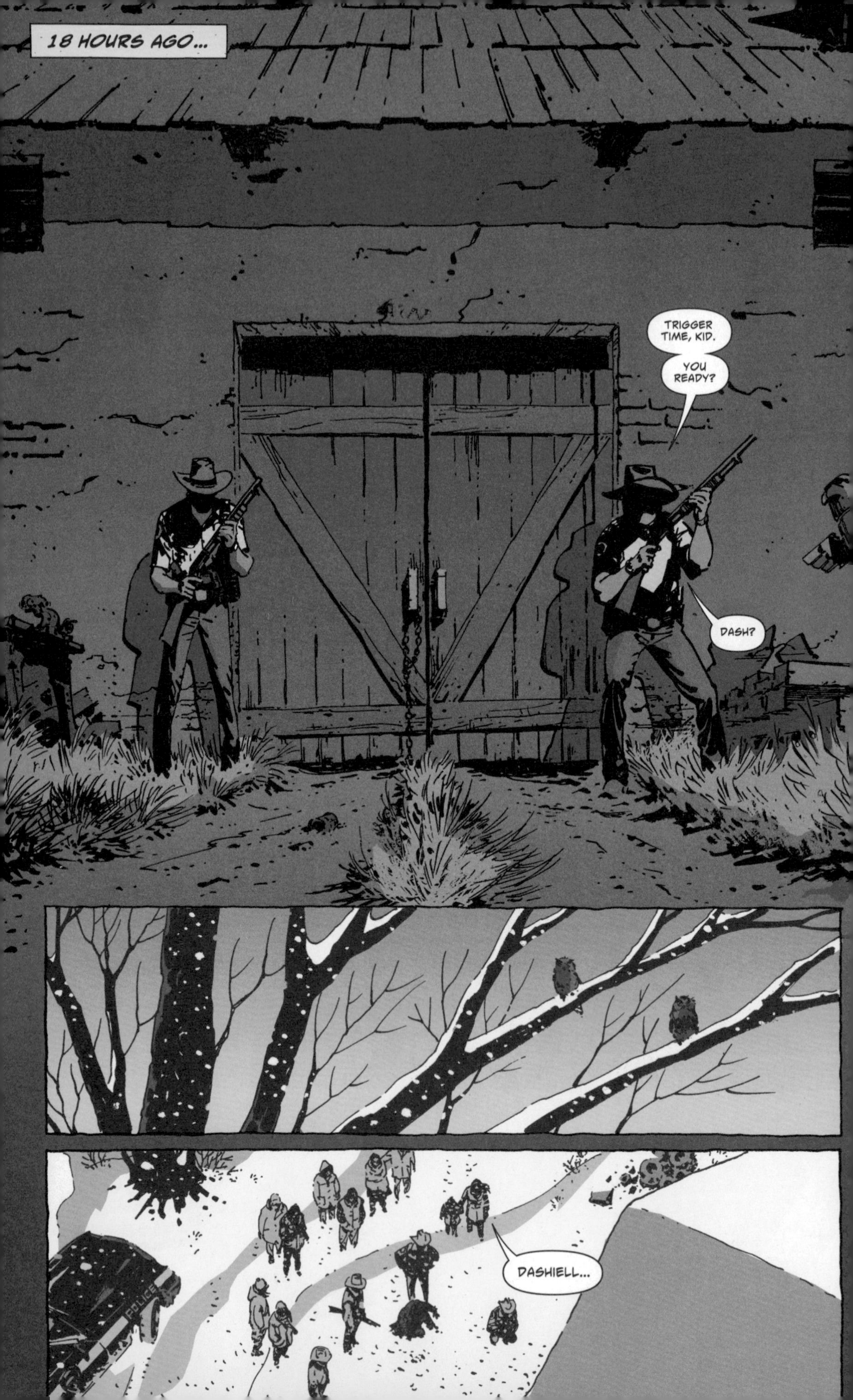
18 HOURS AGO...
TRIGGER TIME, KID.
YOU READY?
DASH?
DASHIELL...

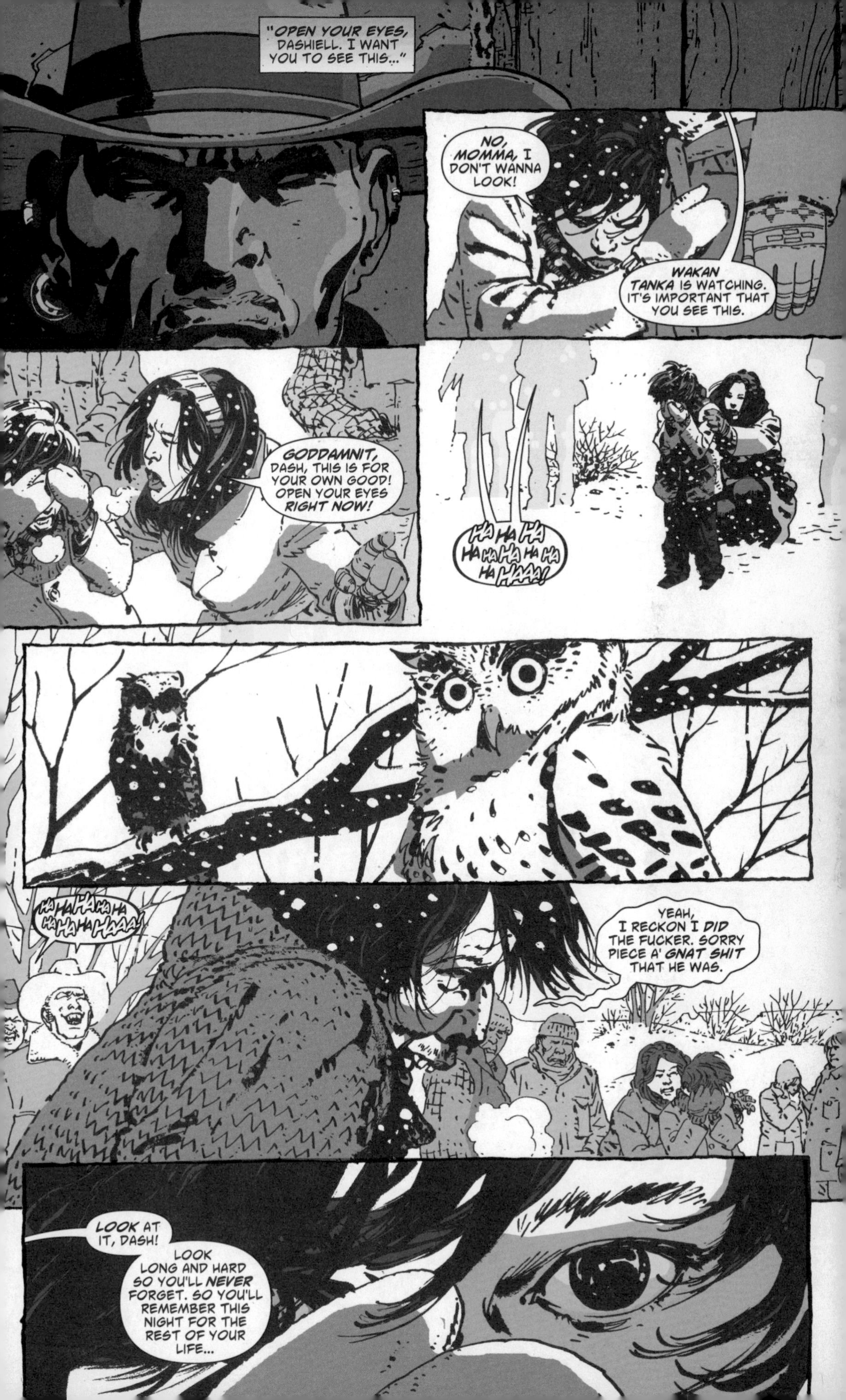
"OPEN YOUR EYES, DASHIELL. I WANT YOU TO SEE THIS..."
NO, MOMMA, I DON'T WANNA LOOK!
WAKAN TANKA IS WATCHING. IT'S IMPORTANT THAT YOU SEE THIS.
GODDAMNIT, DASH, THIS IS FOR YOUR OWN GOOD! OPEN YOUR EYES RIGHT NOW!
HA HA HA HA HA HA HA HA HA HAHAAA!
HA HA HA HA HA HA HA HA HA HAAA!
YEAH, I RECKON I DID THE FUCKER. SORRY PIECE A' GNAT SHIT THAT HE WAS.
LOOK AT IT, DASH!
LOOK LONG AND HARD SO YOU'LL NEVER FORGET. SO YOU'LL REMEMBER THIS NIGHT FOR THE REST OF YOUR LIFE...

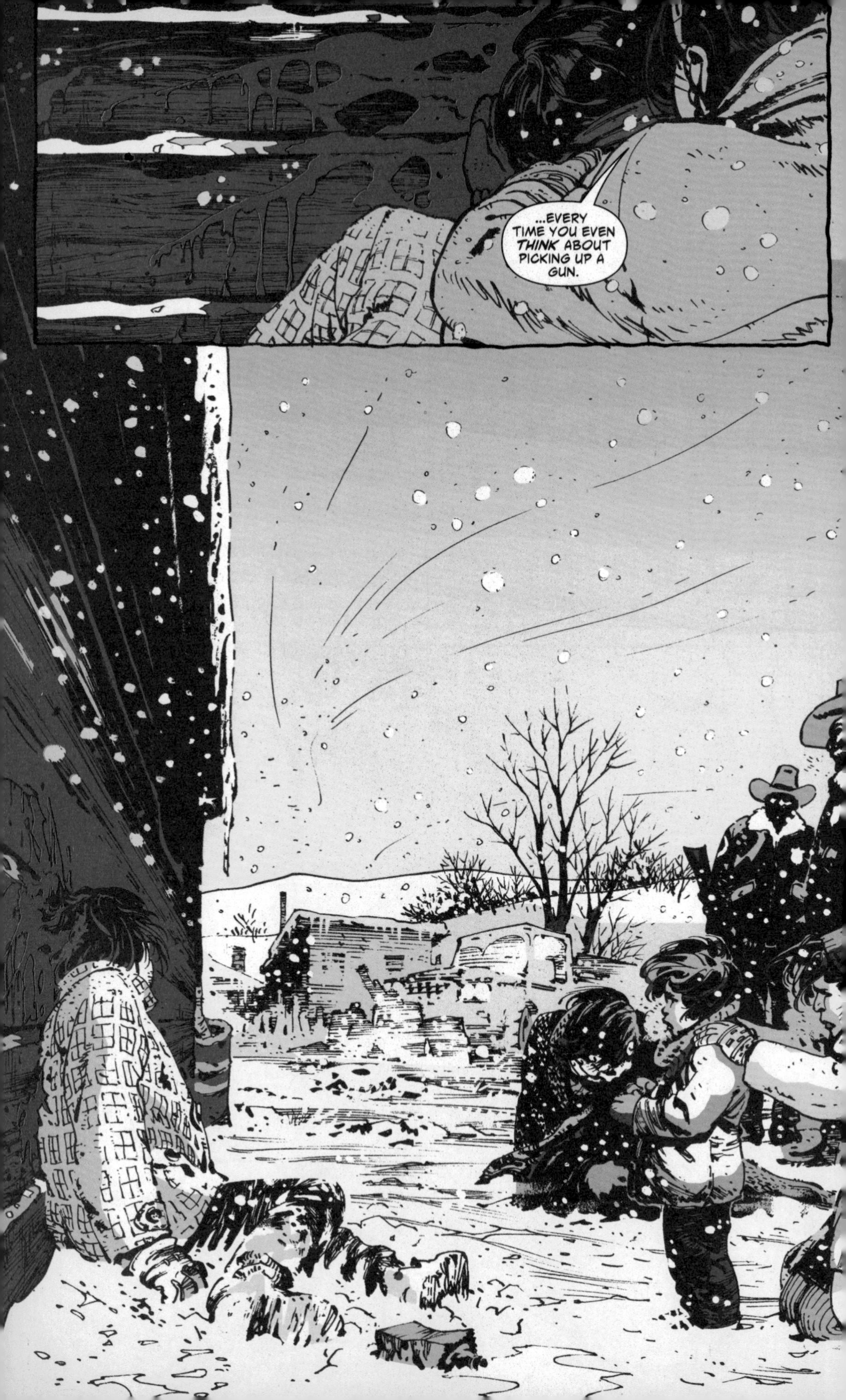
...EVERY TIME YOU EVEN *THINK* ABOUT PICKING UP A GUN.

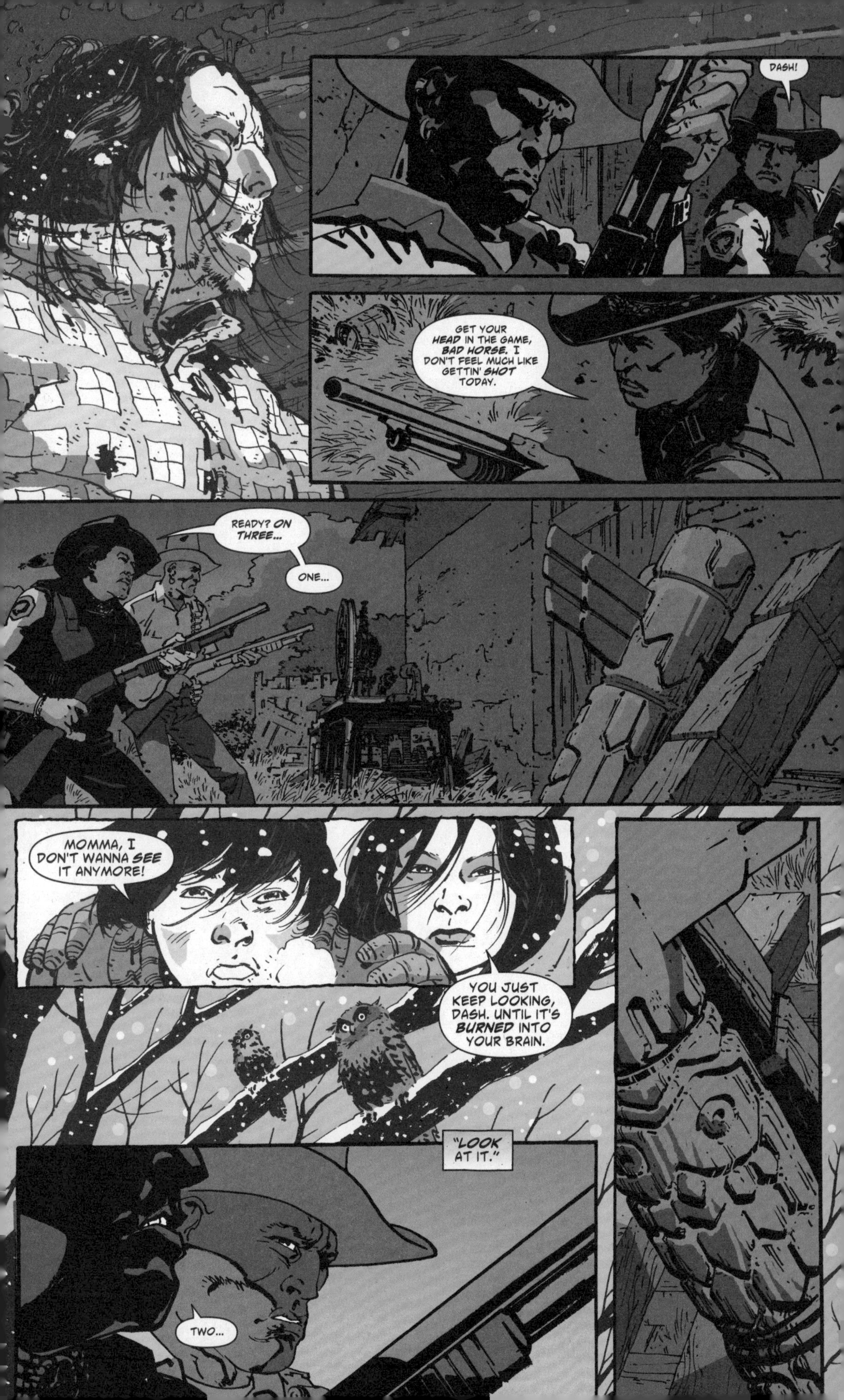
DASH!
GET YOUR HEAD IN THE GAME, BAD HORSE. I DON'T FEEL MUCH LIKE GETTIN' SHOT TODAY.
READY? ON THREE...
ONE...
MOMMA, I DON'T WANNA SEE IT ANYMORE!
YOU JUST KEEP LOOKING, DASH. UNTIL IT'S BURNED INTO YOUR BRAIN.
"LOOK AT IT."
TWO...

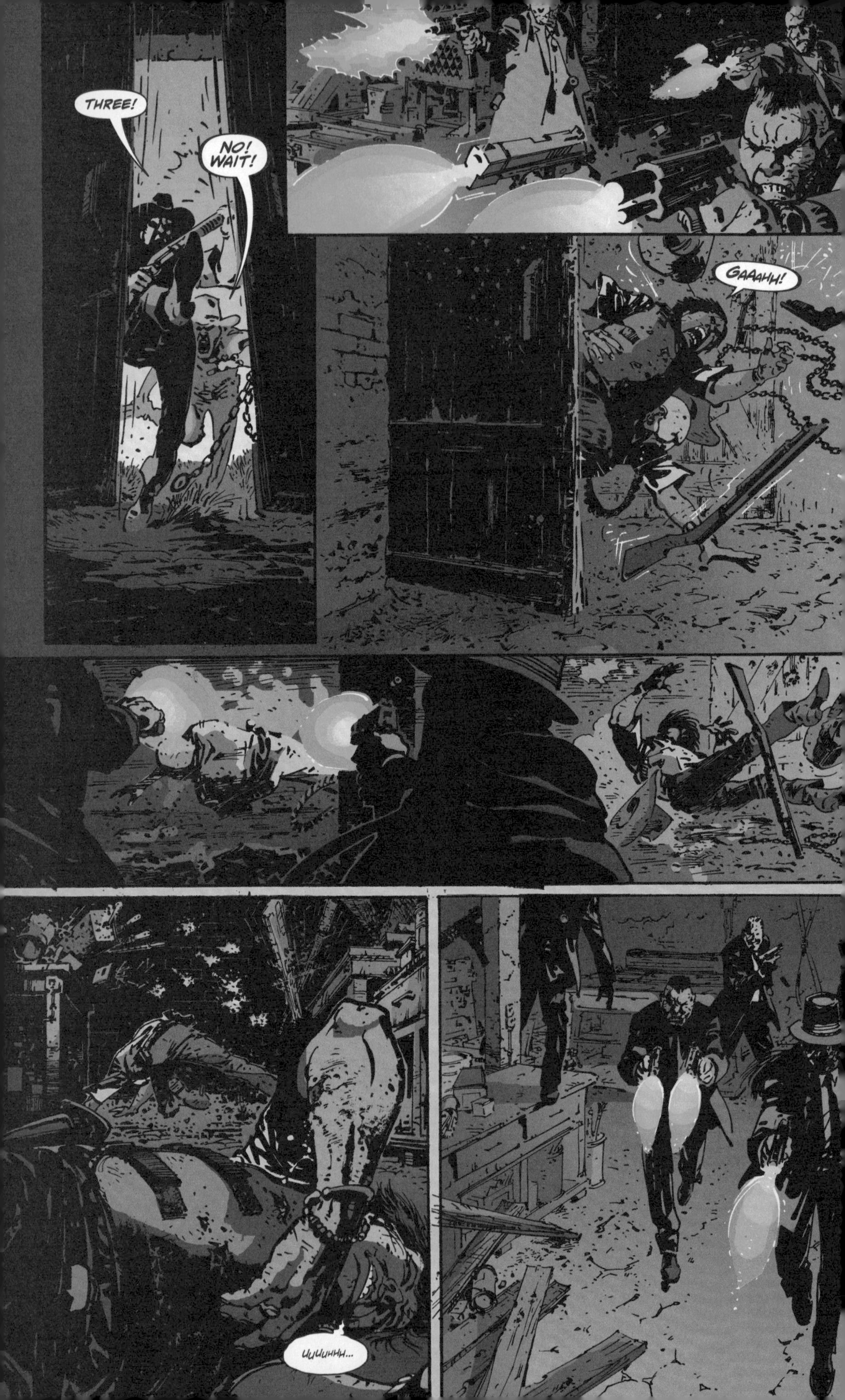
THREE!
NO! WAIT!
GAAAHH!
UUUUHHH...

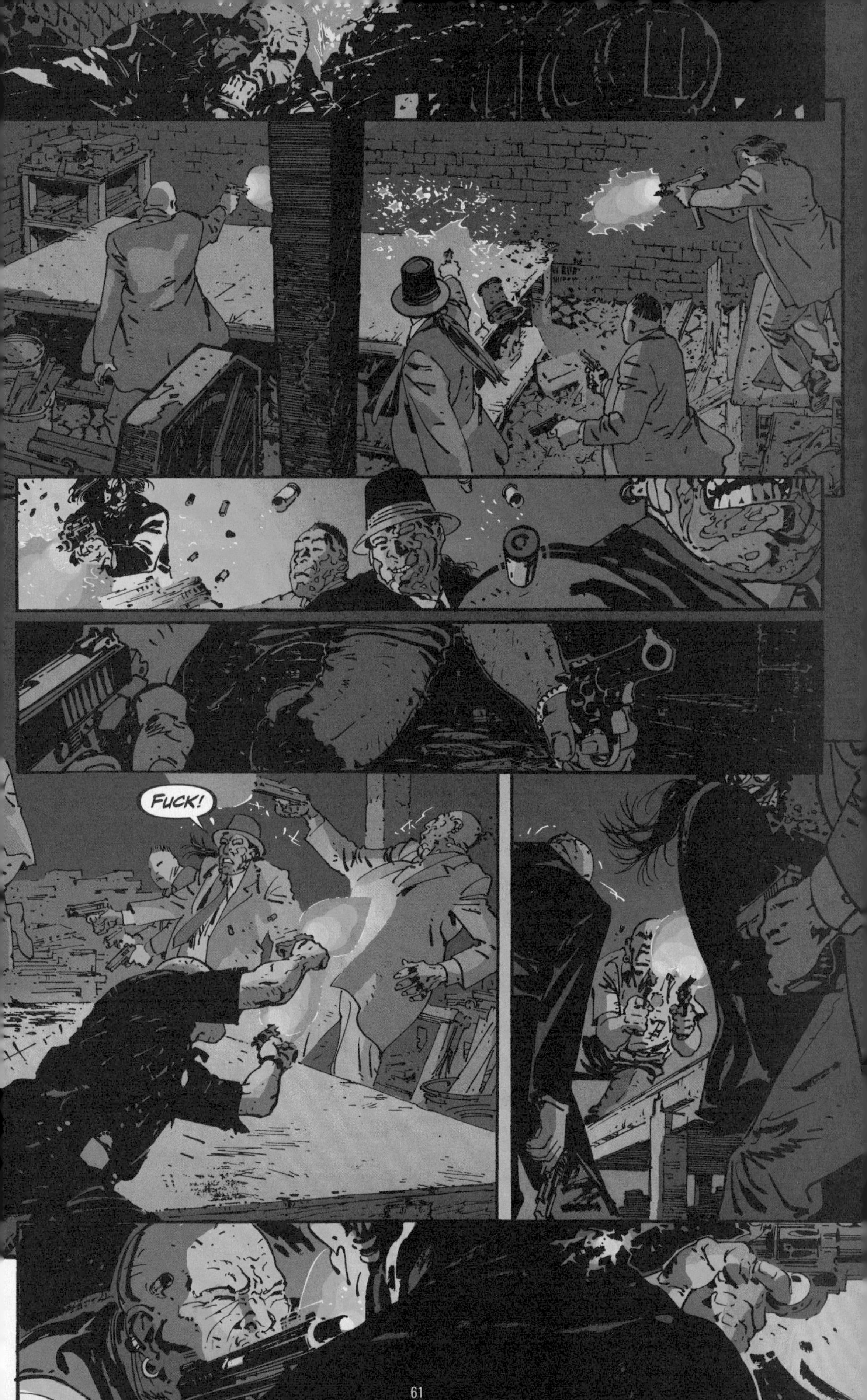
FUCK!

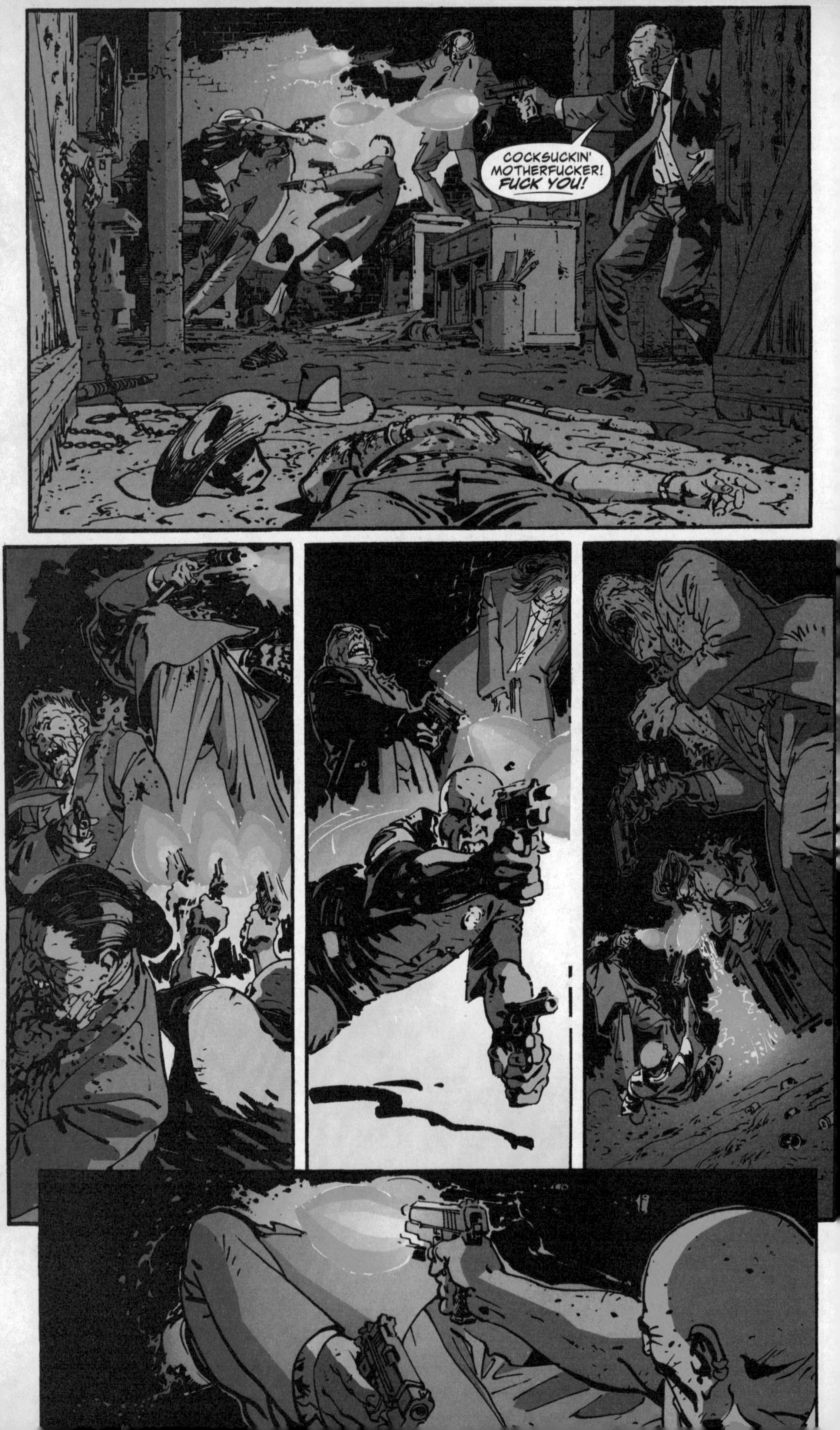
COCKSUCKIN' MOTHERFUCKER! FUCK YOU!

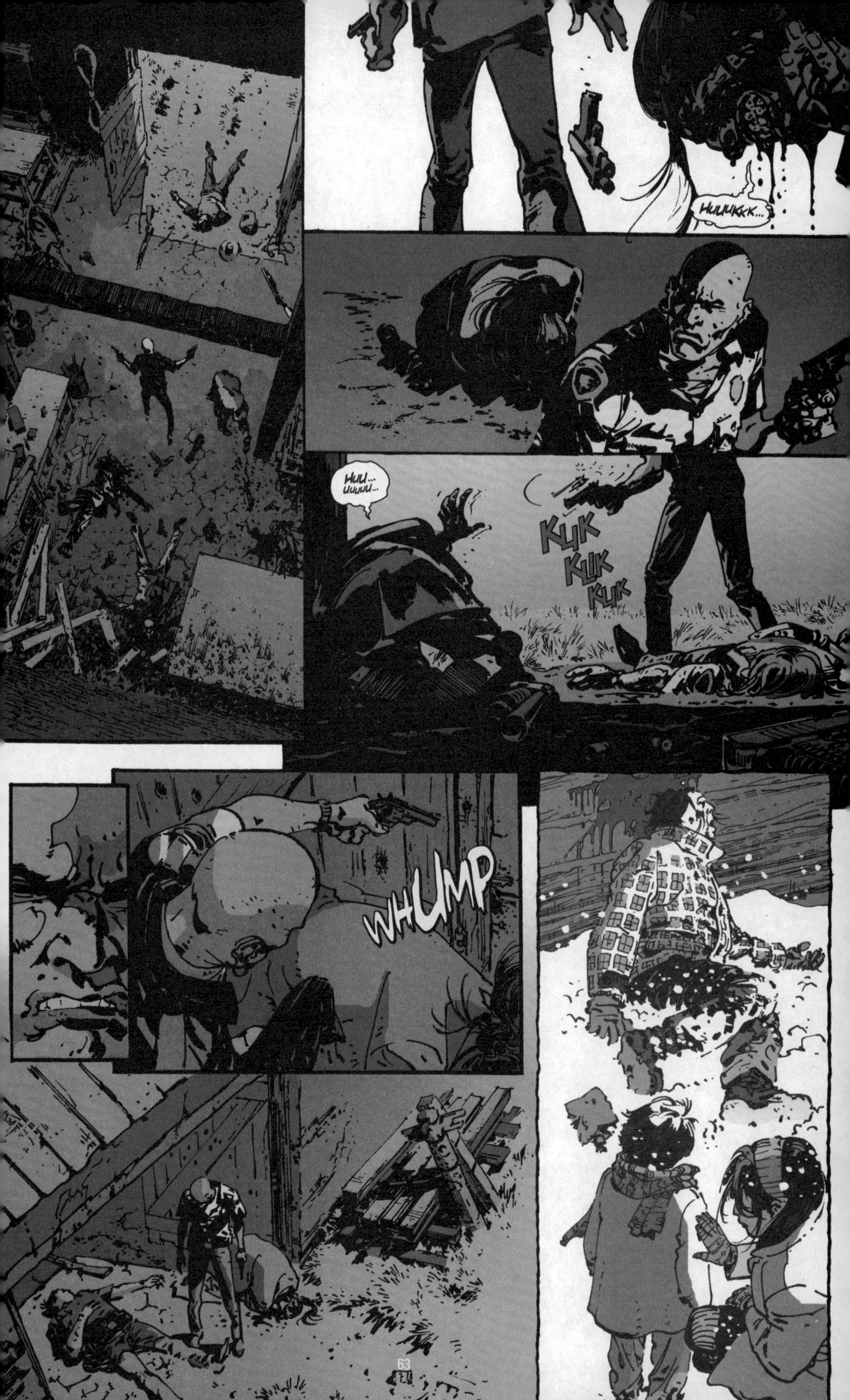
HUUUKKK...
HUU...
UUUUU...
KUK
KUK
KUK
WHUMP

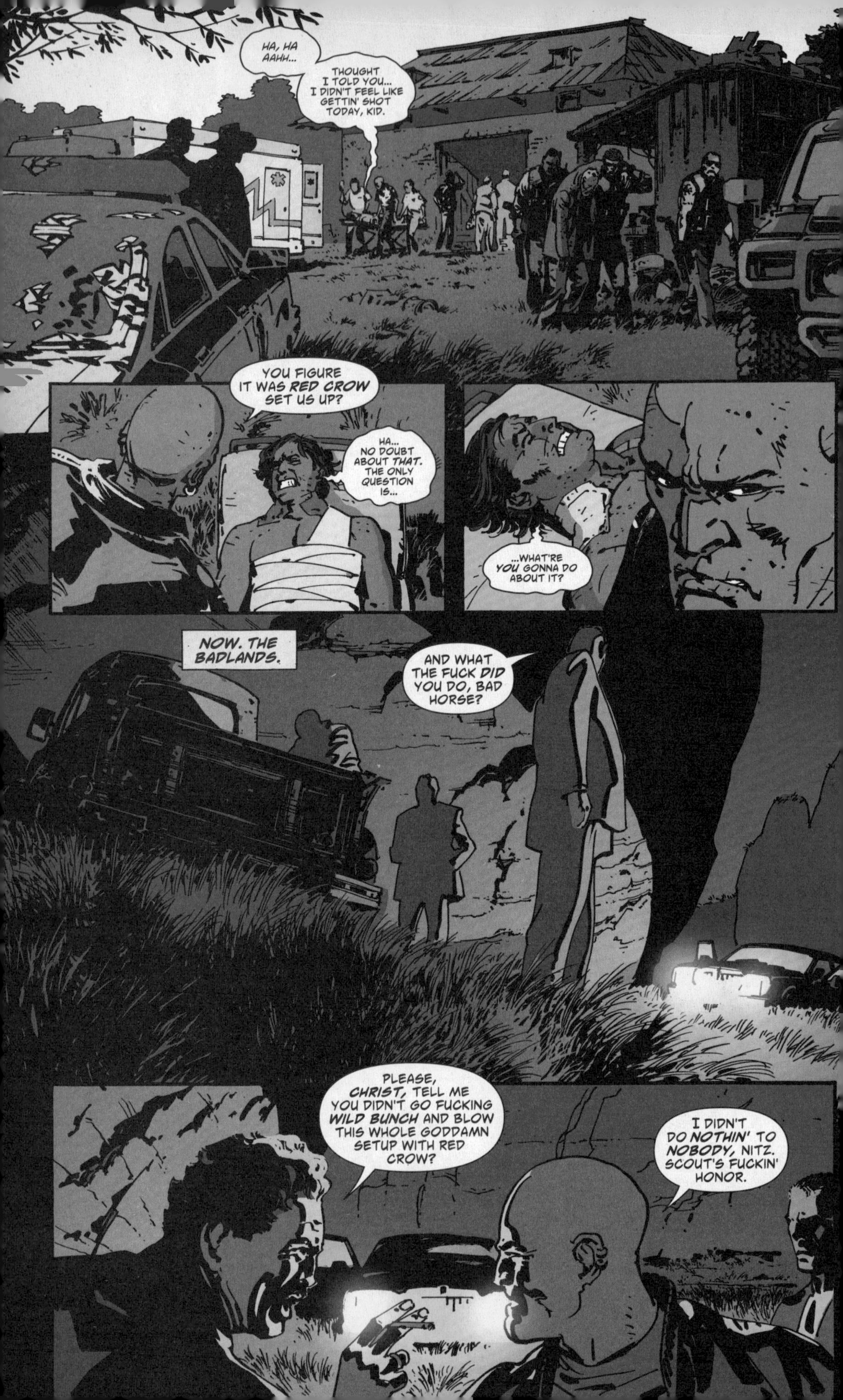
HA, HA AAHH...
THOUGHT I TOLD YOU... I DIDN'T FEEL LIKE GETTIN' SHOT TODAY, KID.
YOU FIGURE IT WAS RED CROW SET US UP?
HA... NO DOUBT ABOUT THAT. THE ONLY QUESTION IS...
...WHAT'RE YOU GONNA DO ABOUT IT?
NOW. THE BADLANDS.
AND WHAT THE FUCK DID YOU DO, BAD HORSE?
PLEASE, CHRIST, TELL ME YOU DIDN'T GO FUCKING WILD BUNCH AND BLOW THIS WHOLE GODDAMN SETUP WITH RED CROW?
I DIDN'T DO NOTHIN' TO NOBODY, NITZ. SCOUT'S FUCKIN' HONOR.

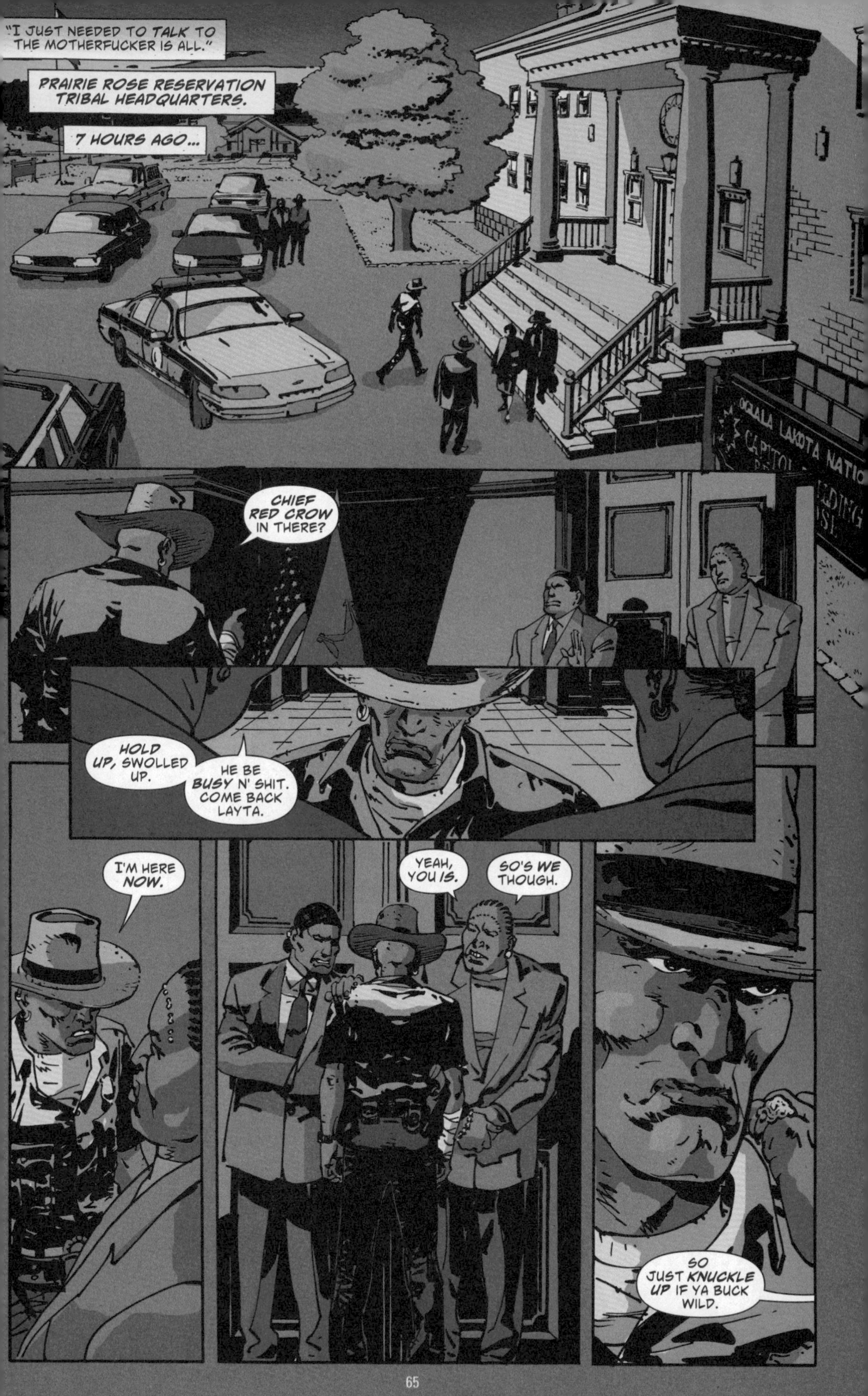
"I JUST NEEDED TO TALK TO THE MOTHERFUCKER IS ALL."
PRAIRIE ROSE RESERVATION TRIBAL HEADQUARTERS.
7 HOURS AGO...
CHIEF RED CROW IN THERE?
HOLD UP, SWOLLED UP.
HE BE BUSY N' SHIT. COME BACK LAYTA.
I'M HERE NOW.
YEAH, YOU IS.
SO'S WE THOUGH.
SO JUST KNUCKLE UP IF YA BUCK WILD.

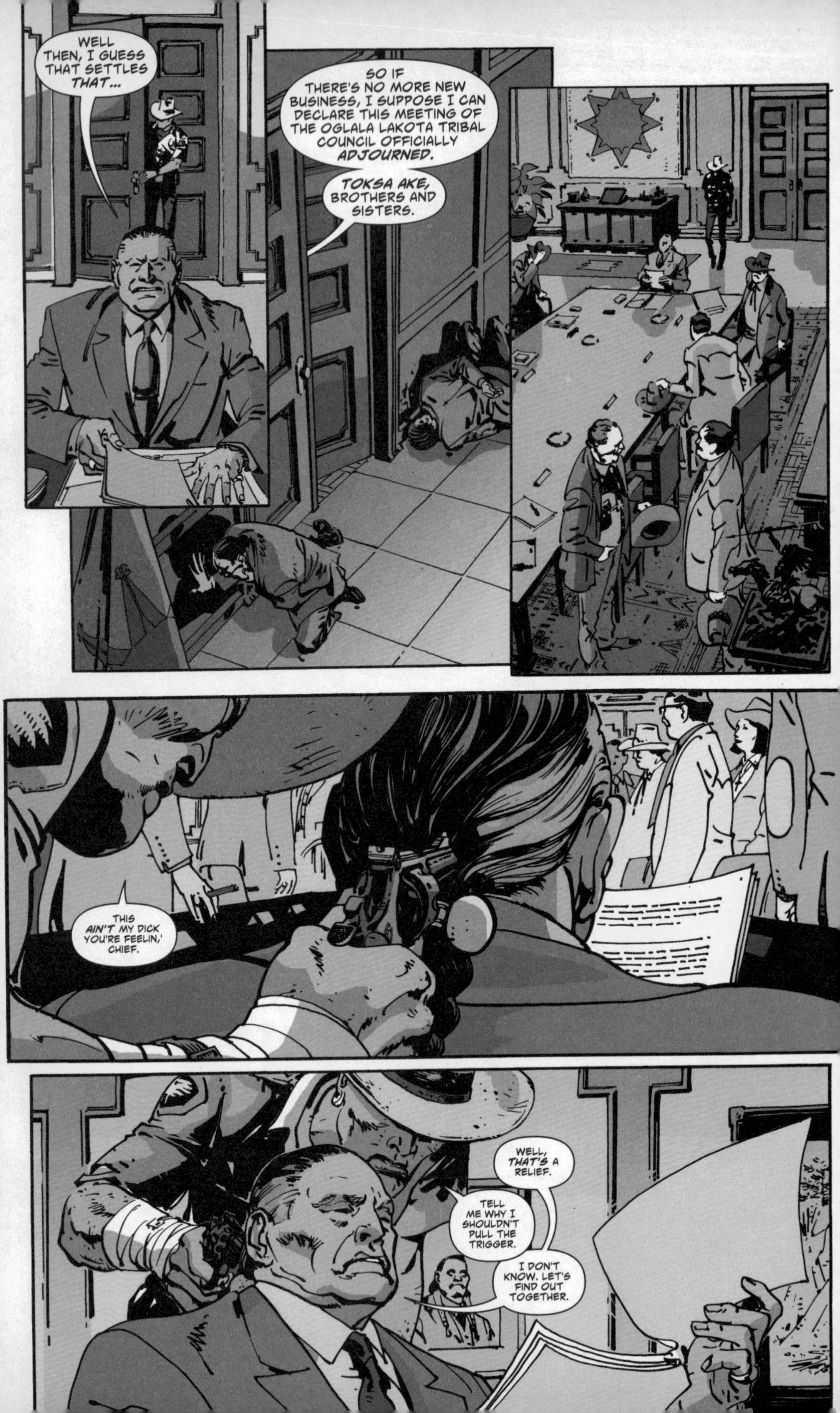
WELL THEN, I GUESS THAT SETTLES THAT...
SO IF THERE'S NO MORE NEW BUSINESS, I SUPPOSE I CAN DECLARE THIS MEETING OF THE OGLALA LAKOTA TRIBAL COUNCIL OFFICIALLY ADJOURNED.
TOKSA AKE, BROTHERS AND SISTERS.
THIS AIN'T MY DICK YOU'RE FEELIN,' CHIEF.
WELL, THAT'S A RELIEF.
TELL ME WHY I SHOULDN'T PULL THE TRIGGER.
I DON'T KNOW. LET'S FIND OUT TOGETHER.

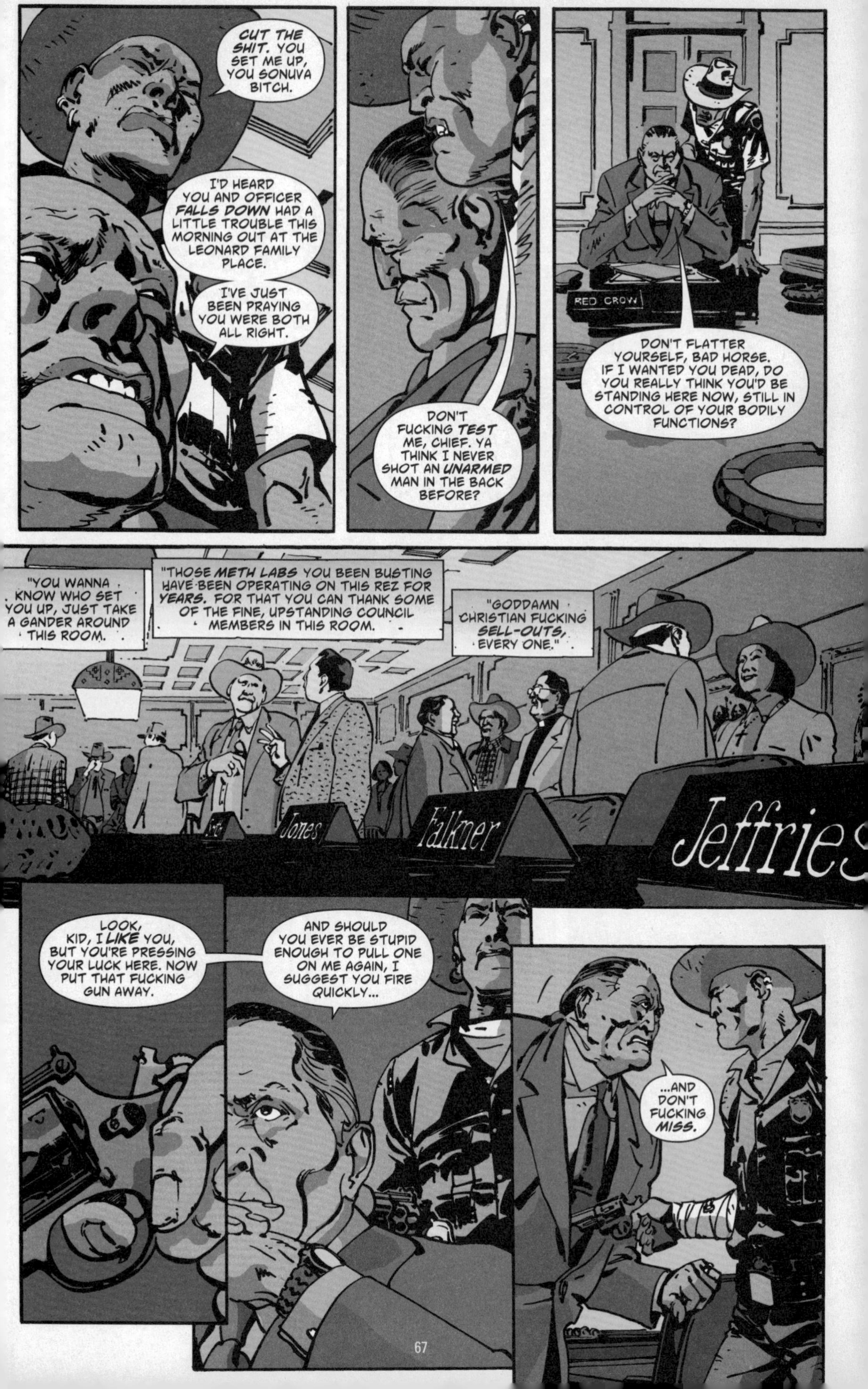
CUT THE SHIT. YOU SET ME UP, YOU SONUVA BITCH.
I'D HEARD YOU AND OFFICER FALLS DOWN HAD A LITTLE TROUBLE THIS MORNING OUT AT THE LEONARD FAMILY PLACE.
I'VE JUST BEEN PRAYING YOU WERE BOTH ALL RIGHT.
DON'T FUCKING TEST ME, CHIEF. YA THINK I NEVER SHOT AN UNARMED MAN IN THE BACK BEFORE?
RED CROW
DON'T FLATTER YOURSELF, BAD HORSE. IF I WANTED YOU DEAD, DO YOU REALLY THINK YOU'D BE STANDING HERE NOW, STILL IN CONTROL OF YOUR BODILY FUNCTIONS?
"YOU WANNA KNOW WHO SET YOU UP, JUST TAKE A GANDER AROUND THIS ROOM.
"THOSE METH LABS YOU BEEN BUSTING HAVE BEEN OPERATING ON THIS REZ FOR YEARS. FOR THAT YOU CAN THANK SOME OF THE FINE, UPSTANDING COUNCIL MEMBERS IN THIS ROOM.
"GODDAMN CHRISTIAN FUCKING SELL-OUTS, EVERY ONE."
Jones
Falkner
Jeffries
LOOK, KID, I LIKE YOU, BUT YOU'RE PRESSING YOUR LUCK HERE. NOW PUT THAT FUCKING GUN AWAY.
AND SHOULD YOU EVER BE STUPID ENOUGH TO PULL ONE ON ME AGAIN, I SUGGEST YOU FIRE QUICKLY...
...AND DON'T FUCKING MISS.

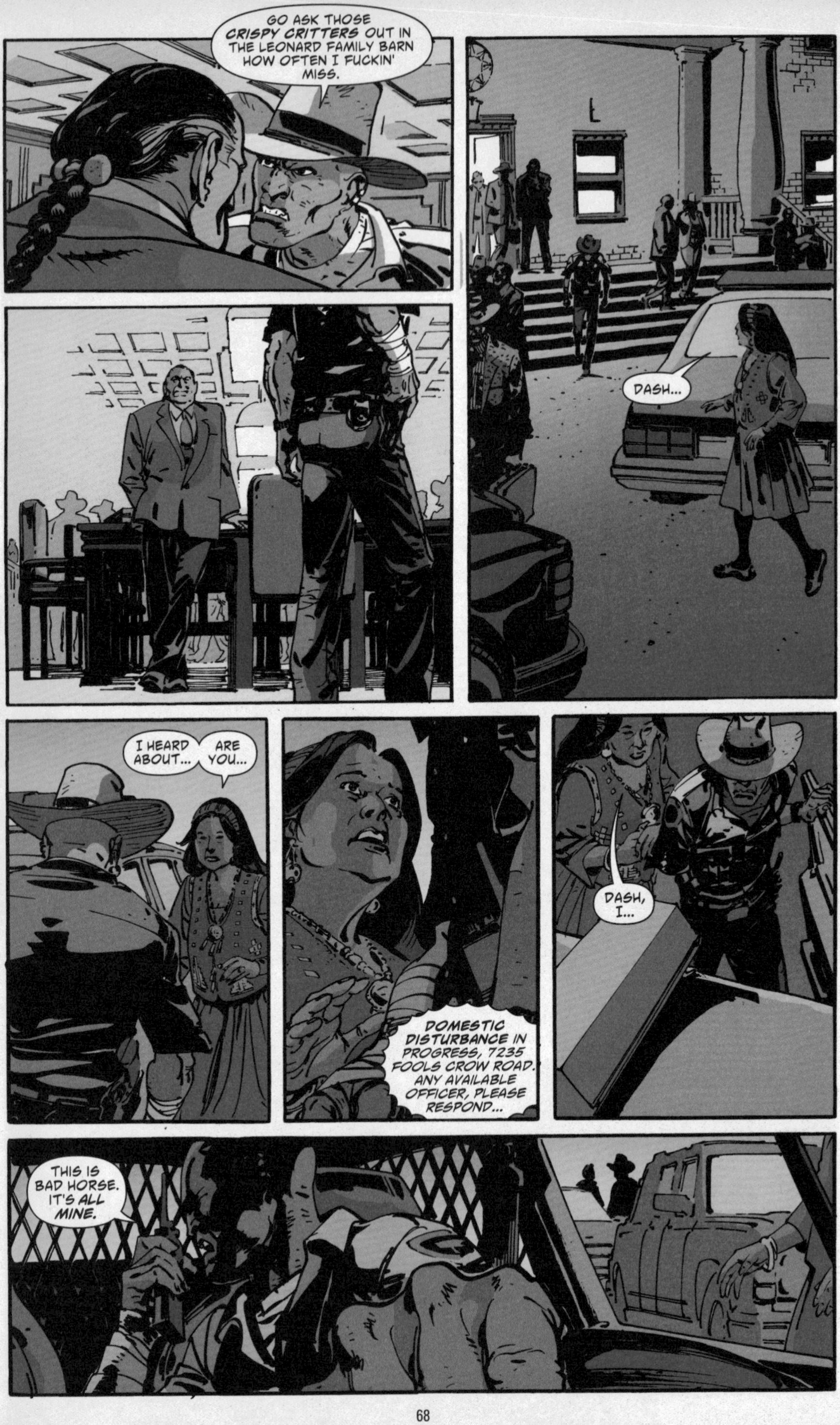
GO ASK THOSE CRISPY CRITTERS OUT IN THE LEONARD FAMILY BARN HOW OFTEN I FUCKIN' MISS.
DASH...
I HEARD ABOUT...
ARE YOU...
DOMESTIC DISTURBANCE IN PROGRESS, 7235 FOOLS CROW ROAD. ANY AVAILABLE OFFICER, PLEASE RESPOND...
DASH, I...
THIS IS BAD HORSE. IT'S ALL MINE.

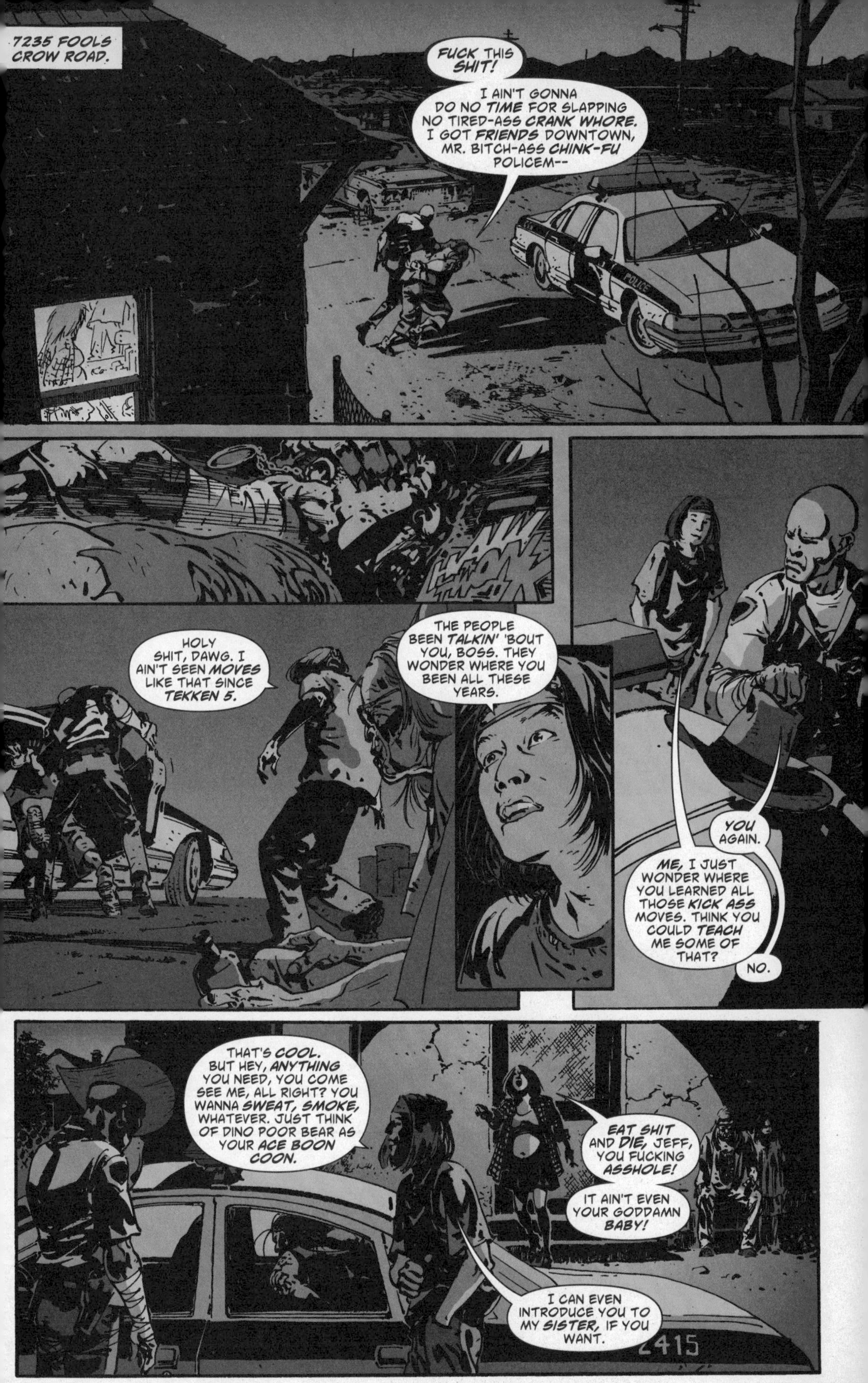
7235 FOOLS CROW ROAD.
FUCK THIS SHIT!
I AIN'T GONNA DO NO TIME FOR SLAPPING NO TIRED-ASS CRANK WHORE. I GOT FRIENDS DOWNTOWN, MR. BITCH-ASS CHINK-FU POLICEM--
POLICE
HOLY SHIT, DAWG. I AIN'T SEEN MOVES LIKE THAT SINCE TEKKEN 5.
THE PEOPLE BEEN TALKIN' 'BOUT YOU, BOSS. THEY WONDER WHERE YOU BEEN ALL THESE YEARS.
YOU AGAIN.
ME, I JUST WONDER WHERE YOU LEARNED ALL THOSE KICK ASS MOVES. THINK YOU COULD TEACH ME SOME OF THAT?
NO.
THAT'S COOL. BUT HEY, ANYTHING YOU NEED, YOU COME SEE ME, ALL RIGHT? YOU WANNA SWEAT, SMOKE, WHATEVER. JUST THINK OF DINO POOR BEAR AS YOUR ACE BOON COON.
EAT SHIT AND DIE, JEFF, YOU FUCKING ASSHOLE!
IT AIN'T EVEN YOUR GODDAMN BABY!
I CAN EVEN INTRODUCE YOU TO MY SISTER, IF YOU WANT.
2415

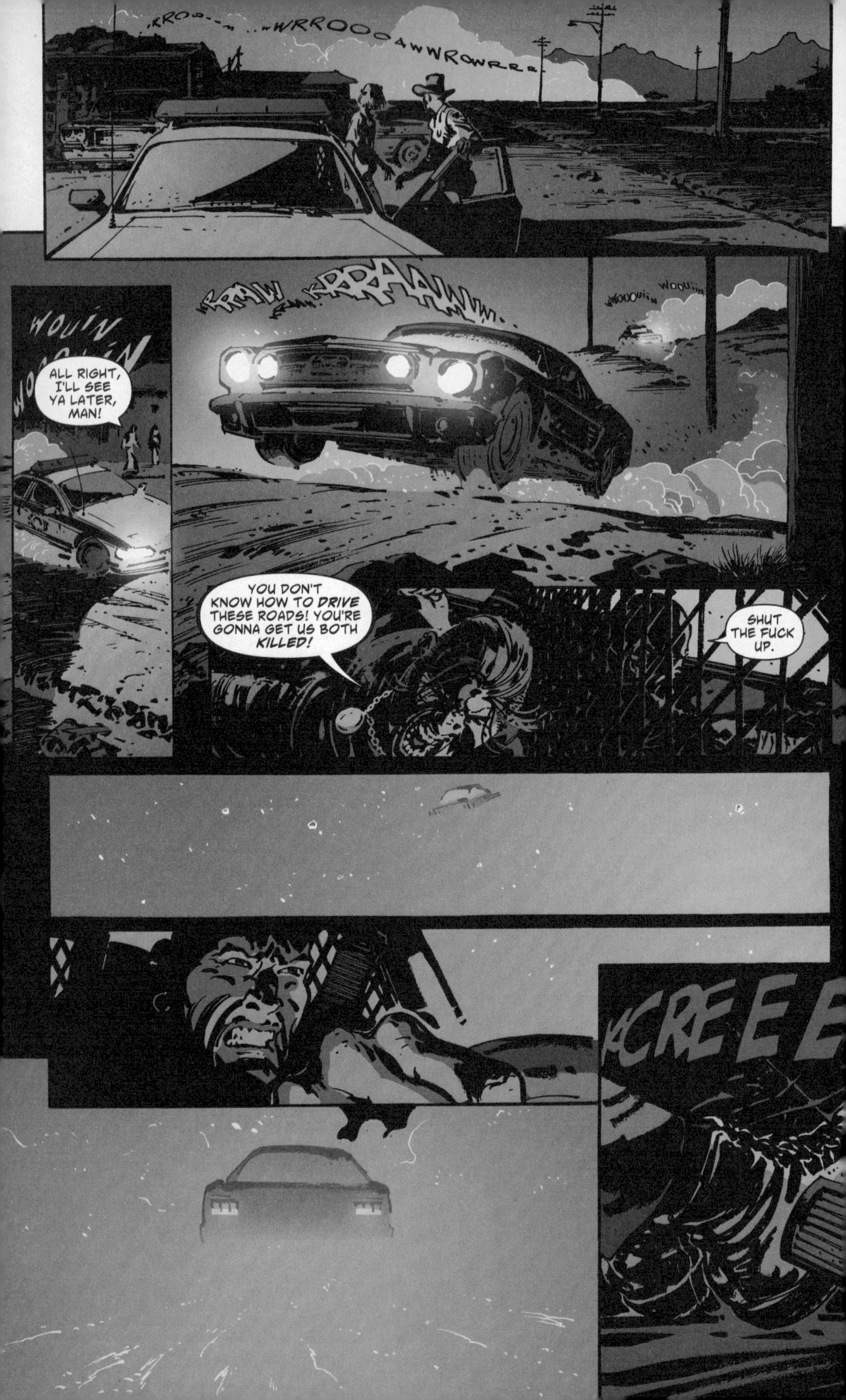
..KROO--.. ..WRROOOOAWWROWRRR..
KRAW KRRAAWWW..
WOOOUII.. WOOUII..
WOUIN WOOOUIN
ALL RIGHT, I'LL SEE YA LATER, MAN!
YOU DON'T KNOW HOW TO DRIVE THESE ROADS! YOU'RE GONNA GET US BOTH KILLED!
SHUT THE FUCK UP.
KCREEE

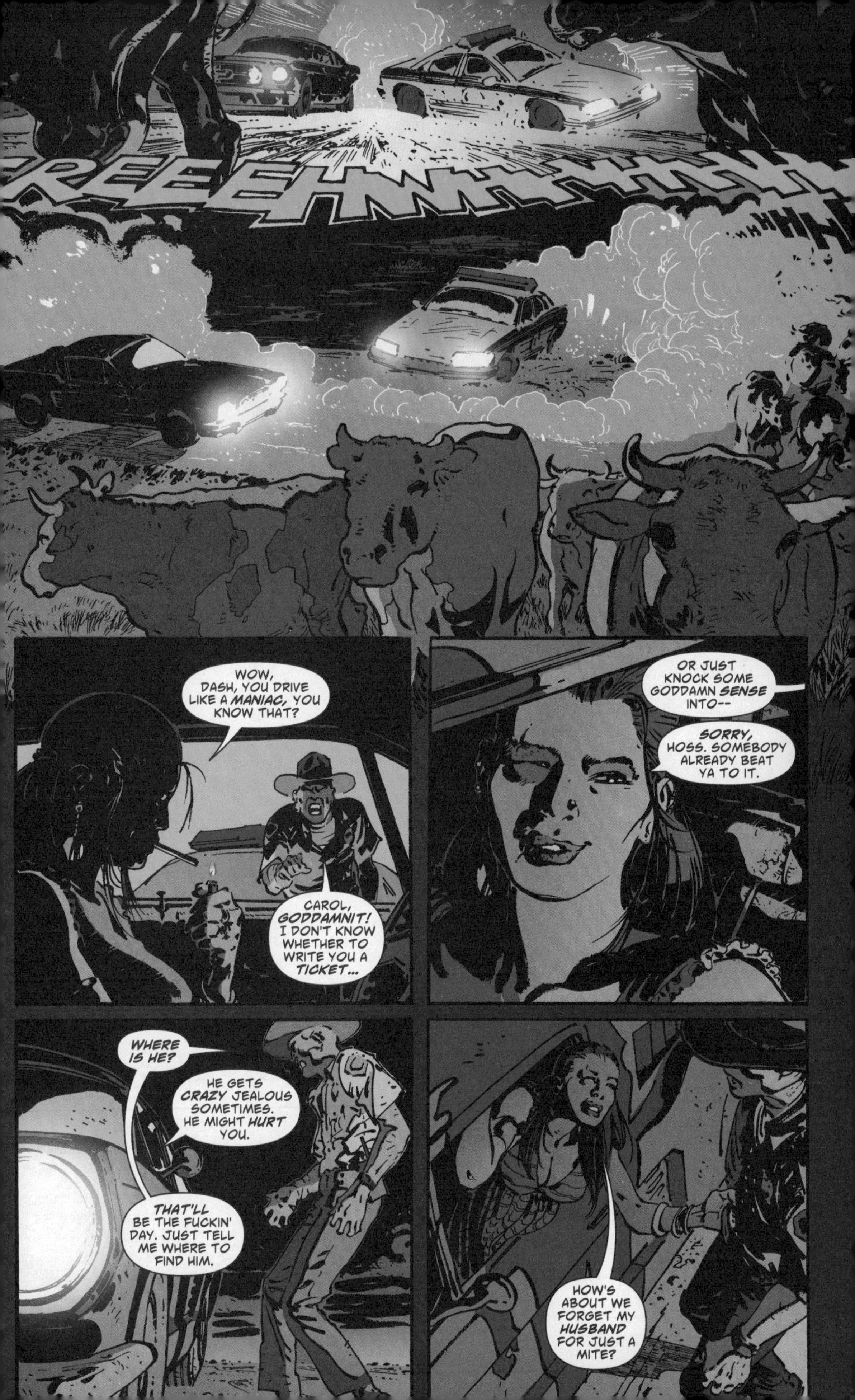
SKREEEEHHHHHHHH
WOW, DASH, YOU DRIVE LIKE A *MANIAC*, YOU KNOW THAT?
CAROL, *GODDAMNIT!* I DON'T KNOW WHETHER TO WRITE YOU A *TICKET...*
OR JUST KNOCK SOME GODDAMN *SENSE* INTO--
SORRY, HOSS. SOMEBODY ALREADY BEAT YA TO IT.
WHERE IS HE?
HE GETS *CRAZY* JEALOUS SOMETIMES. HE MIGHT *HURT* YOU.
THAT'LL BE THE FUCKIN' DAY. JUST TELL ME WHERE TO FIND HIM.
HOW'S ABOUT WE FORGET MY *HUSBAND* FOR JUST A MITE?

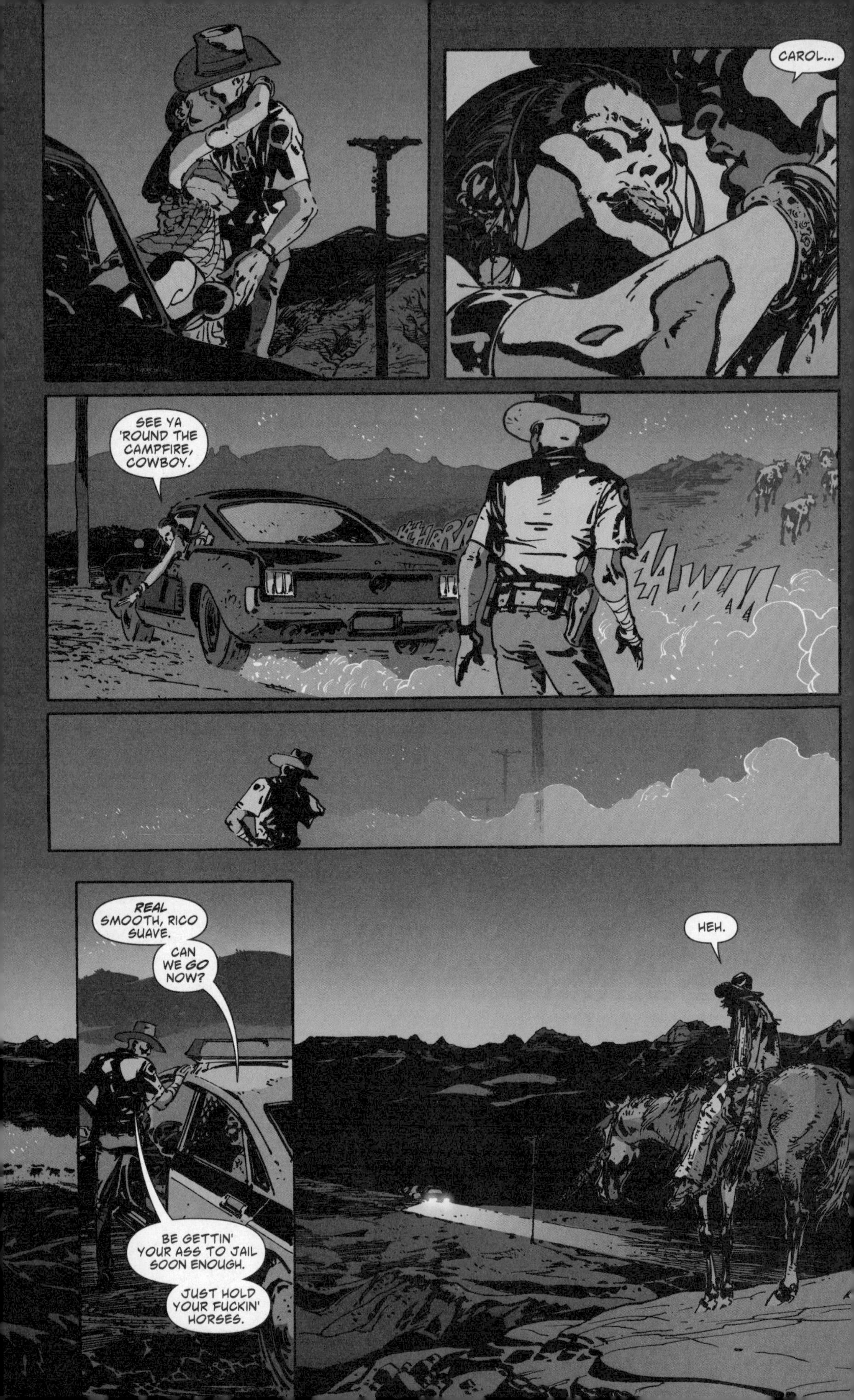
CAROL...
SEE YA 'ROUND THE CAMPFIRE, COWBOY.
WHHRRR
AAWWW AAA
REAL SMOOTH, RICO SUAVE.
CAN WE GO NOW?
HEH.
BE GETTIN' YOUR ASS TO JAIL SOON ENOUGH.
JUST HOLD YOUR FUCKIN' HORSES.

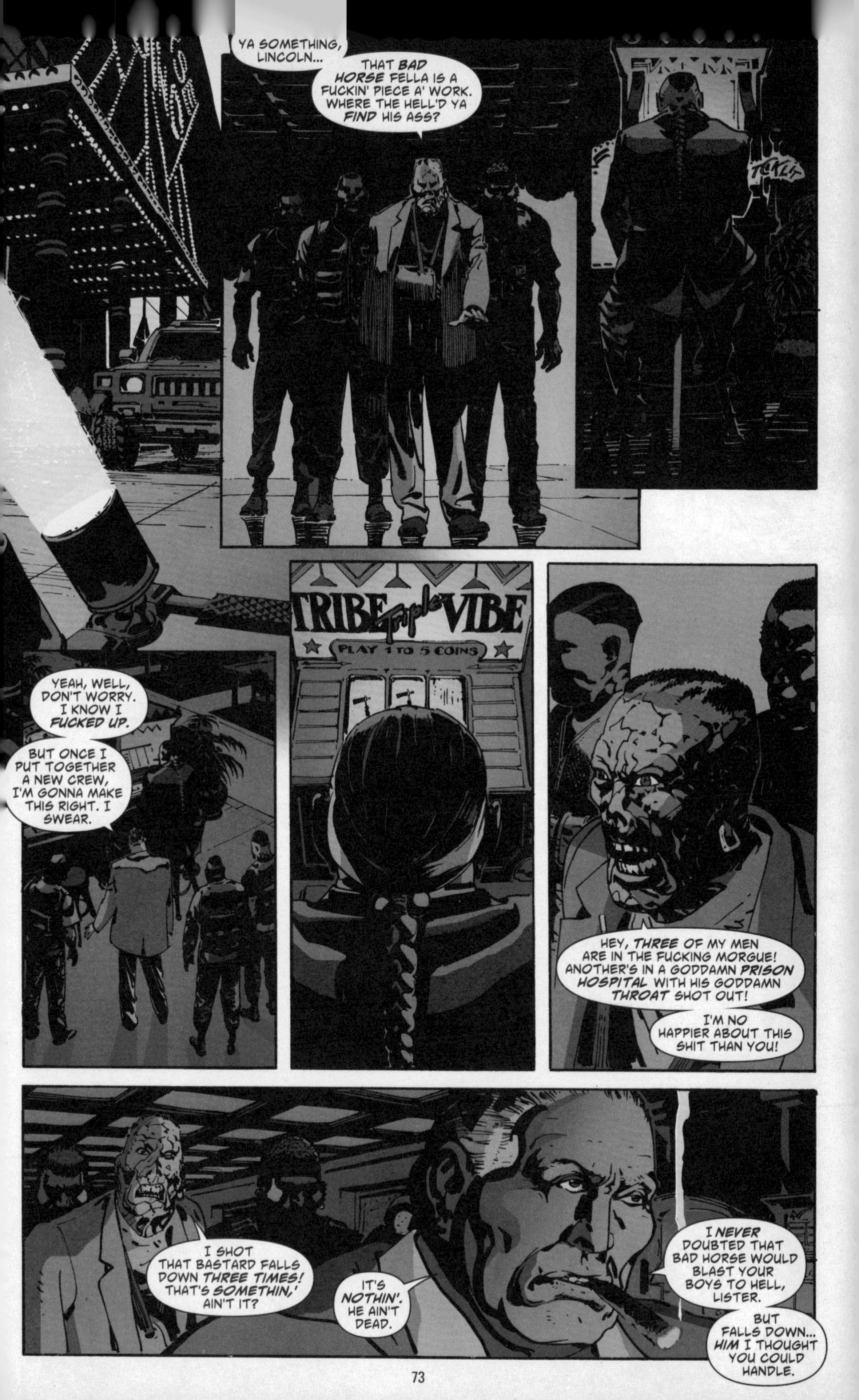
YA SOMETHING, LINCOLN...
THAT BAD HORSE FELLA IS A FUCKIN' PIECE A' WORK. WHERE THE HELL'D YA FIND HIS ASS?
TRIBE triple VIBE
PLAY 1 TO 5 COINS
YEAH, WELL, DON'T WORRY. I KNOW I FUCKED UP.
BUT ONCE I PUT TOGETHER A NEW CREW, I'M GONNA MAKE THIS RIGHT. I SWEAR.
HEY, THREE OF MY MEN ARE IN THE FUCKING MORGUE! ANOTHER'S IN A GODDAMN PRISON HOSPITAL WITH HIS GODDAMN THROAT SHOT OUT!
I'M NO HAPPIER ABOUT THIS SHIT THAN YOU!
I SHOT THAT BASTARD FALLS DOWN THREE TIMES! THAT'S SOMETHIN,' AIN'T IT?
IT'S NOTHIN'. HE AIN'T DEAD.
I NEVER DOUBTED THAT BAD HORSE WOULD BLAST YOUR BOYS TO HELL, LISTER.
BUT FALLS DOWN... HIM I THOUGHT YOU COULD HANDLE.

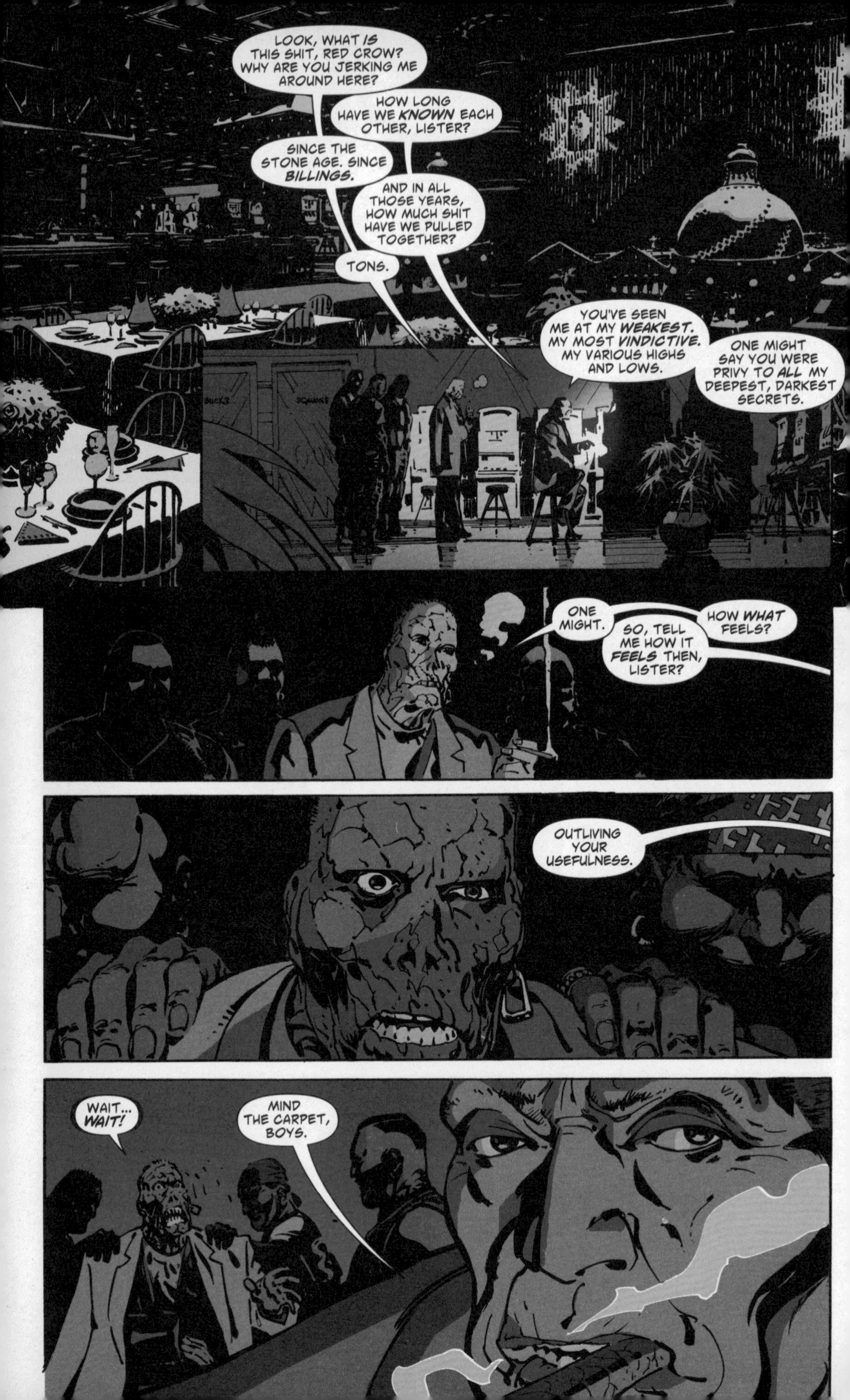
LOOK, WHAT IS THIS SHIT, RED CROW? WHY ARE YOU JERKING ME AROUND HERE?
HOW LONG HAVE WE KNOWN EACH OTHER, LISTER?
SINCE THE STONE AGE. SINCE BILLINGS.
AND IN ALL THOSE YEARS, HOW MUCH SHIT HAVE WE PULLED TOGETHER?
TONS.
YOU'VE SEEN ME AT MY WEAKEST. MY MOST VINDICTIVE. MY VARIOUS HIGHS AND LOWS.
ONE MIGHT SAY YOU WERE PRIVY TO ALL MY DEEPEST, DARKEST SECRETS.
ONE MIGHT.
SO, TELL ME HOW IT FEELS THEN, LISTER?
HOW WHAT FEELS?
OUTLIVING YOUR USEFULNESS.
WAIT... WAIT!
MIND THE CARPET, BOYS.

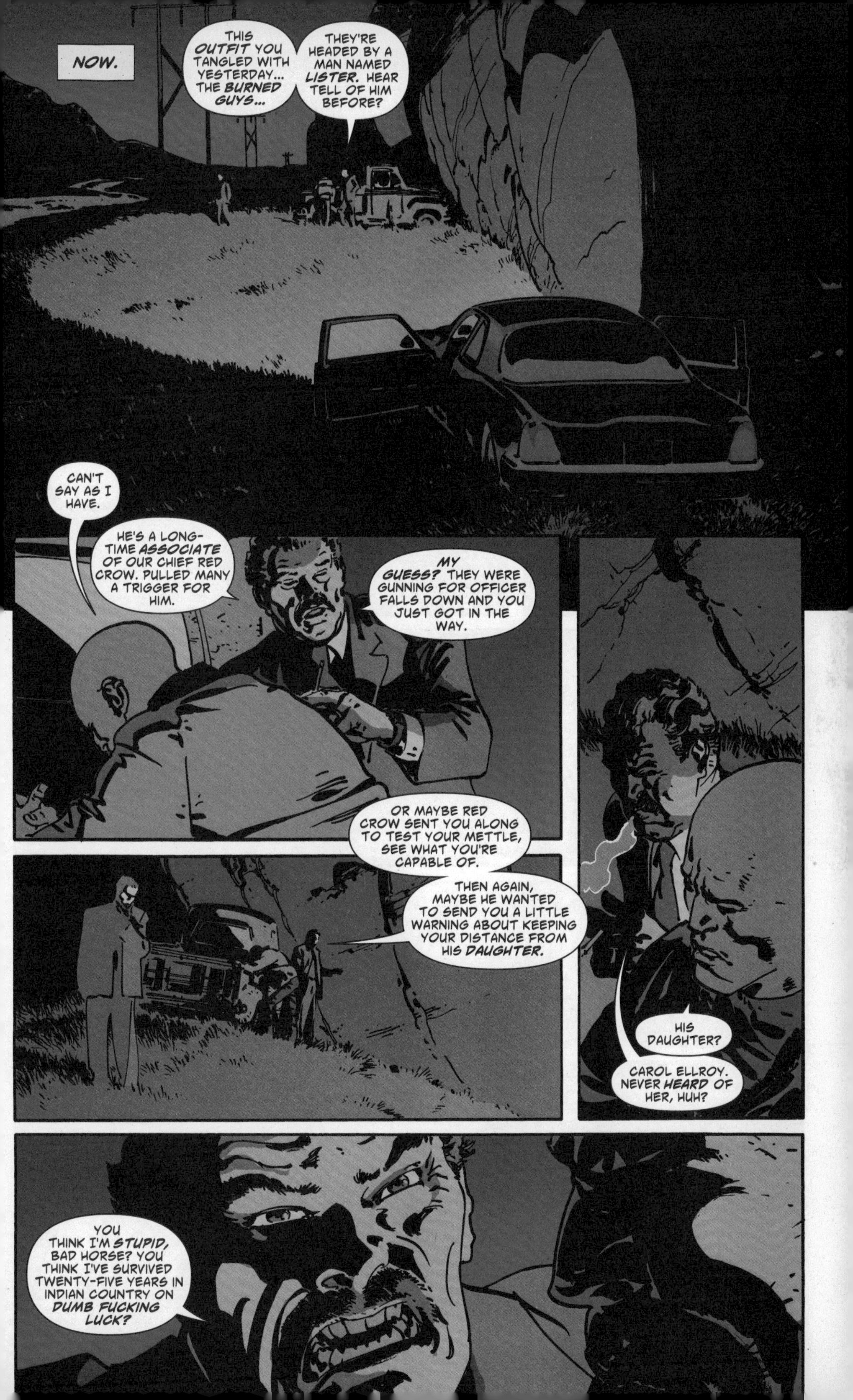
NOW.
THIS OUTFIT YOU TANGLED WITH YESTERDAY... THE BURNED GUYS...
THEY'RE HEADED BY A MAN NAMED LISTER. HEAR TELL OF HIM BEFORE?
CAN'T SAY AS I HAVE.
HE'S A LONG-TIME ASSOCIATE OF OUR CHIEF RED CROW. PULLED MANY A TRIGGER FOR HIM.
MY GUESS? THEY WERE GUNNING FOR OFFICER FALLS DOWN AND YOU JUST GOT IN THE WAY.
OR MAYBE RED CROW SENT YOU ALONG TO TEST YOUR METTLE, SEE WHAT YOU'RE CAPABLE OF.
THEN AGAIN, MAYBE HE WANTED TO SEND YOU A LITTLE WARNING ABOUT KEEPING YOUR DISTANCE FROM HIS DAUGHTER.
HIS DAUGHTER?
CAROL ELLROY. NEVER HEARD OF HER, HUH?
YOU THINK I'M STUPID, BAD HORSE? YOU THINK I'VE SURVIVED TWENTY-FIVE YEARS IN INDIAN COUNTRY ON DUMB FUCKING LUCK?

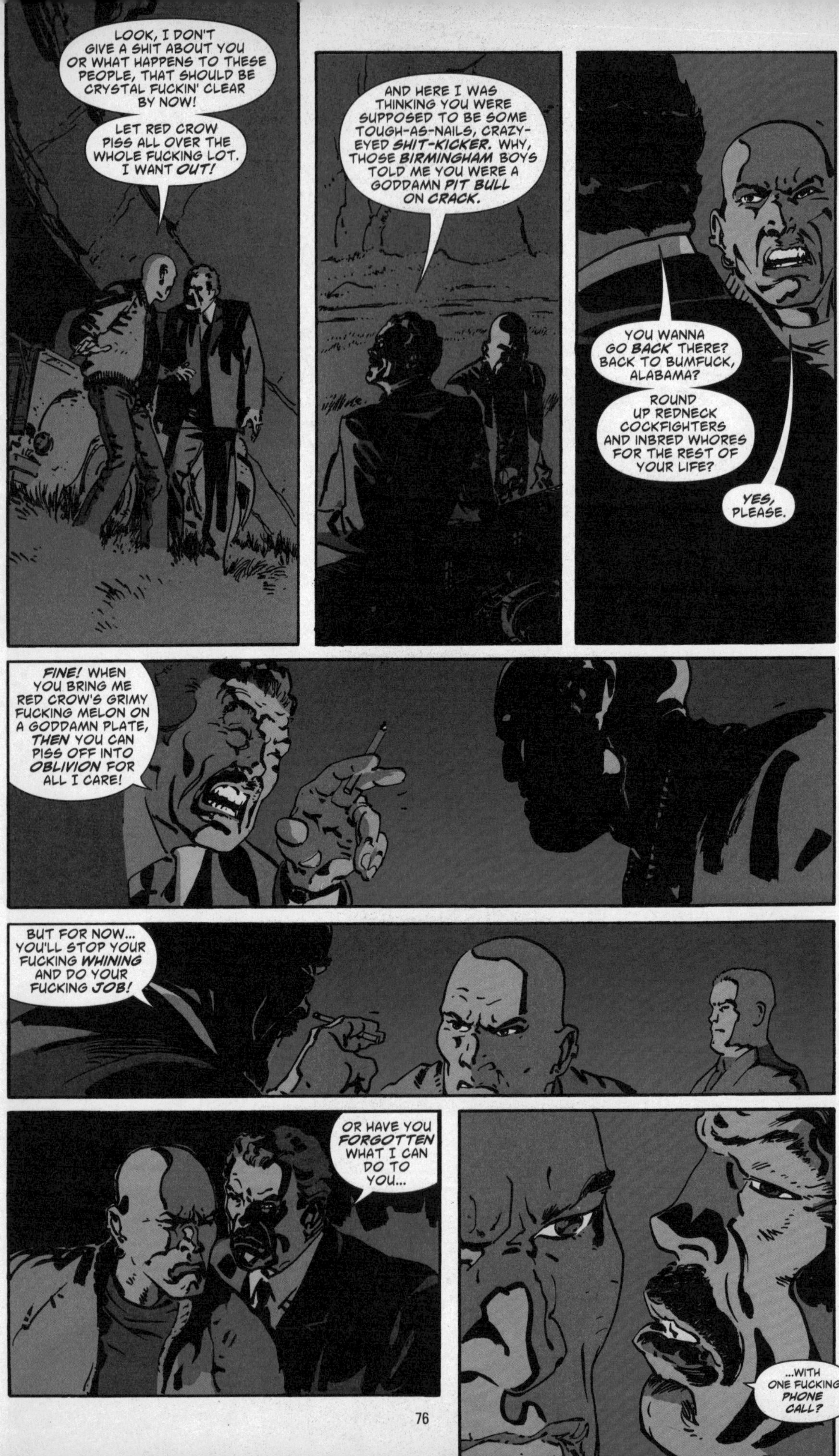
LOOK, I DON'T GIVE A SHIT ABOUT YOU OR WHAT HAPPENS TO THESE PEOPLE, THAT SHOULD BE CRYSTAL FUCKIN' CLEAR BY NOW!
LET RED CROW PISS ALL OVER THE WHOLE FUCKING LOT. I WANT OUT!
AND HERE I WAS THINKING YOU WERE SUPPOSED TO BE SOME TOUGH-AS-NAILS, CRAZY-EYED SHIT-KICKER. WHY, THOSE BIRMINGHAM BOYS TOLD ME YOU WERE A GODDAMN PIT BULL ON CRACK.
YOU WANNA GO BACK THERE? BACK TO BUMFUCK, ALABAMA?
ROUND UP REDNECK COCKFIGHTERS AND INBRED WHORES FOR THE REST OF YOUR LIFE?
YES, PLEASE.
FINE! WHEN YOU BRING ME RED CROW'S GRIMY FUCKING MELON ON A GODDAMN PLATE, THEN YOU CAN PISS OFF INTO OBLIVION FOR ALL I CARE!
BUT FOR NOW... YOU'LL STOP YOUR FUCKING WHINING AND DO YOUR FUCKING JOB!
OR HAVE YOU FORGOTTEN WHAT I CAN DO TO YOU...
...WITH ONE FUCKING PHONE CALL?

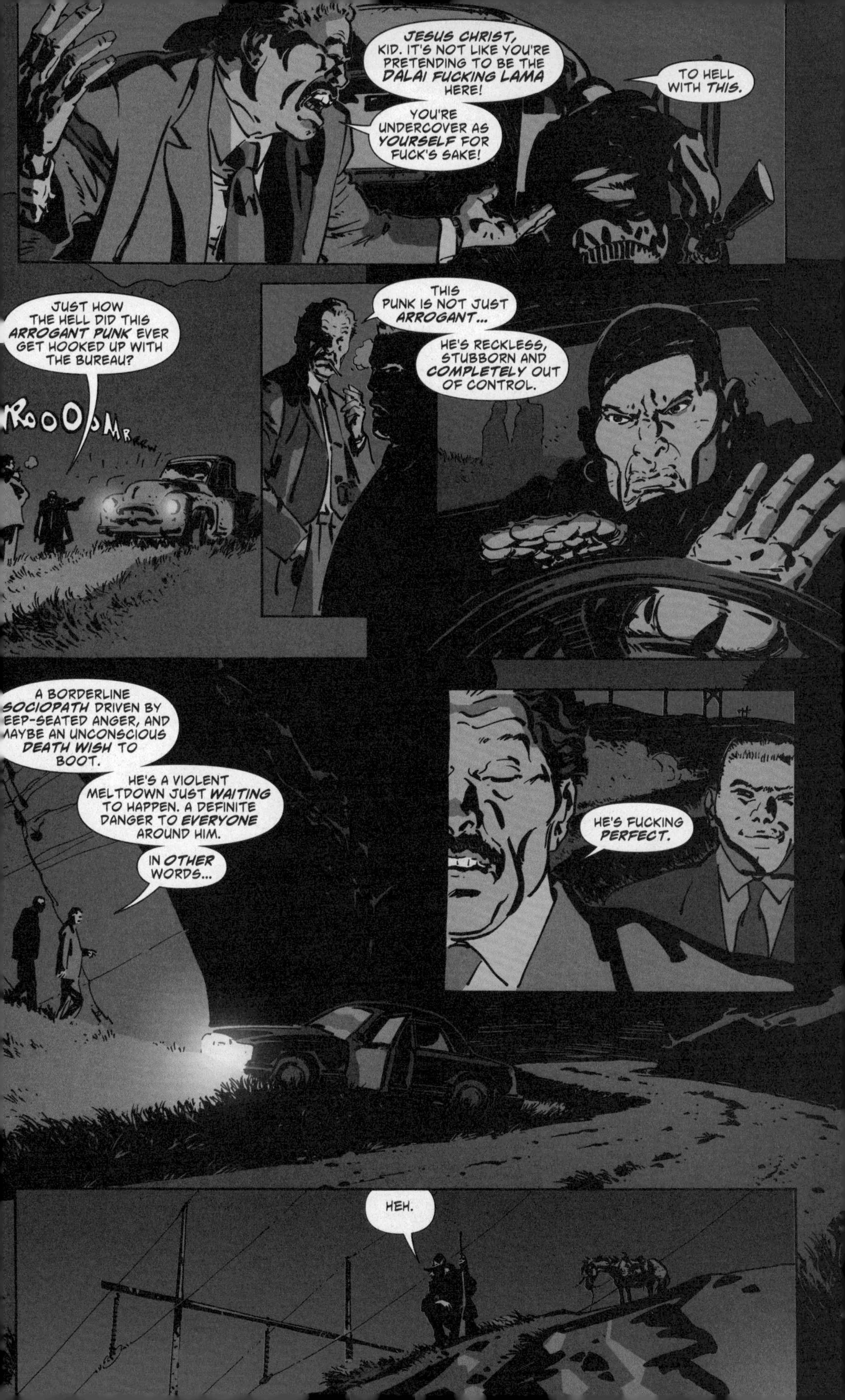
JESUS CHRIST, KID. IT'S NOT LIKE YOU'RE PRETENDING TO BE THE DALAI FUCKING LAMA HERE!
YOU'RE UNDERCOVER AS YOURSELF FOR FUCK'S SAKE!
TO HELL WITH THIS.
JUST HOW THE HELL DID THIS ARROGANT PUNK EVER GET HOOKED UP WITH THE BUREAU?
THIS PUNK IS NOT JUST ARROGANT...
HE'S RECKLESS, STUBBORN AND COMPLETELY OUT OF CONTROL.
A BORDERLINE SOCIOPATH DRIVEN BY EEP-SEATED ANGER, AND AYBE AN UNCONSCIOUS DEATH WISH TO BOOT.
HE'S A VIOLENT MELTDOWN JUST WAITING TO HAPPEN. A DEFINITE DANGER TO EVERYONE AROUND HIM.
IN OTHER WORDS...
HE'S FUCKING PERFECT.
HEH.

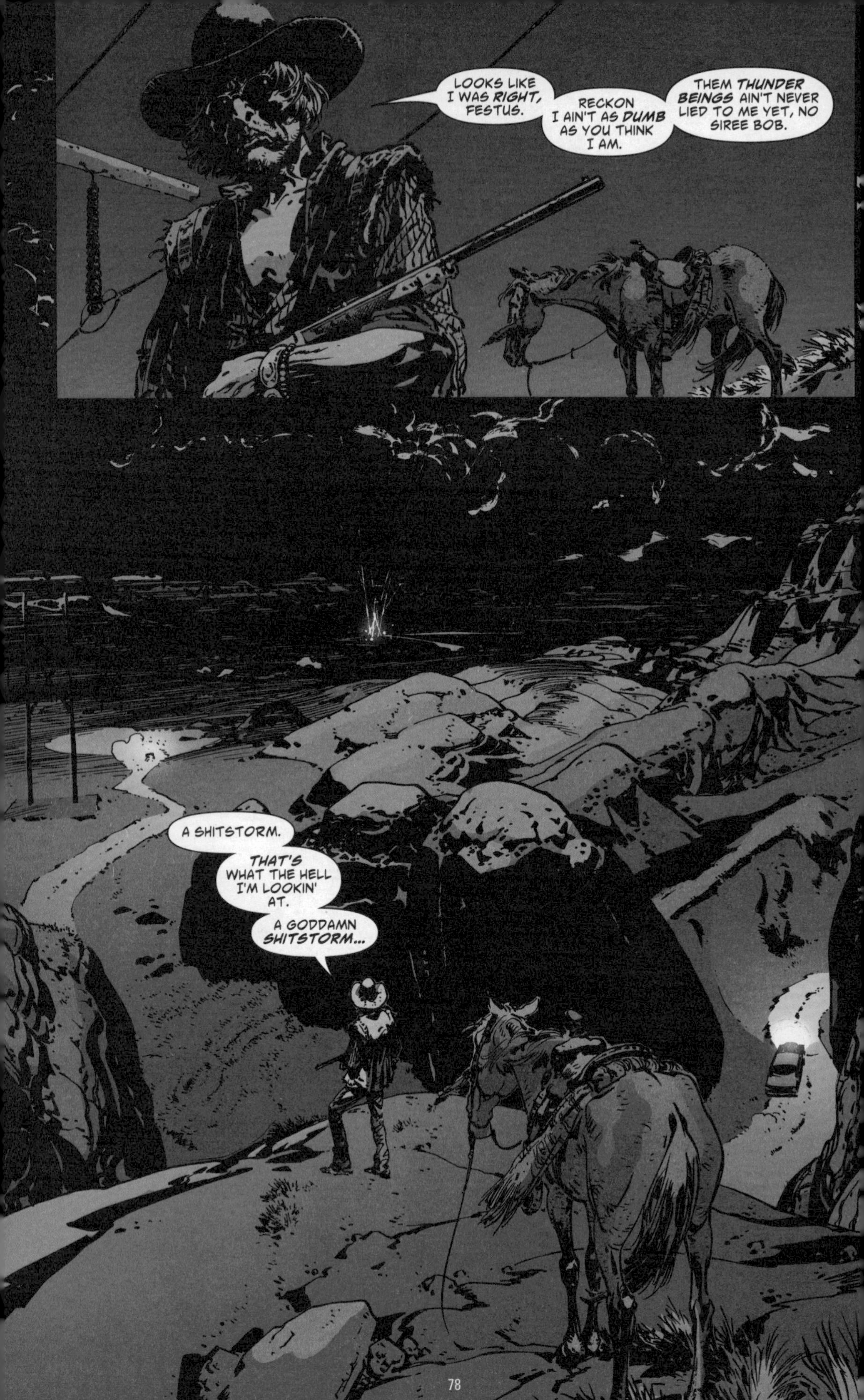
LOOKS LIKE I WAS RIGHT, FESTUS.
RECKON I AIN'T AS DUMB AS YOU THINK I AM.
THEM THUNDER BEINGS AIN'T NEVER LIED TO ME YET, NO SIREE BOB.
A SHITSTORM.
THAT'S WHAT THE HELL I'M LOOKIN' AT.
A GODDAMN SHITSTORM...

HOKA HEY
CHAPTER ONE

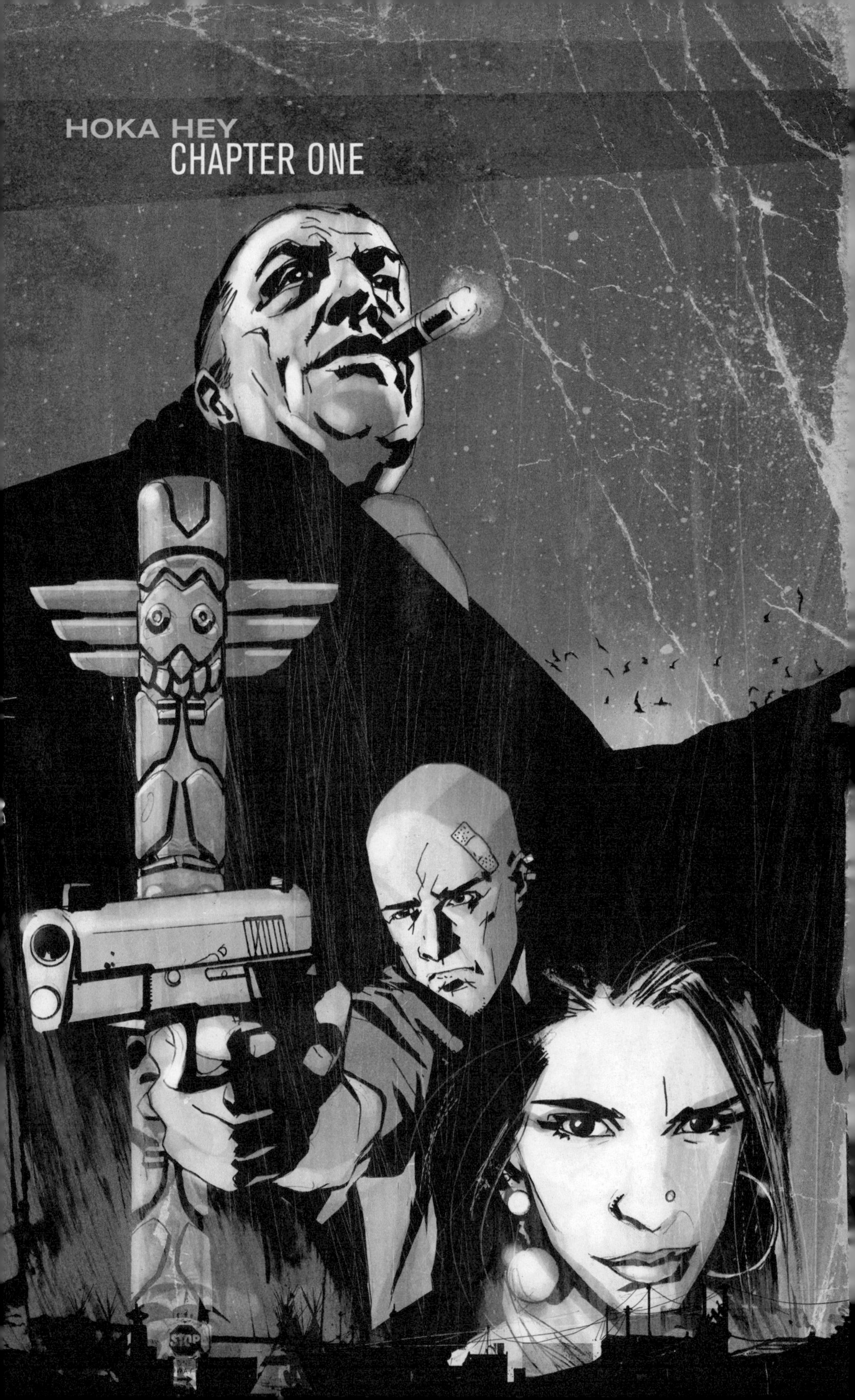
STOP

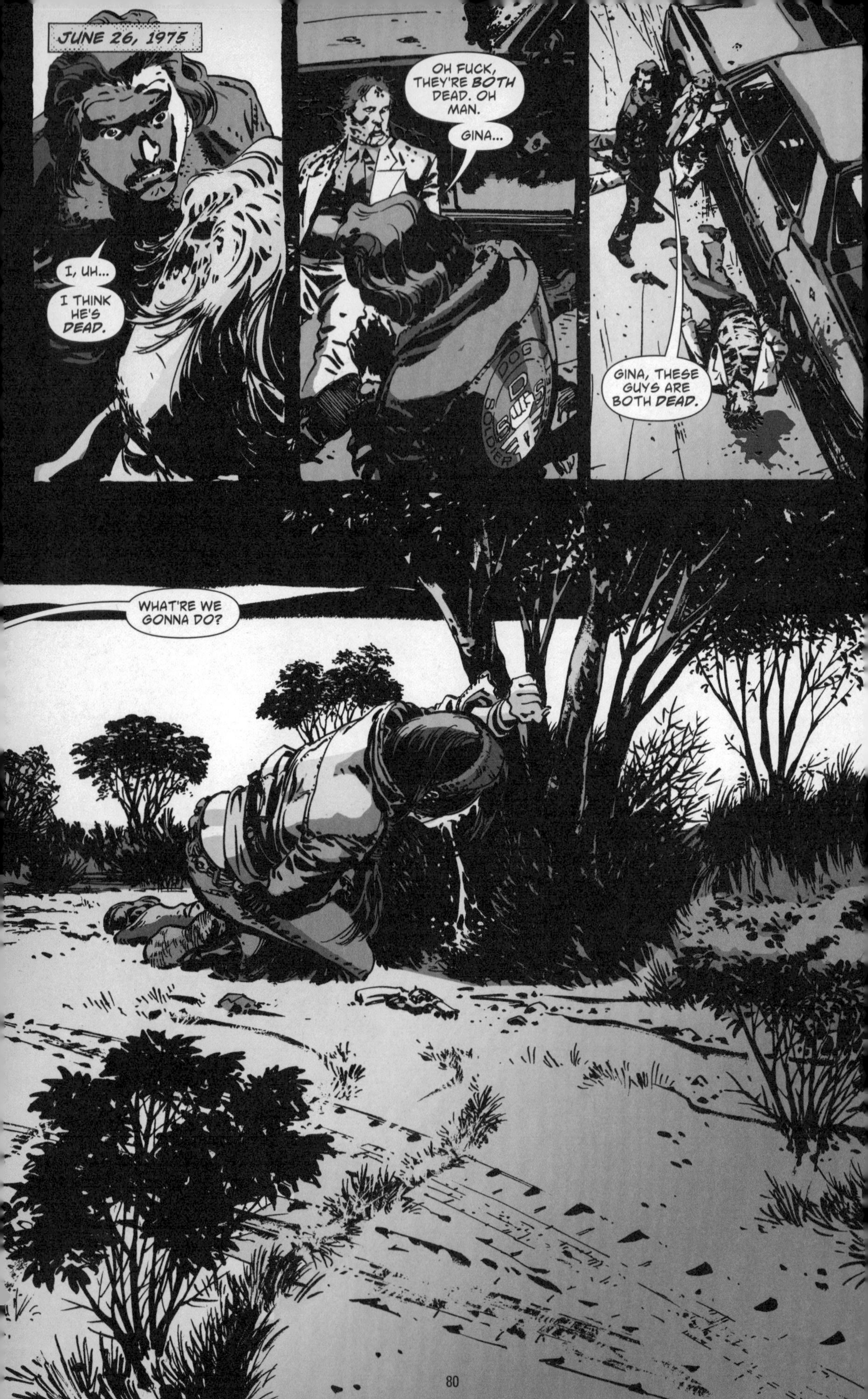

JUNE 26, 1975
I, UH...
I THINK HE'S DEAD.
OH FUCK, THEY'RE BOTH DEAD. OH MAN.
GINA...
DOG SOLDIER
GINA, THESE GUYS ARE BOTH DEAD.
WHAT'RE WE GONNA DO?

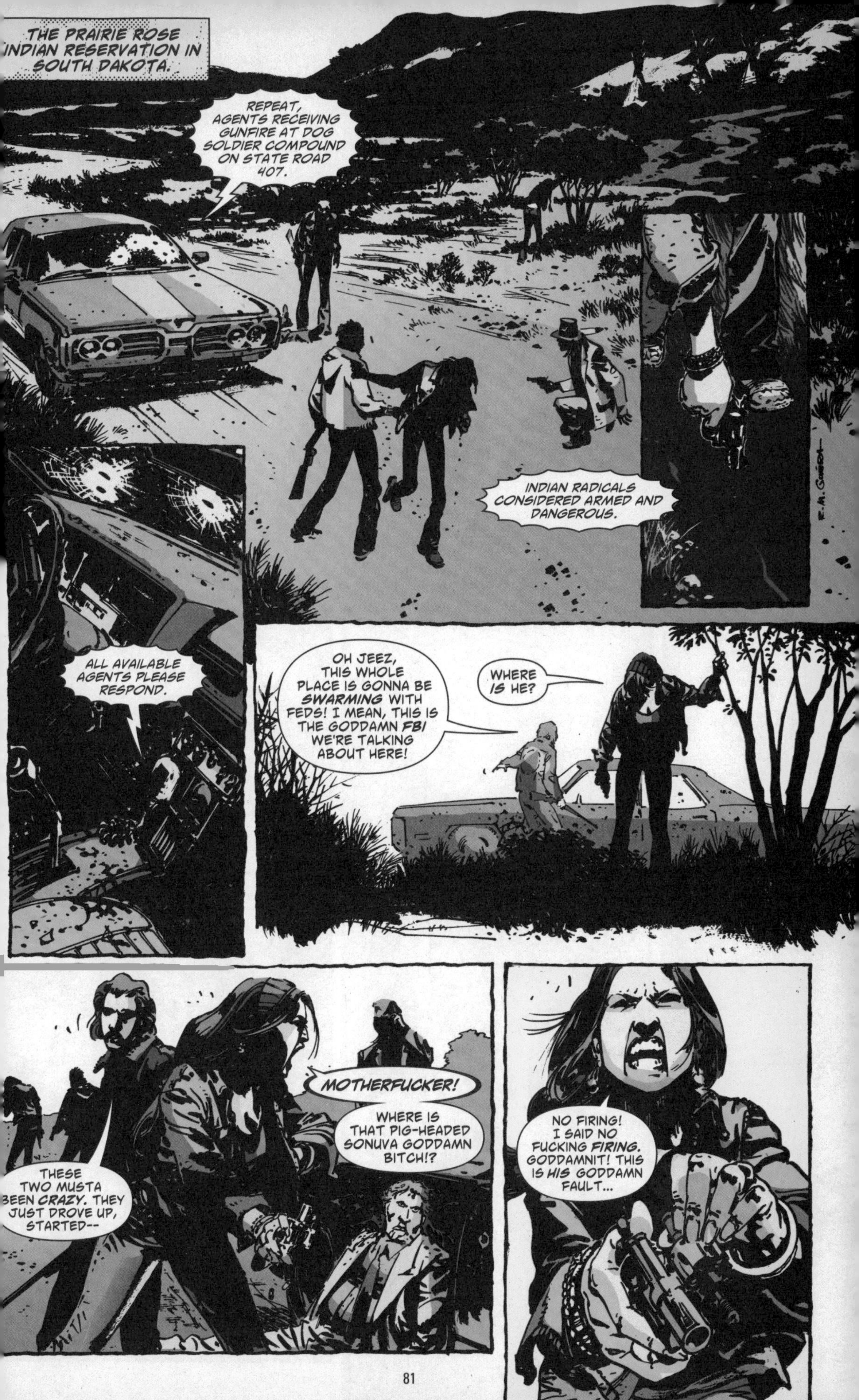
THE PRAIRIE ROSE INDIAN RESERVATION IN SOUTH DAKOTA.
REPEAT, AGENTS RECEIVING GUNFIRE AT DOG SOLDIER COMPOUND ON STATE ROAD 407.
INDIAN RADICALS CONSIDERED ARMED AND DANGEROUS.
ALL AVAILABLE AGENTS PLEASE RESPOND.
OH JEEZ, THIS WHOLE PLACE IS GONNA BE SWARMING WITH FEDS! I MEAN, THIS IS THE GODDAMN FBI WE'RE TALKING ABOUT HERE!
WHERE IS HE?
MOTHERFUCKER!
WHERE IS THAT PIG-HEADED SONUVA GODDAMN BITCH!?
THESE TWO MUSTA BEEN CRAZY. THEY JUST DROVE UP, STARTED--
NO FIRING! I SAID NO FUCKING FIRING. GODDAMNIT! THIS IS HIS GODDAMN FAULT...

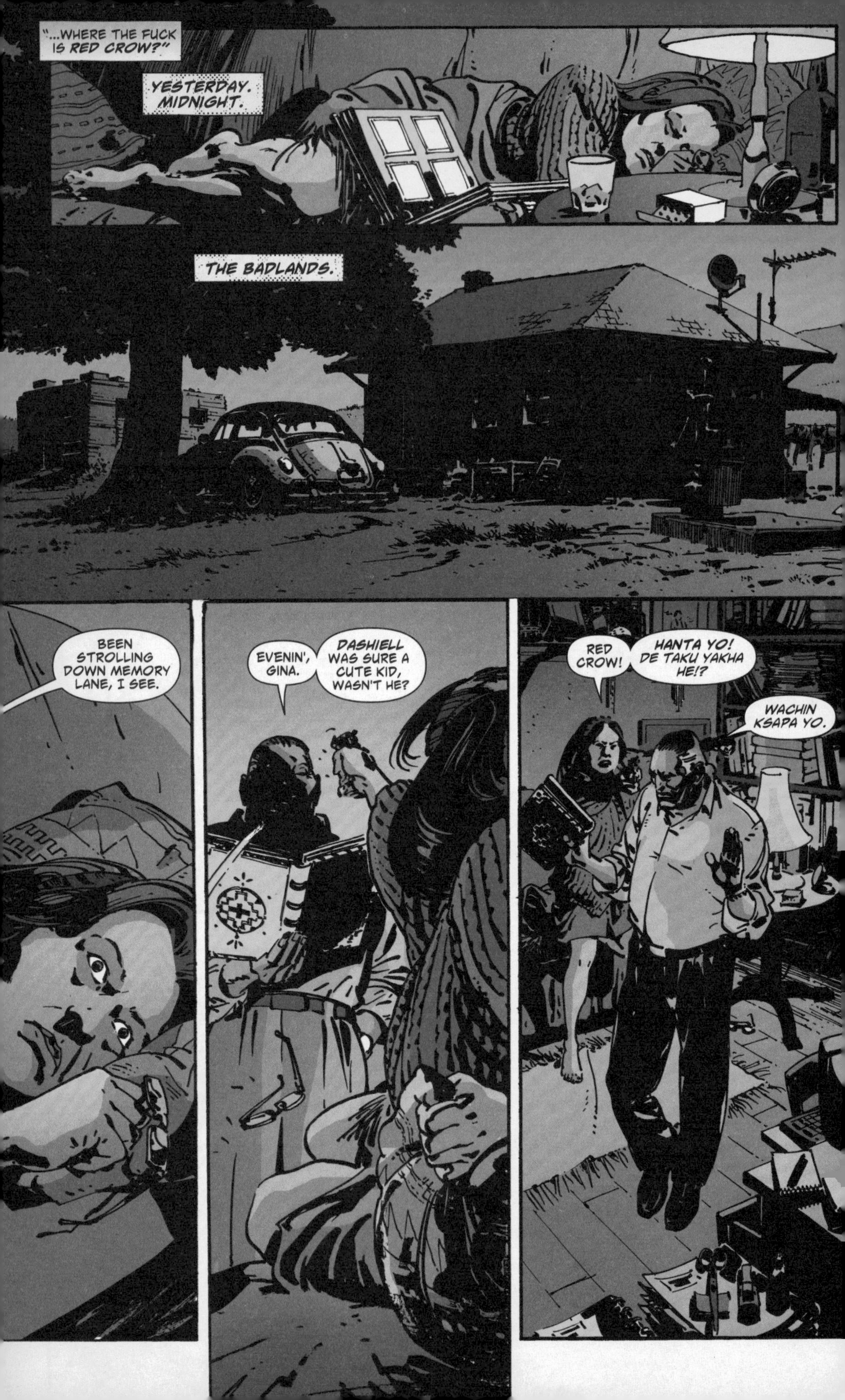
"...WHERE THE FUCK IS RED CROW?"
YESTERDAY. MIDNIGHT.
THE BADLANDS.
BEEN STROLLING DOWN MEMORY LANE, I SEE.
EVENIN', GINA.
DASHIELL WAS SURE A CUTE KID, WASN'T HE?
RED CROW!
HANTA YO! DE TAKU YAKHA HE!?
WACHIN KSAPA YO.

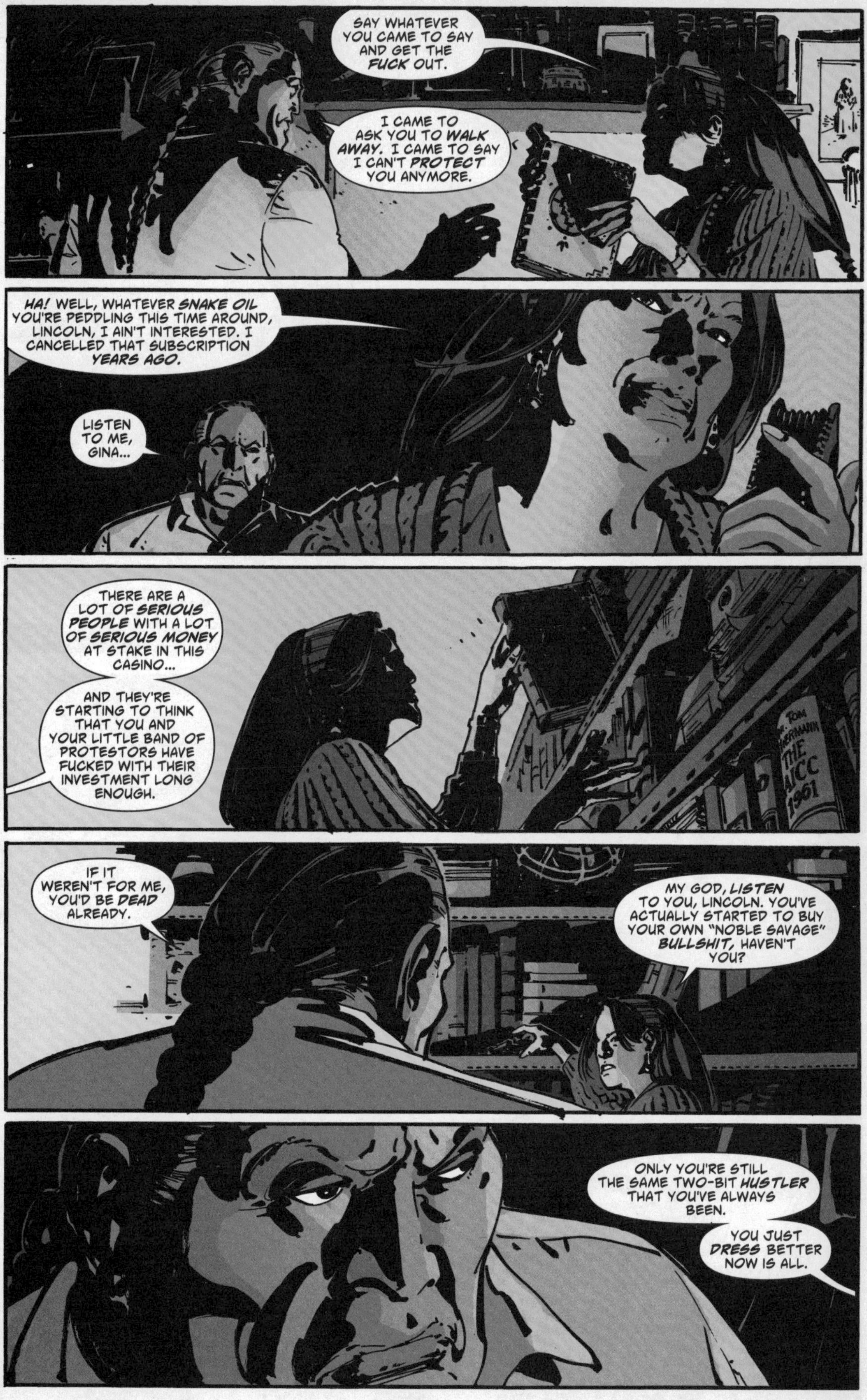
SAY WHATEVER YOU CAME TO SAY AND GET THE FUCK OUT.
I CAME TO ASK YOU TO WALK AWAY. I CAME TO SAY I CAN'T PROTECT YOU ANYMORE.
HA! WELL, WHATEVER SNAKE OIL YOU'RE PEDDLING THIS TIME AROUND, LINCOLN, I AIN'T INTERESTED. I CANCELLED THAT SUBSCRIPTION YEARS AGO.
LISTEN TO ME, GINA...
THERE ARE A LOT OF SERIOUS PEOPLE WITH A LOT OF SERIOUS MONEY AT STAKE IN THIS CASINO...
AND THEY'RE STARTING TO THINK THAT YOU AND YOUR LITTLE BAND OF PROTESTORS HAVE FUCKED WITH THEIR INVESTMENT LONG ENOUGH.
IF IT WEREN'T FOR ME, YOU'D BE DEAD ALREADY.
MY GOD, LISTEN TO YOU, LINCOLN. YOU'VE ACTUALLY STARTED TO BUY YOUR OWN "NOBLE SAVAGE" BULLSHIT, HAVEN'T YOU?
ONLY YOU'RE STILL THE SAME TWO-BIT HUSTLER THAT YOU'VE ALWAYS BEEN.
YOU JUST DRESS BETTER NOW IS ALL.

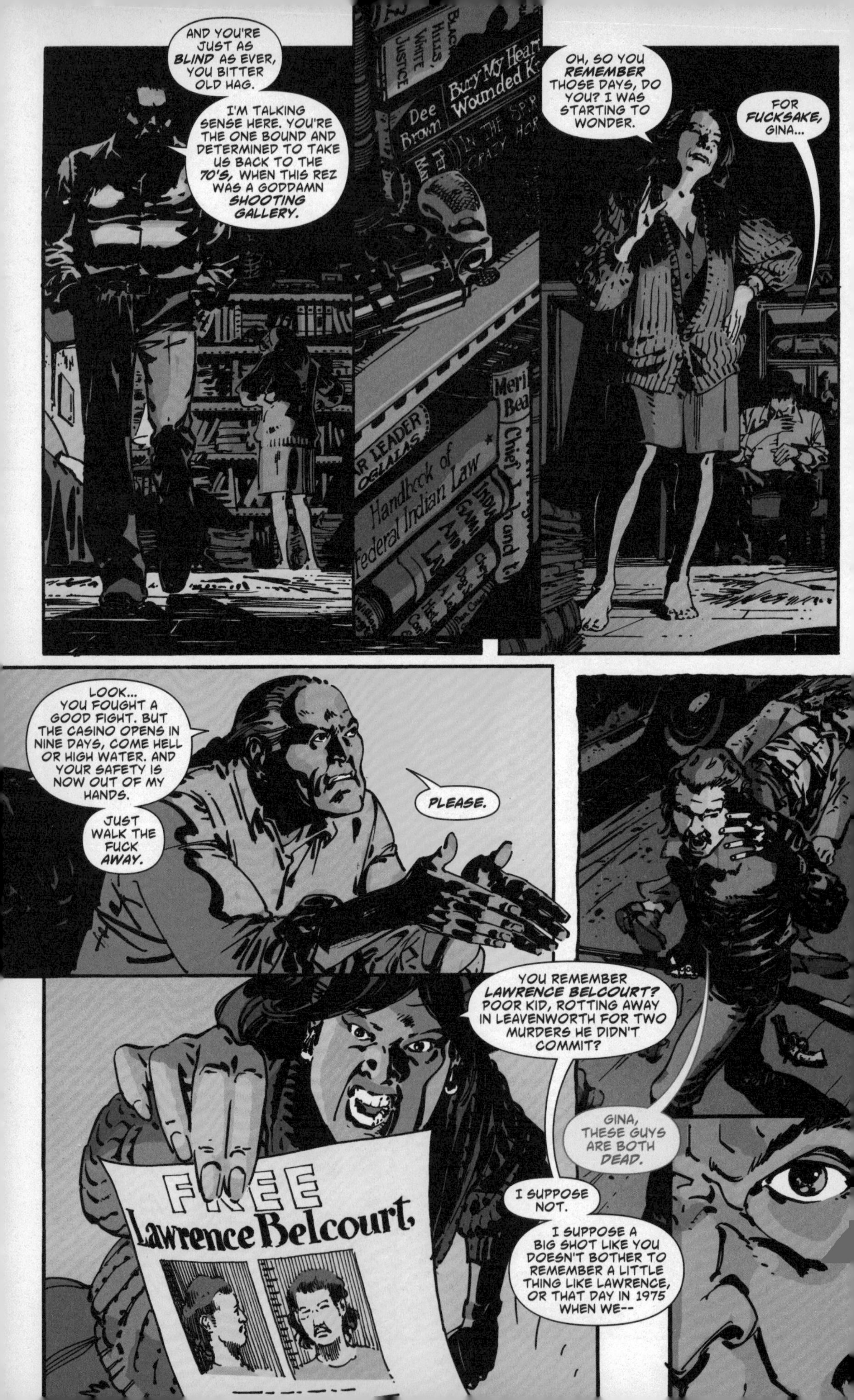
AND YOU'RE JUST AS BLIND AS EVER, YOU BITTER OLD HAG.
I'M TALKING SENSE HERE. YOU'RE THE ONE BOUND AND DETERMINED TO TAKE US BACK TO THE 70'S, WHEN THIS REZ WAS A GODDAMN SHOOTING GALLERY.
Black Hills, White Justice
Bury My Heart at Wounded Knee
Dee Brown
Handbook of Federal Indian Law
OH, SO YOU REMEMBER THOSE DAYS, DO YOU? I WAS STARTING TO WONDER.
FOR FUCKSAKE, GINA...
LOOK... YOU FOUGHT A GOOD FIGHT. BUT THE CASINO OPENS IN NINE DAYS, COME HELL OR HIGH WATER. AND YOUR SAFETY IS NOW OUT OF MY HANDS.
JUST WALK THE FUCK AWAY.
PLEASE.
YOU REMEMBER LAWRENCE BELCOURT? POOR KID, ROTTING AWAY IN LEAVENWORTH FOR TWO MURDERS HE DIDN'T COMMIT?
FREE Lawrence Belcourt
GINA, THESE GUYS ARE BOTH DEAD.
I SUPPOSE NOT.
I SUPPOSE A BIG SHOT LIKE YOU DOESN'T BOTHER TO REMEMBER A LITTLE THING LIKE LAWRENCE, OR THAT DAY IN 1975 WHEN WE--

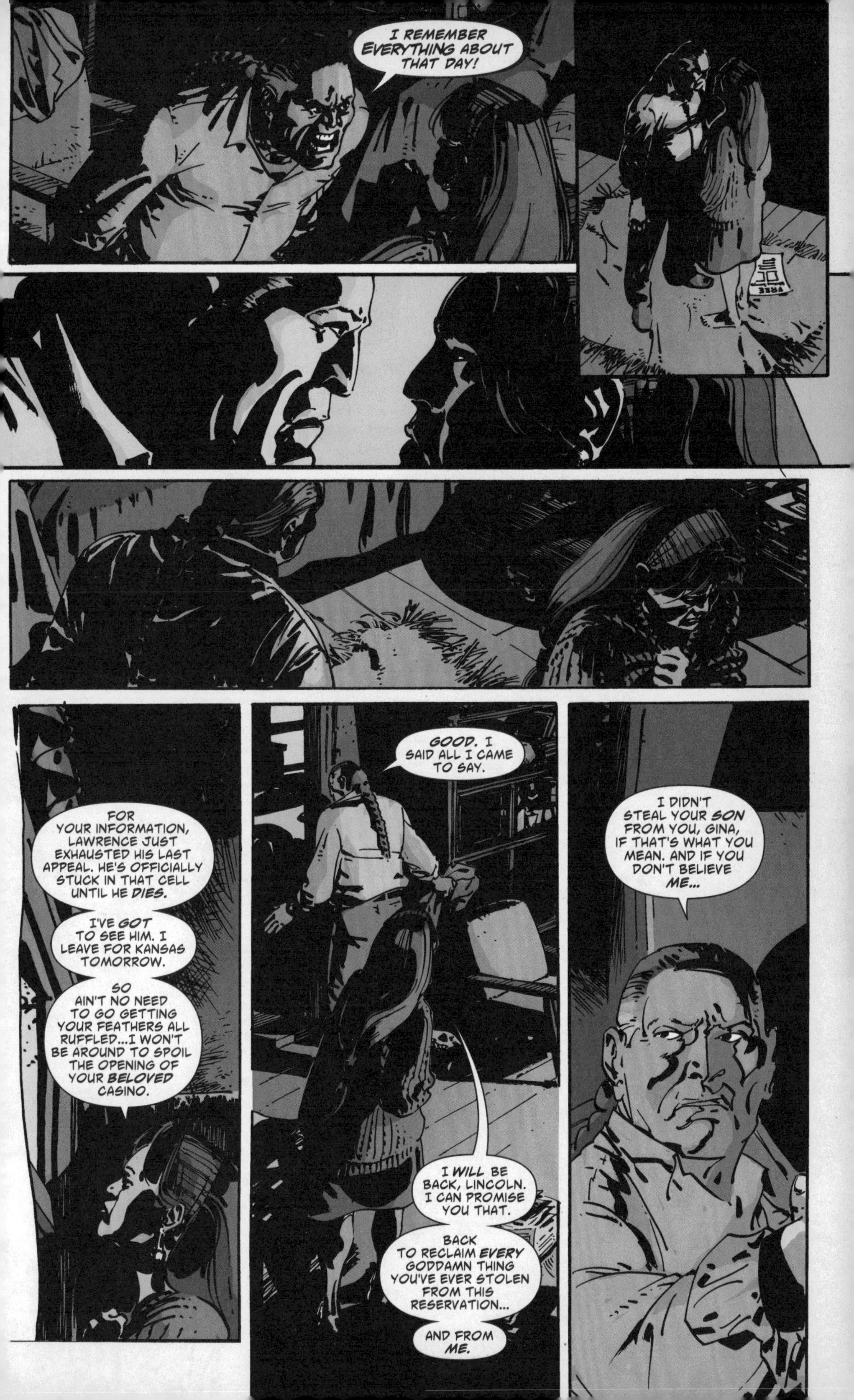
I REMEMBER EVERYTHING ABOUT THAT DAY!
FOR YOUR INFORMATION, LAWRENCE JUST EXHAUSTED HIS LAST APPEAL. HE'S OFFICIALLY STUCK IN THAT CELL UNTIL HE DIES.
I'VE GOT TO SEE HIM. I LEAVE FOR KANSAS TOMORROW.
SO AIN'T NO NEED TO GO GETTING YOUR FEATHERS ALL RUFFLED...I WON'T BE AROUND TO SPOIL THE OPENING OF YOUR BELOVED CASINO.
GOOD. I SAID ALL I CAME TO SAY.
I WILL BE BACK, LINCOLN. I CAN PROMISE YOU THAT.
BACK TO RECLAIM EVERY GODDAMN THING YOU'VE EVER STOLEN FROM THIS RESERVATION...
AND FROM ME.
I DIDN'T STEAL YOUR SON FROM YOU, GINA, IF THAT'S WHAT YOU MEAN. AND IF YOU DON'T BELIEVE ME...

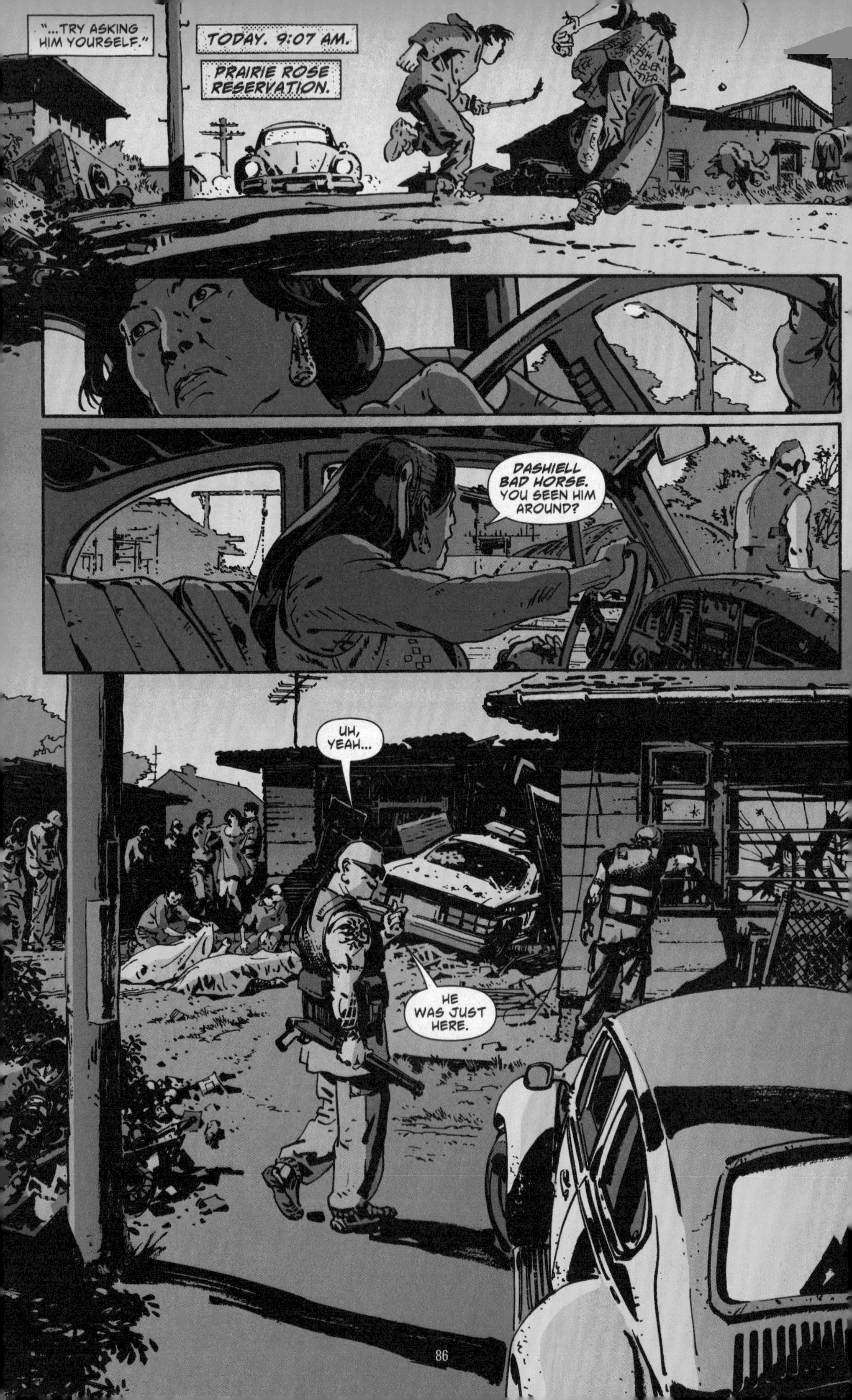
"...TRY ASKING HIM YOURSELF."
TODAY. 9:07 AM.
PRAIRIE ROSE RESERVATION.
DASHIELL BAD HORSE. YOU SEEN HIM AROUND?
UH, YEAH...
HE WAS JUST HERE.

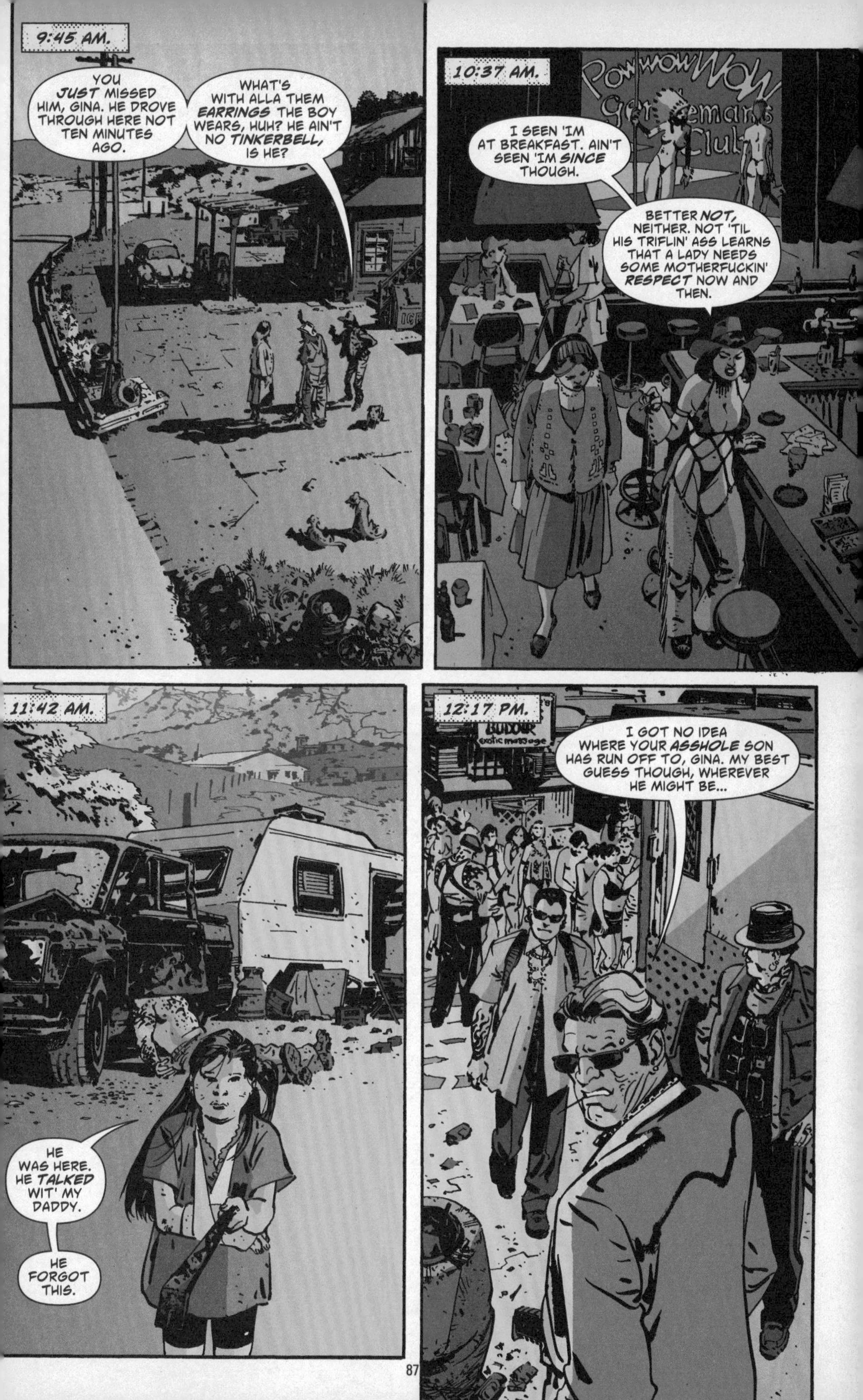
9:45 AM.
YOU JUST MISSED HIM, GINA. HE DROVE THROUGH HERE NOT TEN MINUTES AGO.
WHAT'S WITH ALLA THEM EARRINGS THE BOY WEARS, HUH? HE AIN'T NO TINKERBELL, IS HE?
10:37 AM.
PowwowWOW Gentlemans Club
I SEEN 'IM AT BREAKFAST. AIN'T SEEN 'IM SINCE THOUGH.
BETTER NOT, NEITHER. NOT 'TIL HIS TRIFLIN' ASS LEARNS THAT A LADY NEEDS SOME MOTHERFUCKIN' RESPECT NOW AND THEN.
11:42 AM.
HE WAS HERE. HE TALKED WIT' MY DADDY.
HE FORGOT THIS.
12:17 PM.
BOUDOIR exotic massage
I GOT NO IDEA WHERE YOUR ASSHOLE SON HAS RUN OFF TO, GINA. MY BEST GUESS THOUGH, WHEREVER HE MIGHT BE...

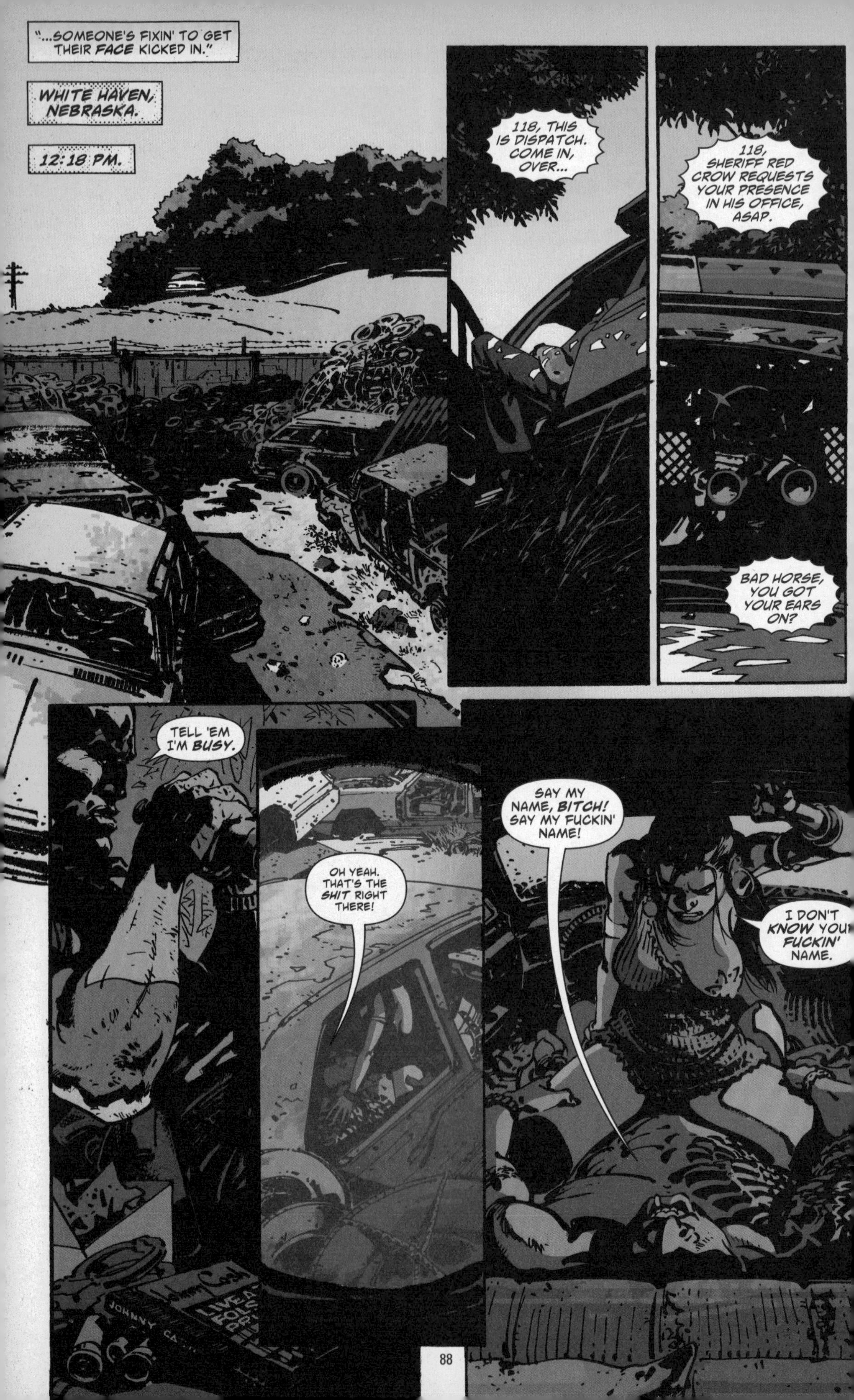
"...SOMEONE'S FIXIN' TO GET THEIR FACE KICKED IN."
WHITE HAVEN, NEBRASKA.
12:18 PM.
118, THIS IS DISPATCH. COME IN, OVER...
118, SHERIFF RED CROW REQUESTS YOUR PRESENCE IN HIS OFFICE, ASAP.
BAD HORSE, YOU GOT YOUR EARS ON?
TELL 'EM I'M BUSY.
OH YEAH. THAT'S THE SHIT RIGHT THERE!
SAY MY NAME, BITCH! SAY MY FUCKIN' NAME!
I DON'T KNOW YOUR FUCKIN' NAME.

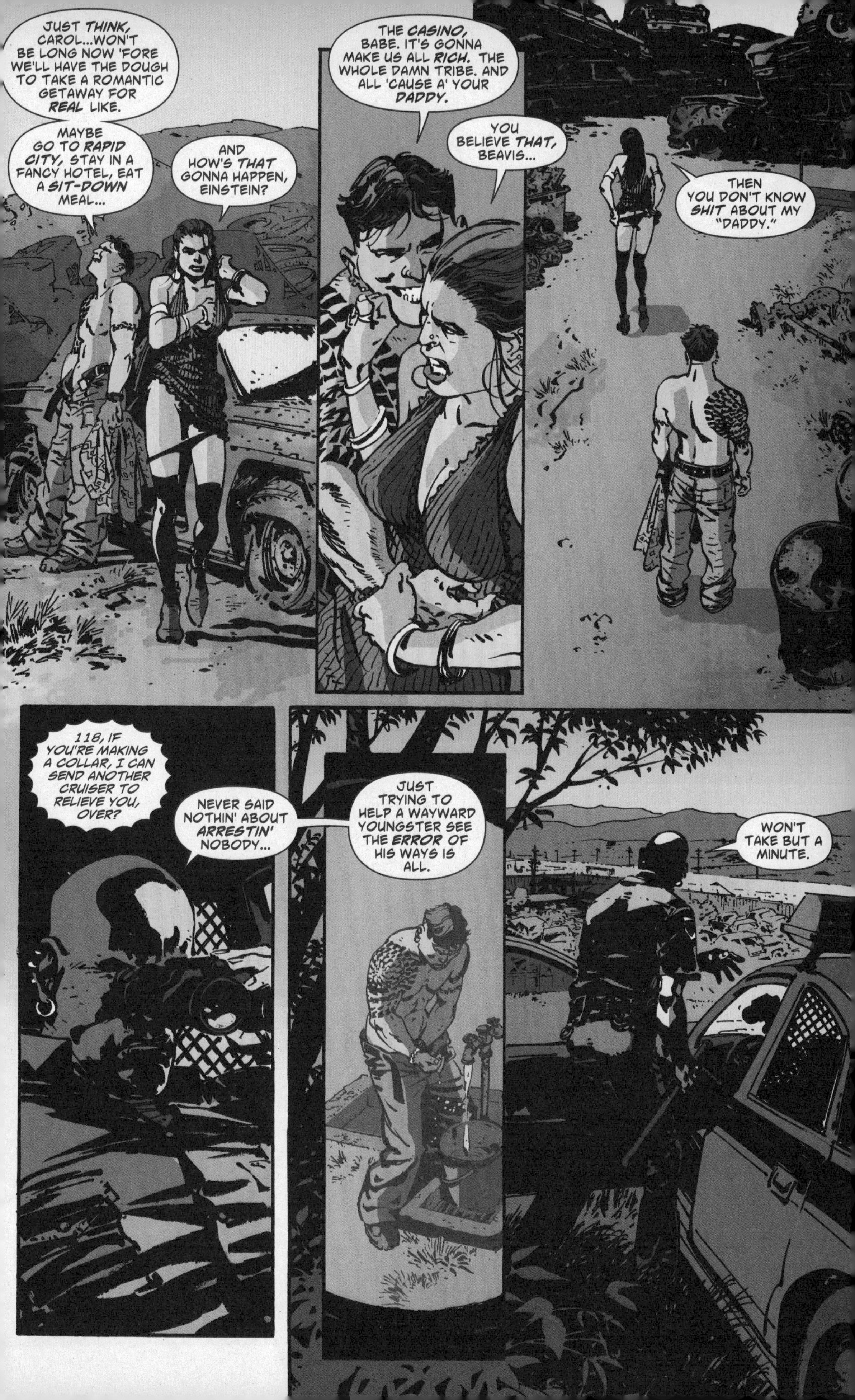
JUST THINK, CAROL...WON'T BE LONG NOW 'FORE WE'LL HAVE THE DOUGH TO TAKE A ROMANTIC GETAWAY FOR REAL LIKE.
MAYBE GO TO RAPID CITY, STAY IN A FANCY HOTEL, EAT A SIT-DOWN MEAL...
AND HOW'S THAT GONNA HAPPEN, EINSTEIN?
THE CASINO, BABE. IT'S GONNA MAKE US ALL RICH. THE WHOLE DAMN TRIBE. AND ALL 'CAUSE A' YOUR DADDY.
YOU BELIEVE THAT, BEAVIS...
THEN YOU DON'T KNOW SHIT ABOUT MY "DADDY."
118, IF YOU'RE MAKING A COLLAR, I CAN SEND ANOTHER CRUISER TO RELIEVE YOU, OVER?
NEVER SAID NOTHIN' ABOUT ARRESTIN' NOBODY...
JUST TRYING TO HELP A WAYWARD YOUNGSTER SEE THE ERROR OF HIS WAYS IS ALL.
WON'T TAKE BUT A MINUTE.

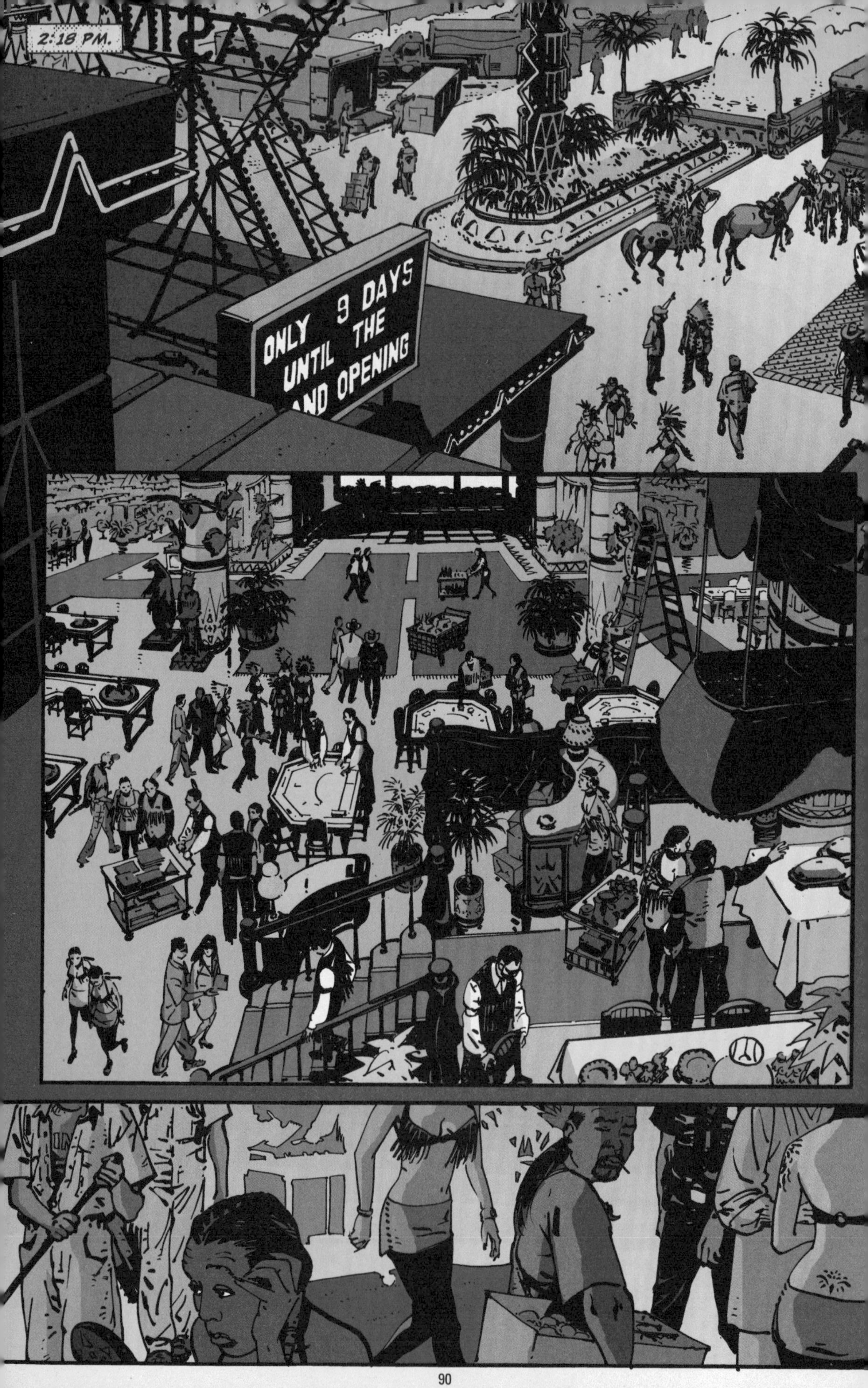
2:18 P.M.
ONLY 9 DAYS
UNTIL THE
AND OPENING

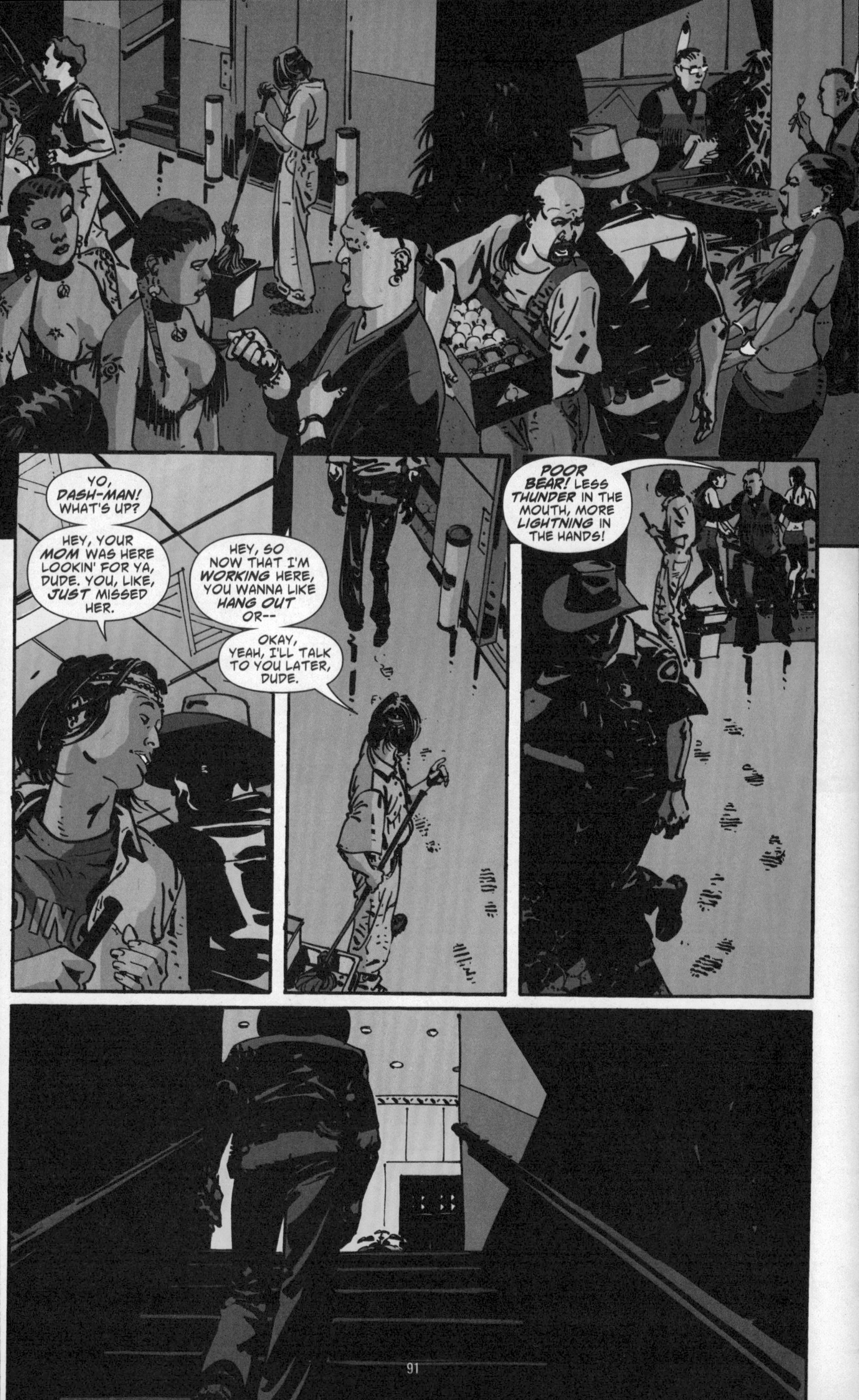
YO, DASH-MAN! WHAT'S UP?
HEY, YOUR MOM WAS HERE LOOKIN' FOR YA, DUDE. YOU, LIKE, JUST MISSED HER.
HEY, SO NOW THAT I'M WORKING HERE, YOU WANNA LIKE HANG OUT OR--
OKAY, YEAH, I'LL TALK TO YOU LATER, DUDE.
POOR BEAR! LESS THUNDER IN THE MOUTH, MORE LIGHTNING IN THE HANDS!

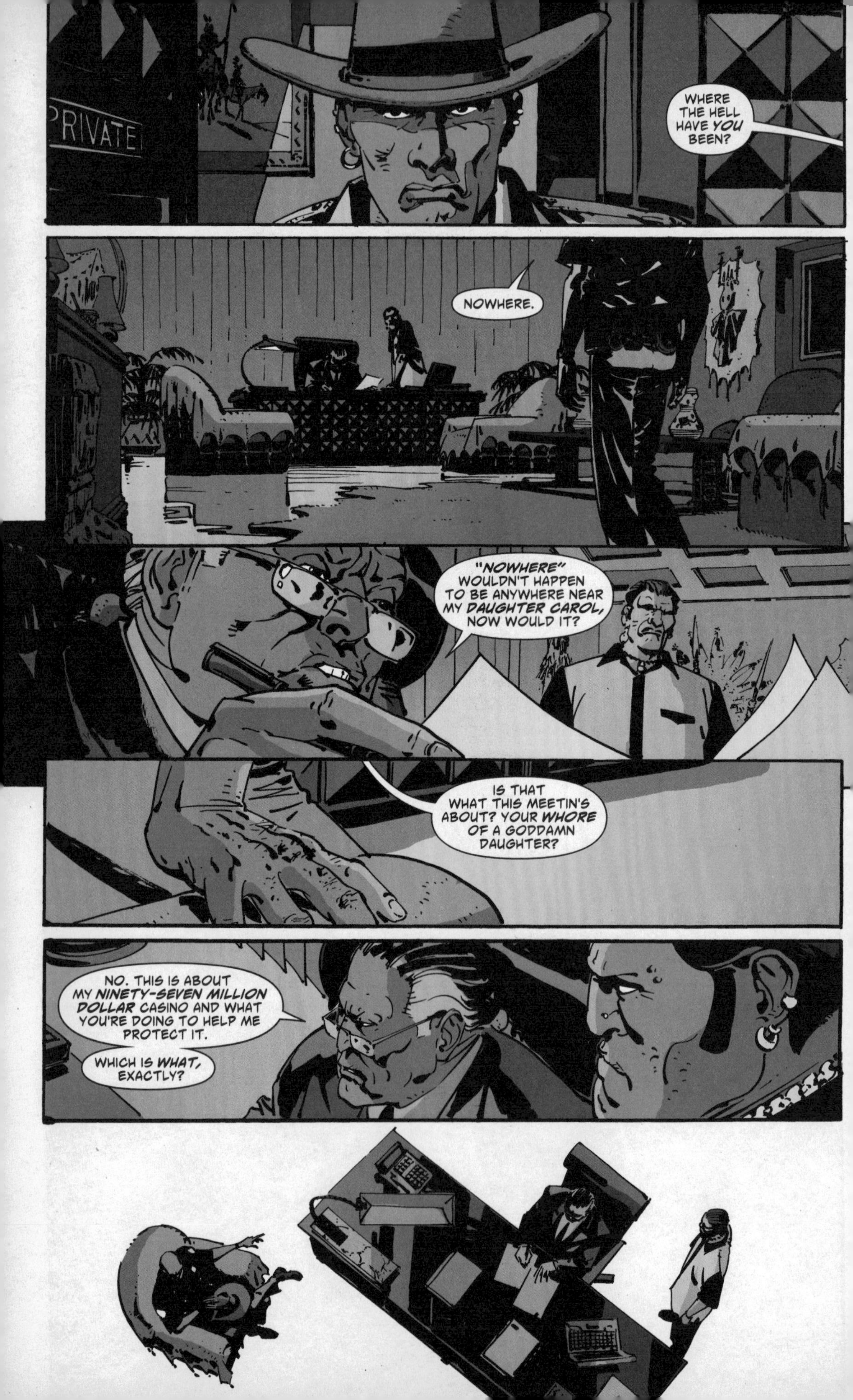
PRIVATE
WHERE THE HELL HAVE YOU BEEN?
NOWHERE.
"NOWHERE" WOULDN'T HAPPEN TO BE ANYWHERE NEAR MY DAUGHTER CAROL, NOW WOULD IT?
IS THAT WHAT THIS MEETIN'S ABOUT? YOUR WHORE OF A GODDAMN DAUGHTER?
NO. THIS IS ABOUT MY NINETY-SEVEN MILLION DOLLAR CASINO AND WHAT YOU'RE DOING TO HELP ME PROTECT IT.
WHICH IS WHAT, EXACTLY?

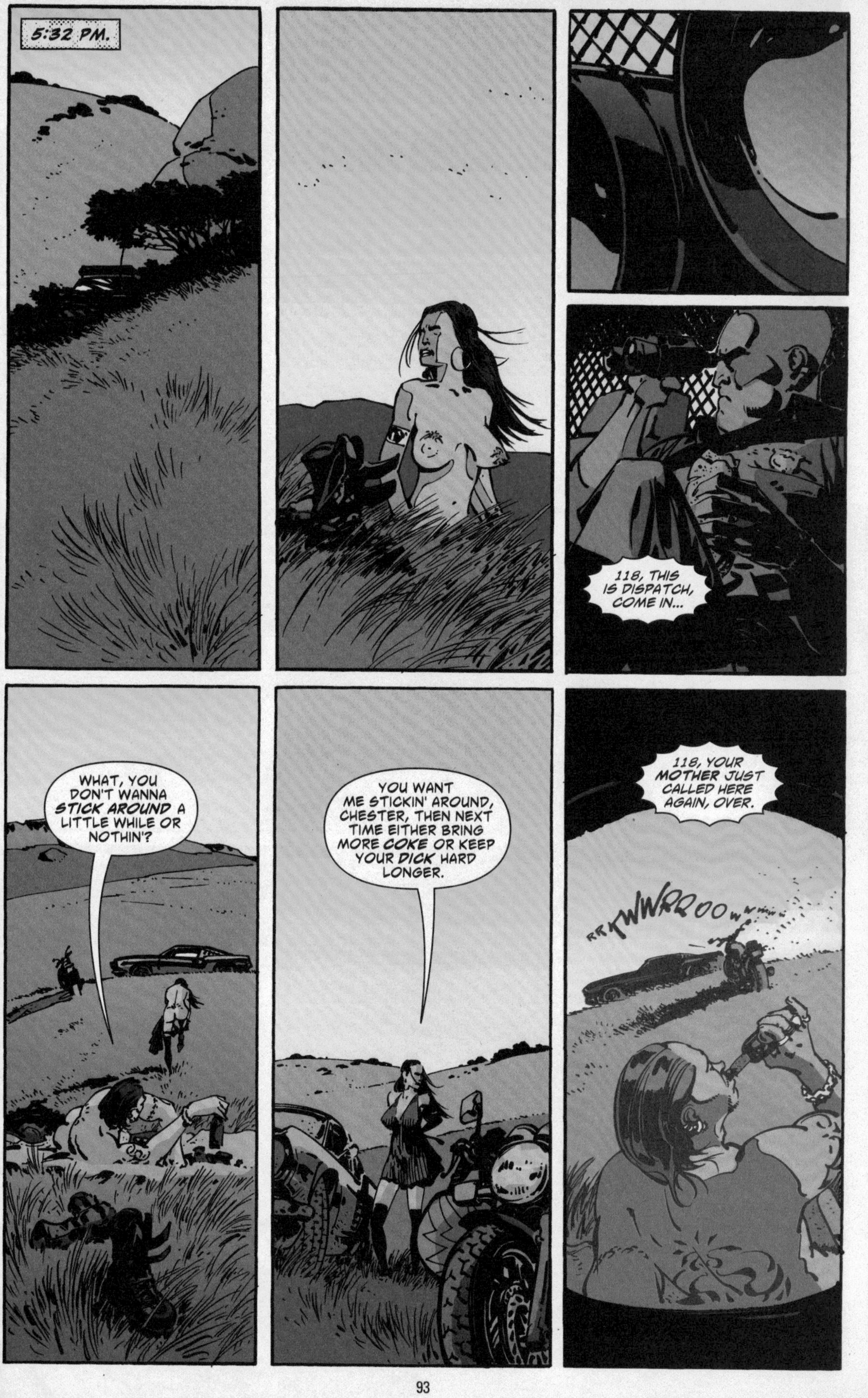
5:32 PM.
118, THIS IS DISPATCH, COME IN...
WHAT, YOU DON'T WANNA STICK AROUND A LITTLE WHILE OR NOTHIN'?
YOU WANT ME STICKIN' AROUND, CHESTER, THEN NEXT TIME EITHER BRING MORE COKE OR KEEP YOUR DICK HARD LONGER.
118, YOUR MOTHER JUST CALLED HERE AGAIN, OVER.
RRRWWRRROOOWWW

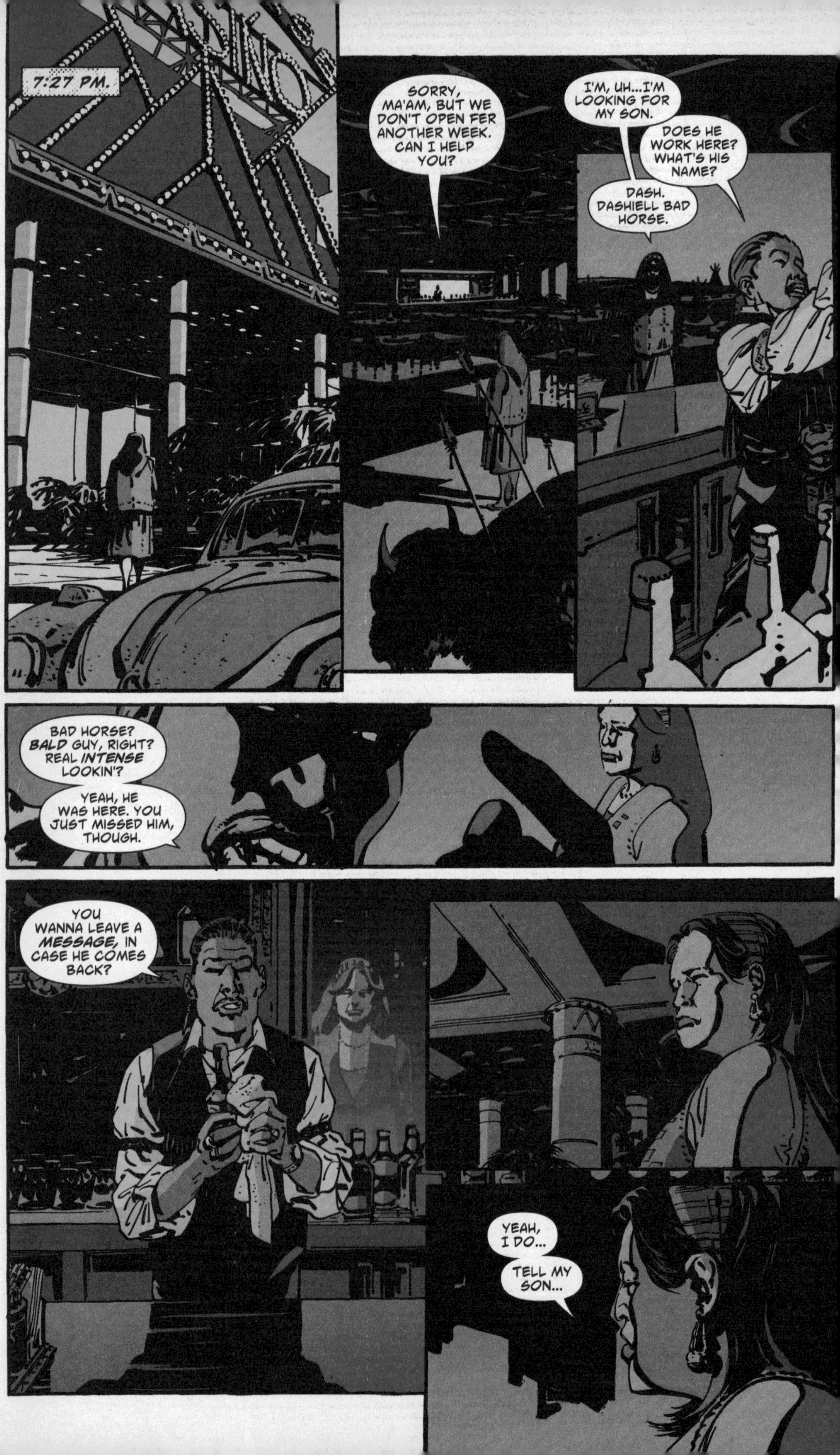
7:27 PM.
SORRY, MA'AM, BUT WE DON'T OPEN FER ANOTHER WEEK. CAN I HELP YOU?
I'M, UH...I'M LOOKING FOR MY SON.
DOES HE WORK HERE? WHAT'S HIS NAME?
DASH. DASHIELL BAD HORSE.
BAD HORSE? BALD GUY, RIGHT? REAL INTENSE LOOKIN'?
YEAH, HE WAS HERE. YOU JUST MISSED HIM, THOUGH.
YOU WANNA LEAVE A MESSAGE, IN CASE HE COMES BACK?
YEAH, I DO...
TELL MY SON...

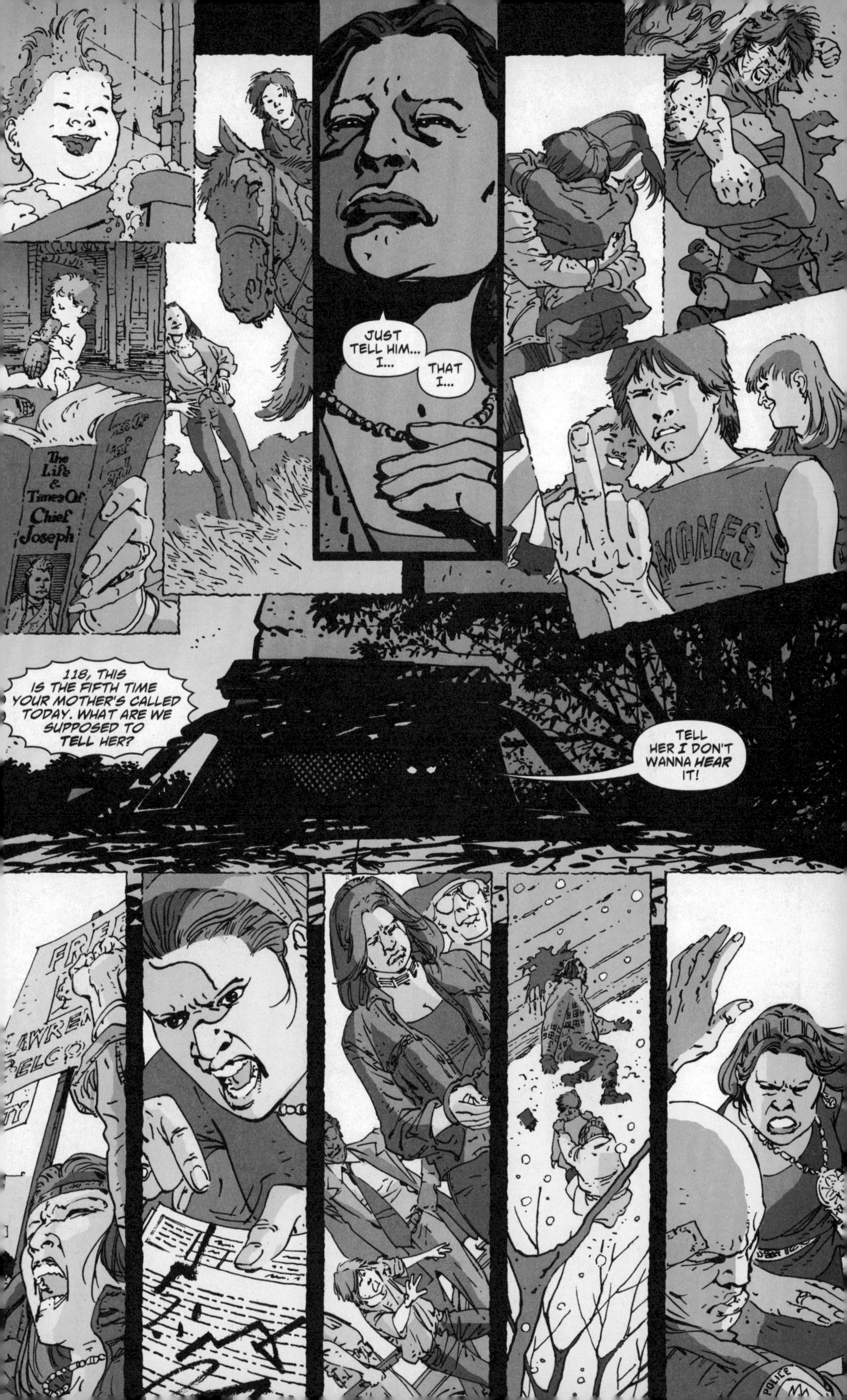

The Life & Times Of Chief Joseph
JUST TELL HIM... I...
THAT I...
MONES
118, THIS IS THE FIFTH TIME YOUR MOTHER'S CALLED TODAY. WHAT ARE WE SUPPOSED TO TELL HER?
TELL HER I DON'T WANNA HEAR IT!

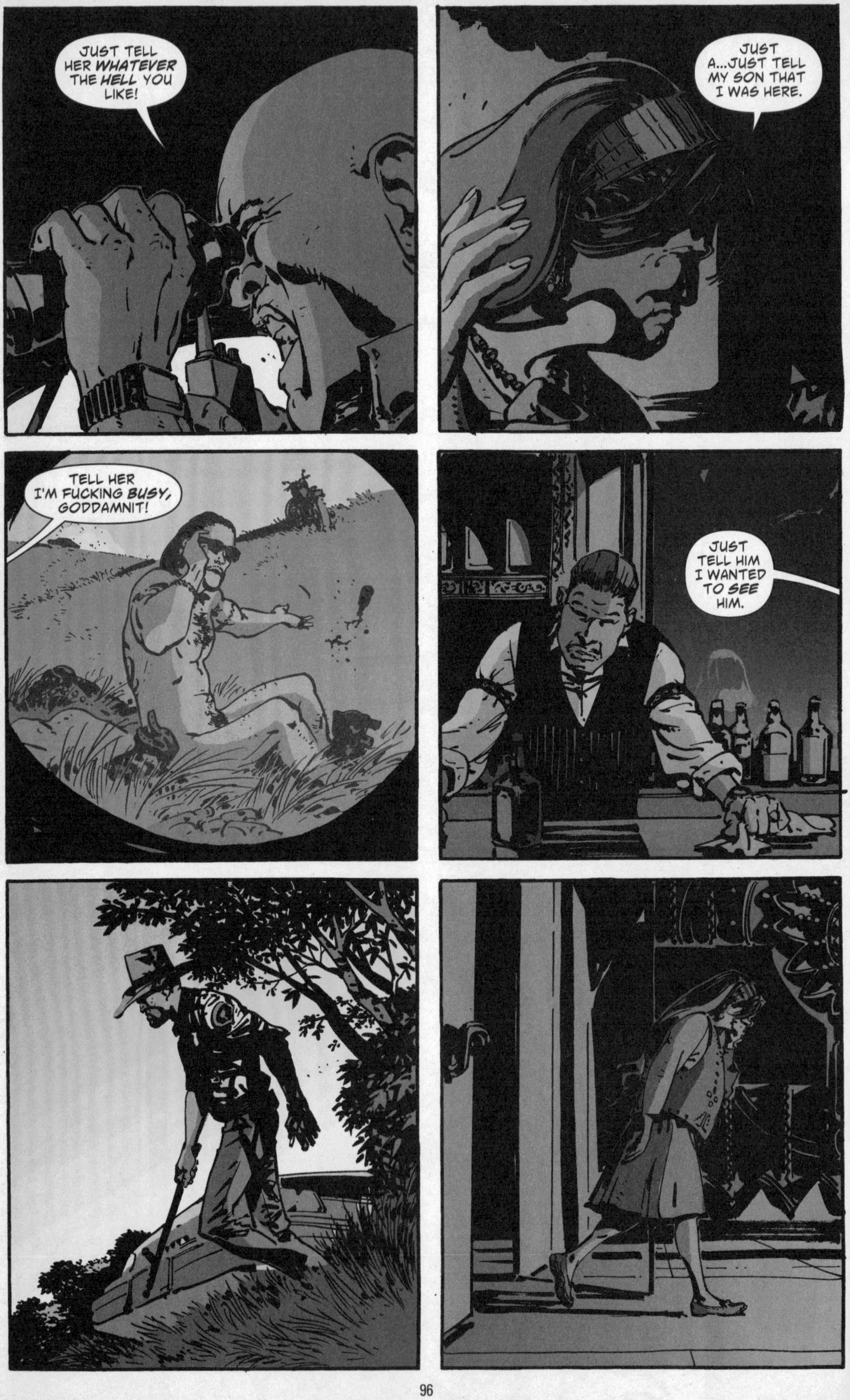
JUST TELL HER *WHATEVER* THE *HELL* YOU LIKE!
JUST A...JUST TELL MY SON THAT I WAS HERE.
TELL HER I'M FUCKING *BUSY*, GODDAMNIT!
JUST TELL HIM I WANTED TO *SEE* HIM.

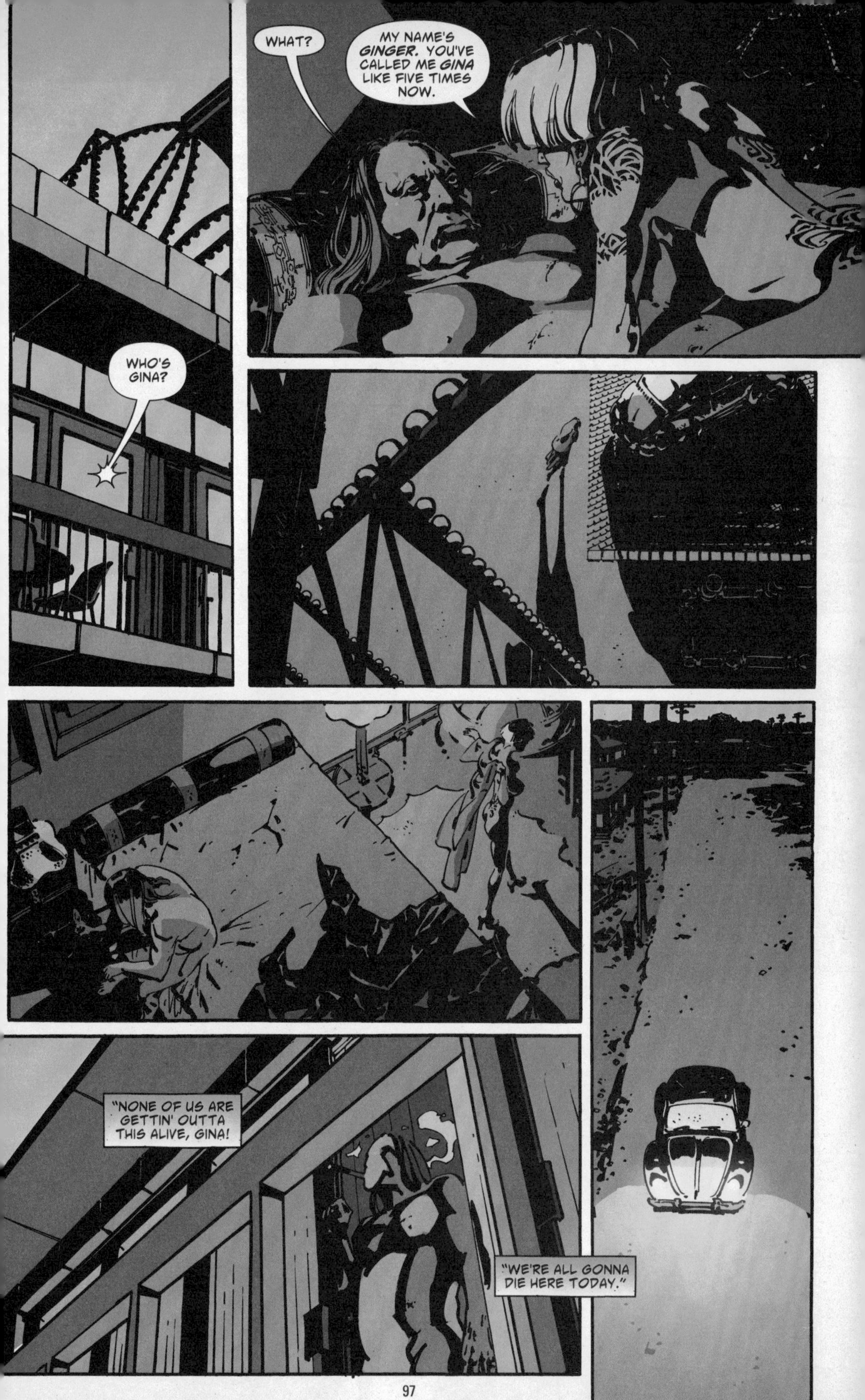
WHO'S GINA?
WHAT?
MY NAME'S GINGER. YOU'VE CALLED ME GINA LIKE FIVE TIMES NOW.
"NONE OF US ARE GETTIN' OUTTA THIS ALIVE, GINA!
"WE'RE ALL GONNA DIE HERE TODAY."

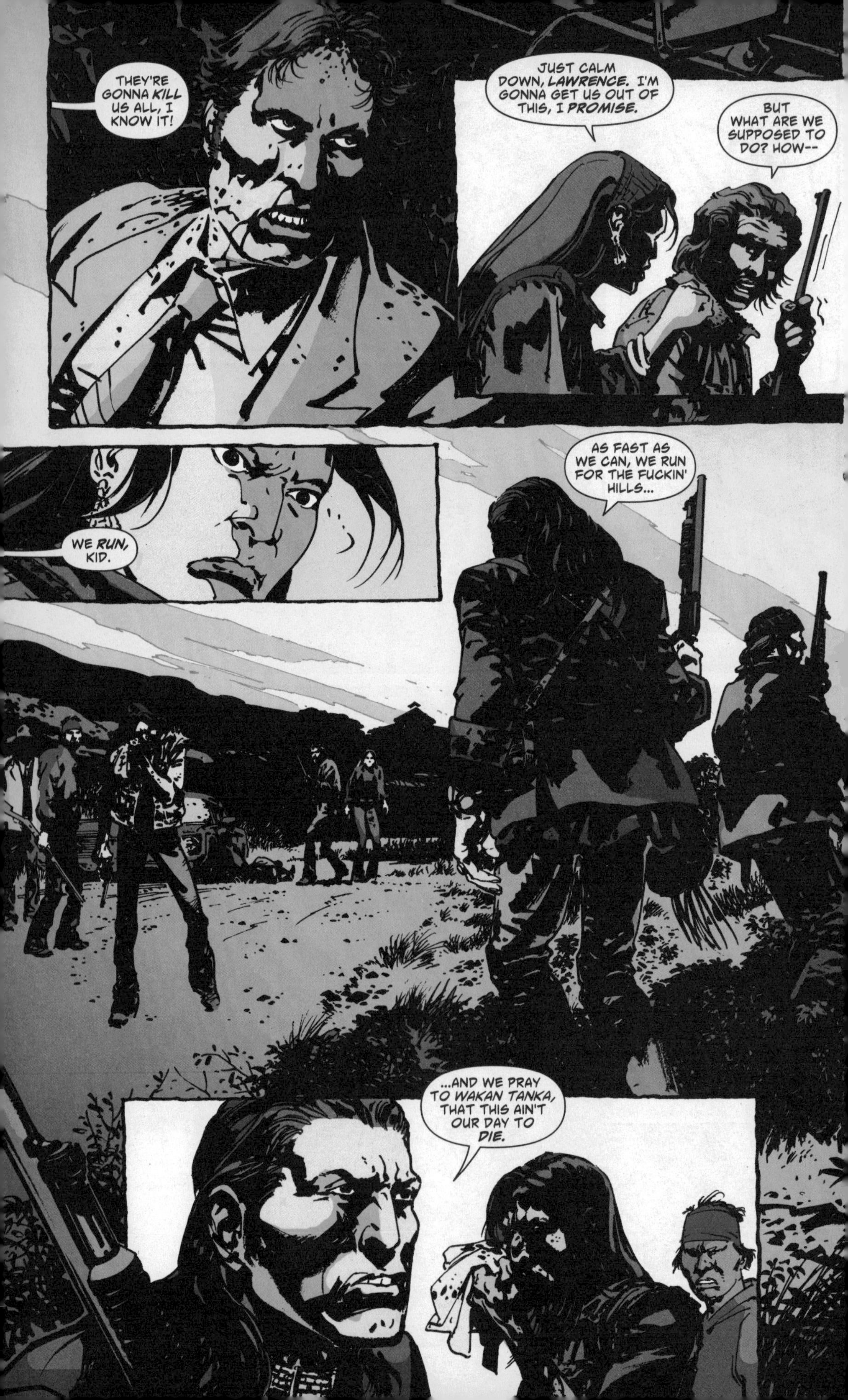
THEY'RE GONNA KILL US ALL, I KNOW IT!
JUST CALM DOWN, LAWRENCE. I'M GONNA GET US OUT OF THIS, I PROMISE.
BUT WHAT ARE WE SUPPOSED TO DO? HOW--
WE RUN, KID.
AS FAST AS WE CAN, WE RUN FOR THE FUCKIN' HILLS...
...AND WE PRAY TO WAKAN TANKA, THAT THIS AIN'T OUR DAY TO DIE.

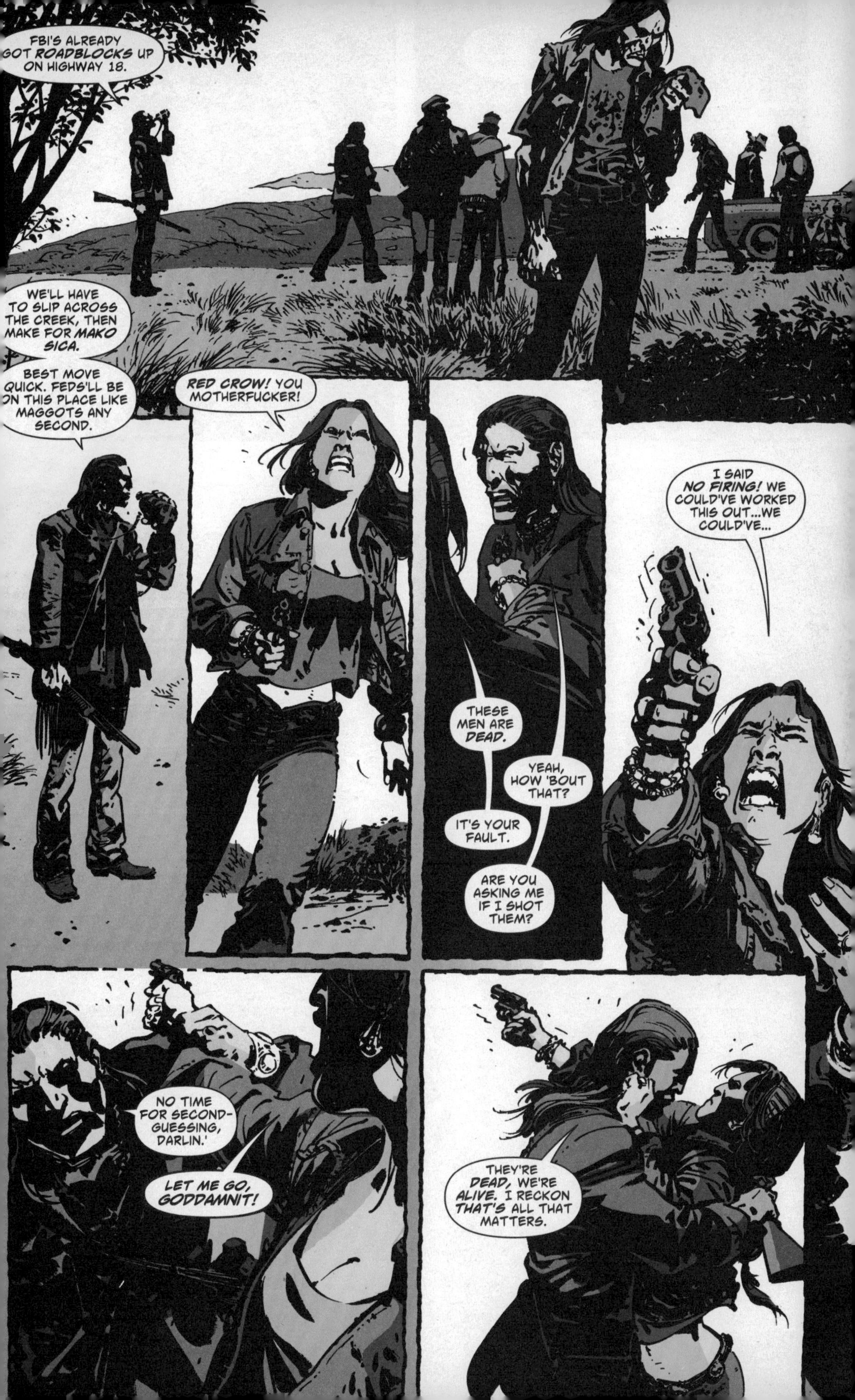
FBI'S ALREADY GOT *ROADBLOCKS* UP ON HIGHWAY 18.
WE'LL HAVE TO SLIP ACROSS THE CREEK, THEN MAKE FOR *MAKO SICA.*
BEST MOVE QUICK. FEDS'LL BE ON THIS PLACE LIKE MAGGOTS ANY SECOND.
RED CROW! YOU MOTHERFUCKER!
THESE MEN ARE *DEAD.*
IT'S YOUR FAULT.
YEAH, HOW 'BOUT THAT?
ARE YOU ASKING ME IF I SHOT THEM?
I SAID *NO FIRING!* WE COULD'VE WORKED THIS OUT...WE COULD'VE...
NO TIME FOR SECOND-GUESSING, DARLIN.'
LET ME GO, GODDAMNIT!
THEY'RE *DEAD,* WE'RE *ALIVE.* I RECKON *THAT'S* ALL THAT MATTERS.

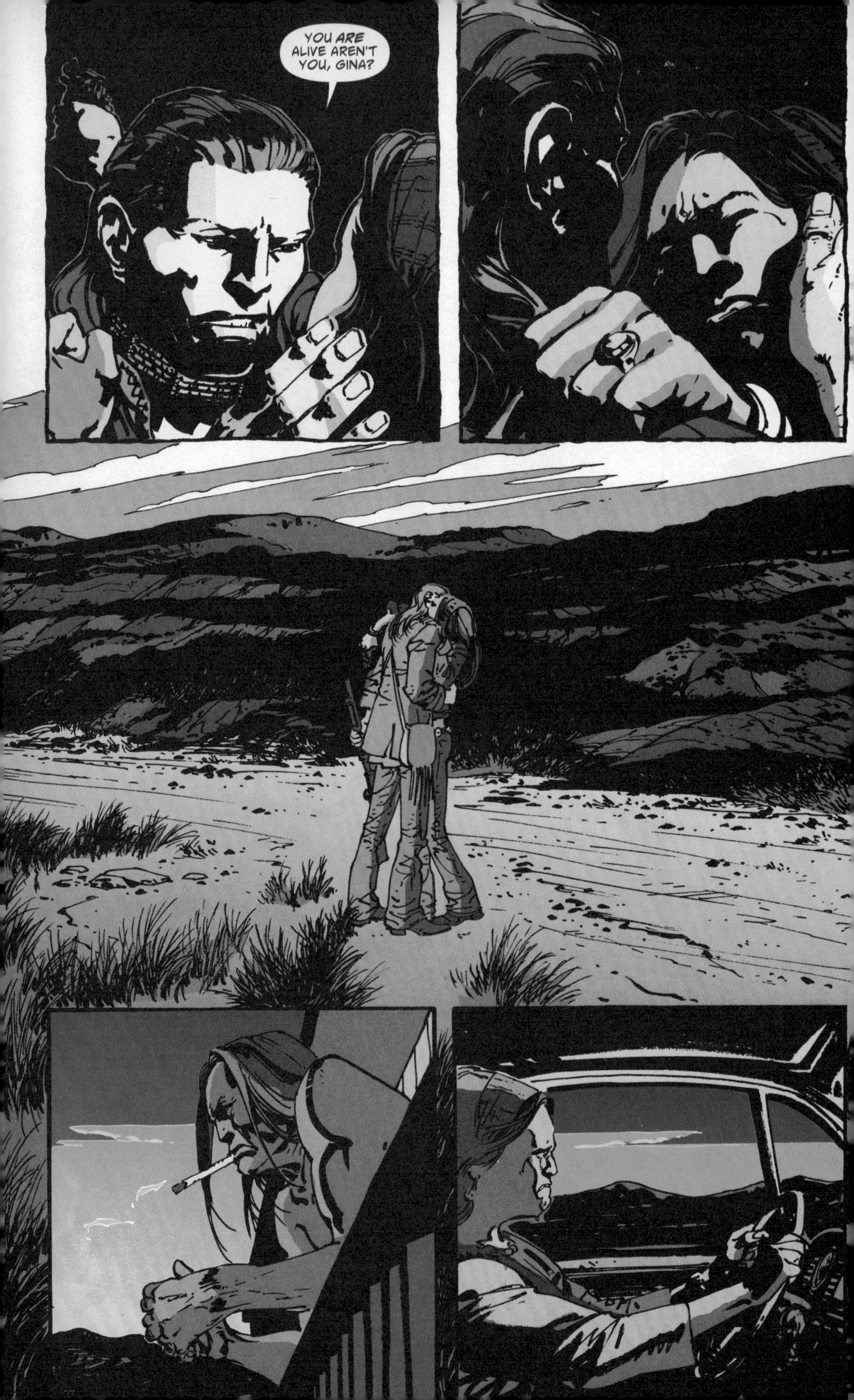
YOU ARE ALIVE AREN'T YOU, GINA?

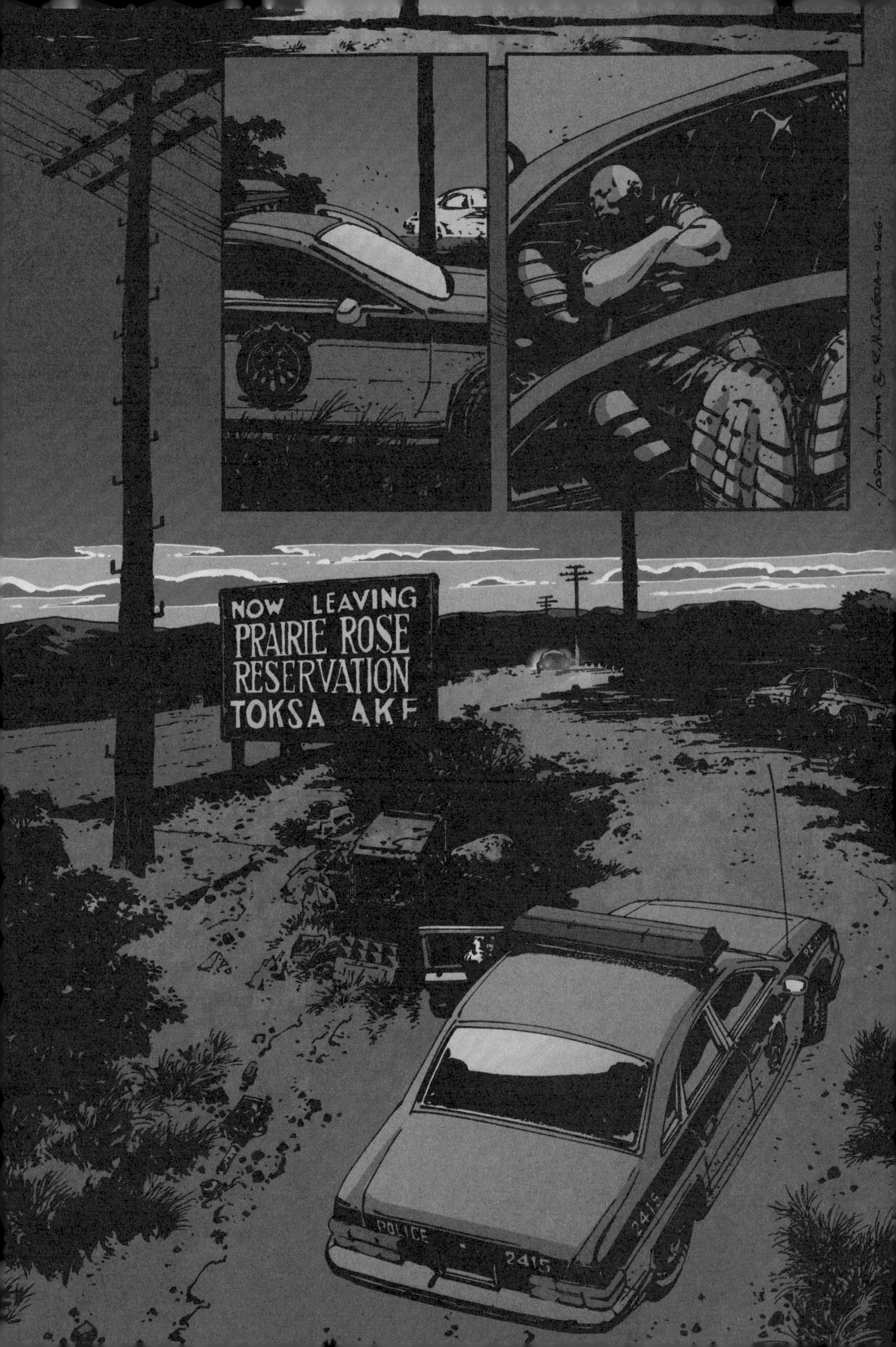
NOW LEAVING
PRAIRIE ROSE
RESERVATION
TOKSA AKE
POLICE
2415
2415

HOKA HEY
CHAPTER TWO

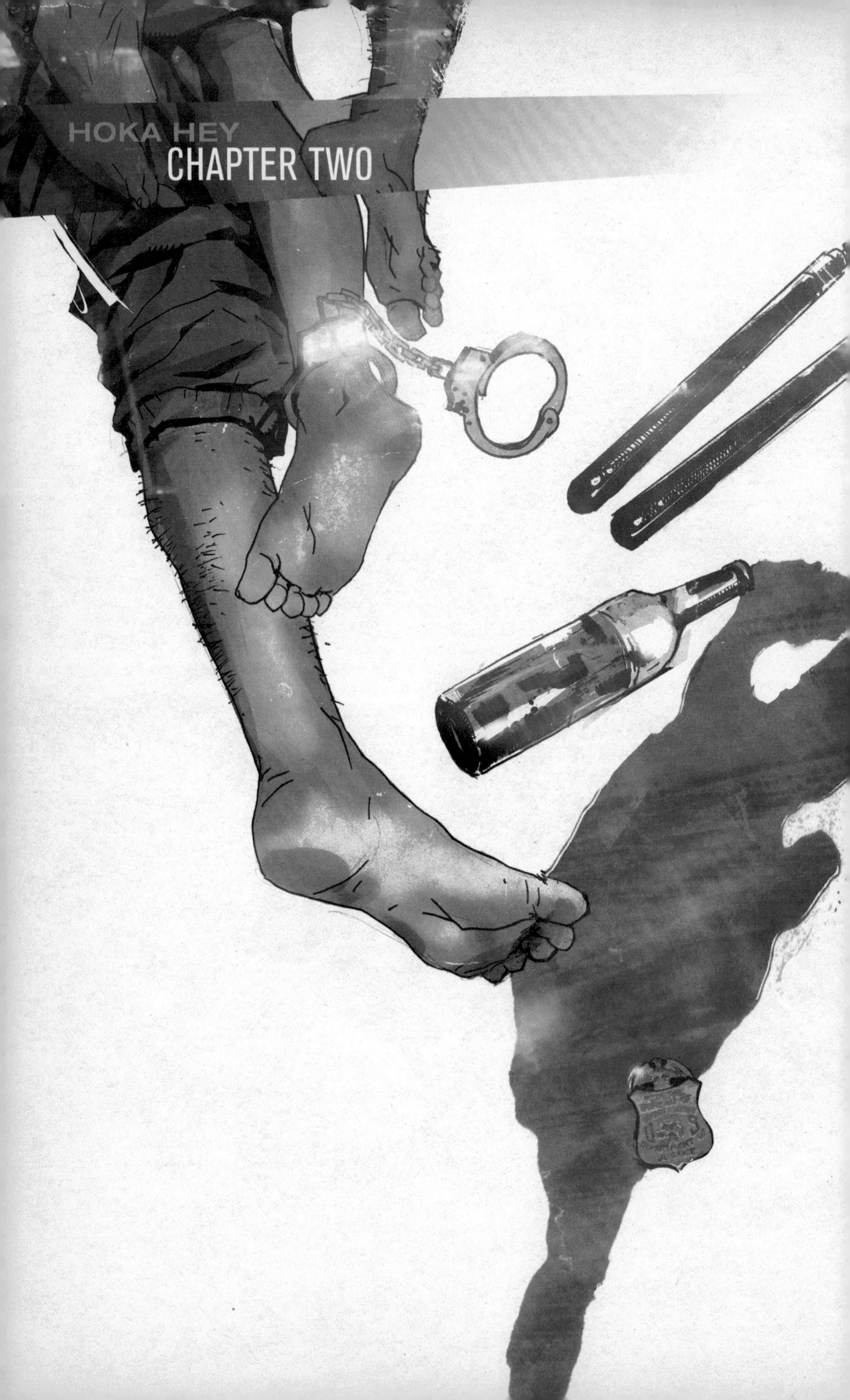

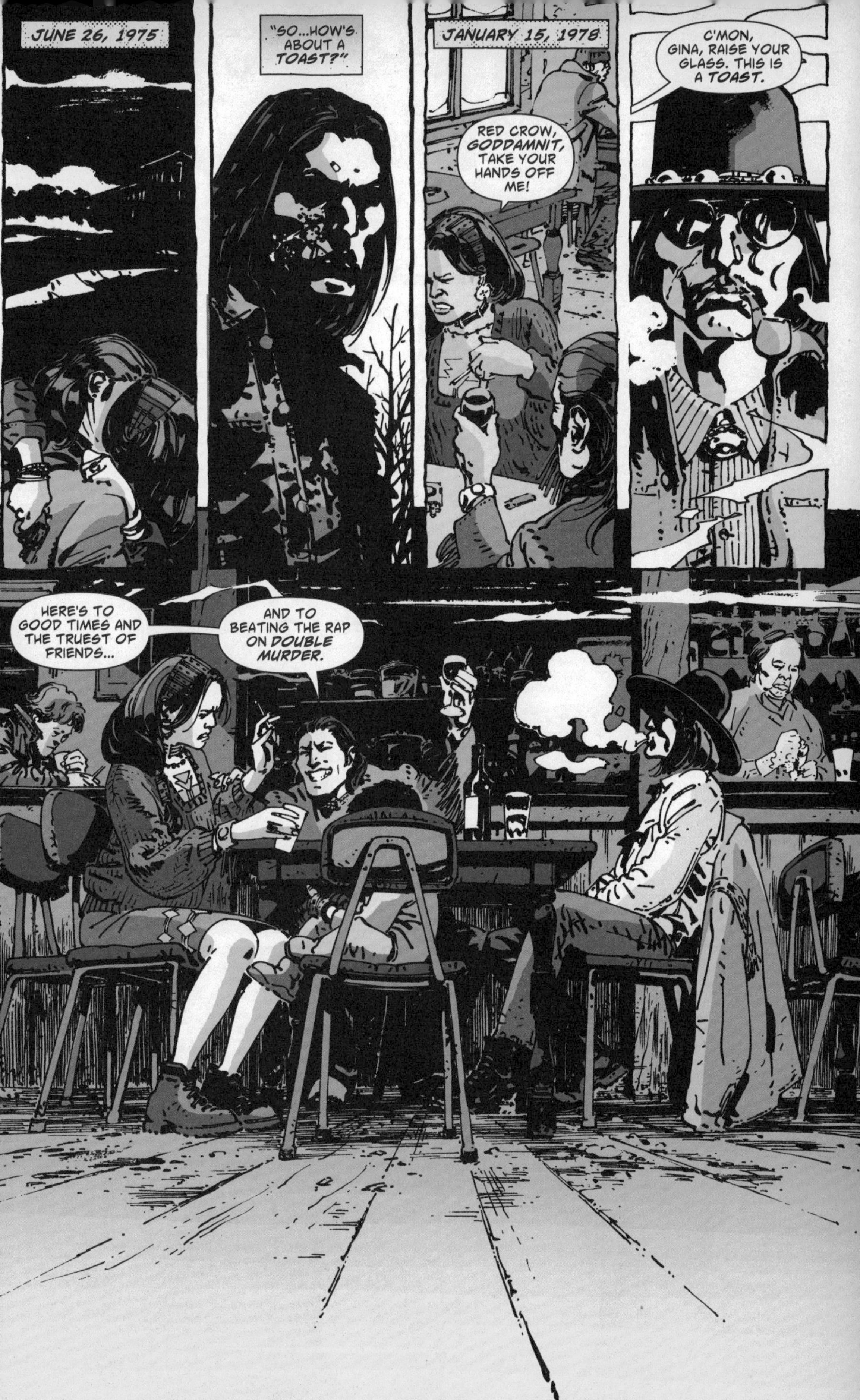

JUNE 26, 1975
"SO...HOW'S ABOUT A TOAST?"
JANUARY 15, 1978
RED CROW, GODDAMNIT, TAKE YOUR HANDS OFF ME!
C'MON, GINA, RAISE YOUR GLASS. THIS IS A TOAST.
HERE'S TO GOOD TIMES AND THE TRUEST OF FRIENDS...
AND TO BEATING THE RAP ON DOUBLE MURDER.

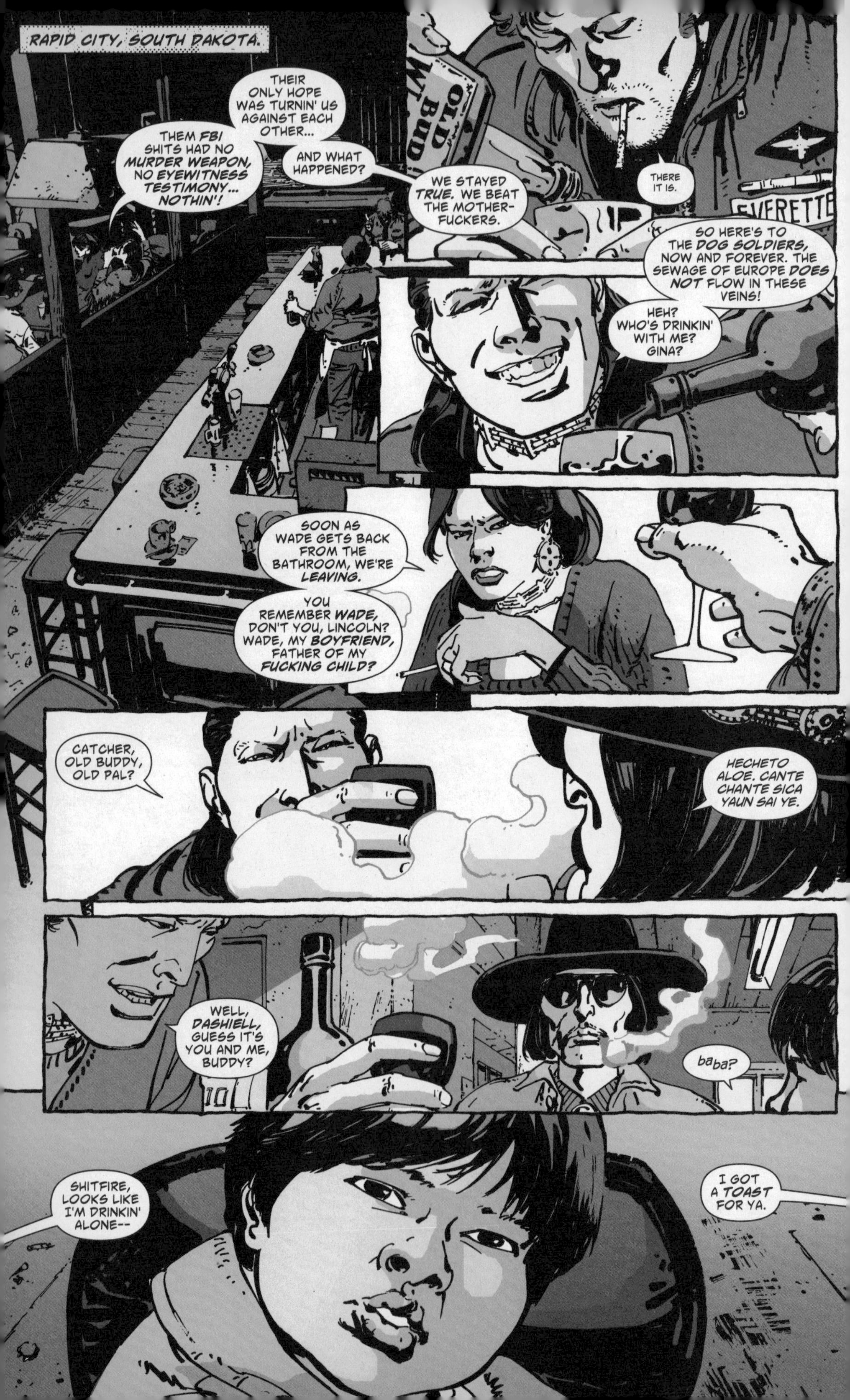
RAPID CITY, SOUTH DAKOTA.
THEM FBI SHITS HAD NO MURDER WEAPON, NO EYEWITNESS TESTIMONY... NOTHIN'!
THEIR ONLY HOPE WAS TURNIN' US AGAINST EACH OTHER...
AND WHAT HAPPENED?
WE STAYED TRUE. WE BEAT THE MOTHER-FUCKERS.
OLD W BUD
THERE IT IS.
EVERETTE
SO HERE'S TO THE DOG SOLDIERS, NOW AND FOREVER. THE SEWAGE OF EUROPE DOES NOT FLOW IN THESE VEINS!
HEH? WHO'S DRINKIN' WITH ME? GINA?
SOON AS WADE GETS BACK FROM THE BATHROOM, WE'RE LEAVING.
YOU REMEMBER WADE, DON'T YOU, LINCOLN? WADE, MY BOYFRIEND, FATHER OF MY FUCKING CHILD?
CATCHER, OLD BUDDY, OLD PAL?
HECHETO ALOE. CANTE CHANTE SICA YAUN SAI YE.
WELL, DASHIELL, GUESS IT'S YOU AND ME, BUDDY?
baba?
SHITFIRE, LOOKS LIKE I'M DRINKIN' ALONE--
I GOT A TOAST FOR YA.

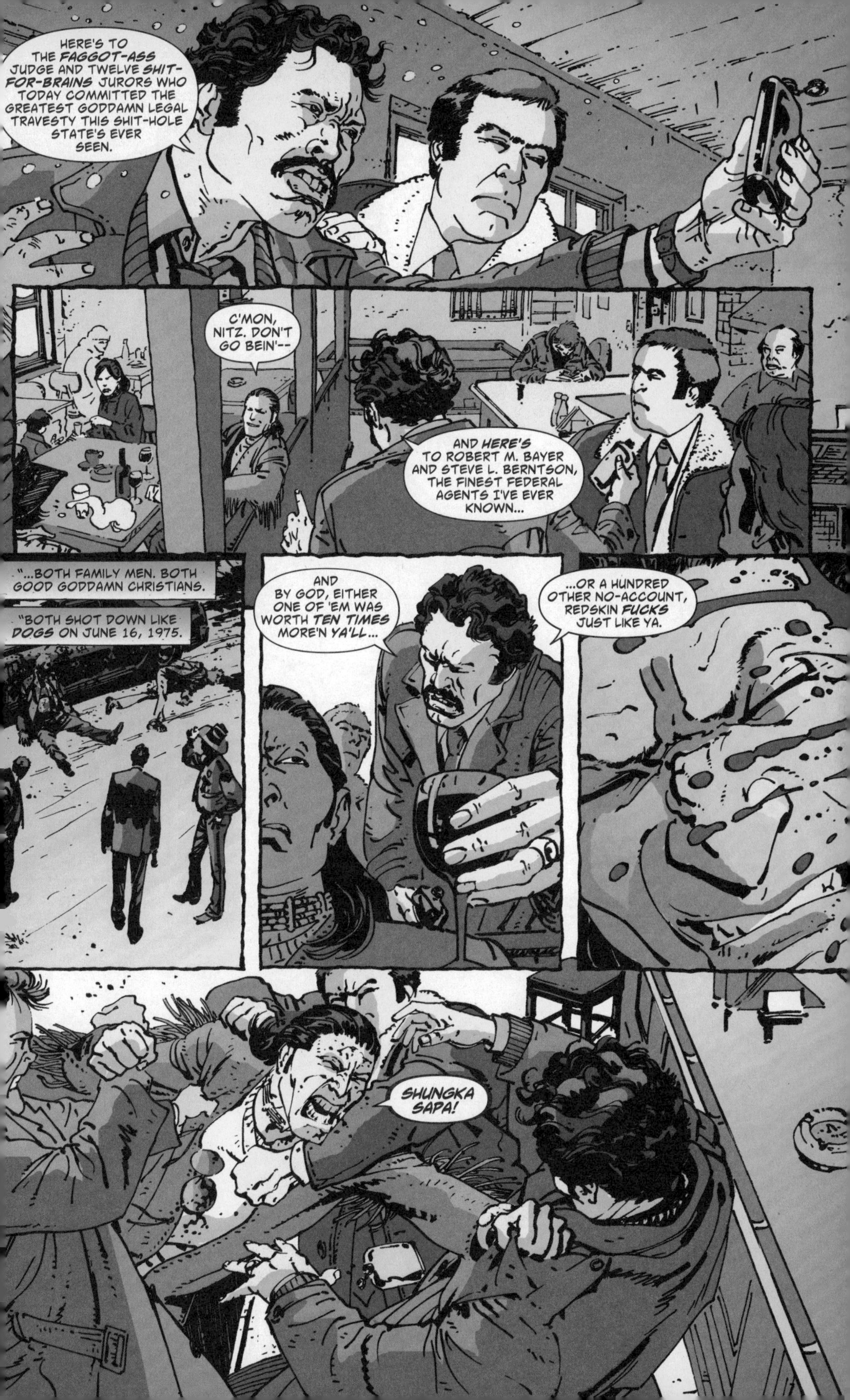
HERE'S TO THE FAGGOT-ASS JUDGE AND TWELVE SHIT-FOR-BRAINS JURORS WHO TODAY COMMITTED THE GREATEST GODDAMN LEGAL TRAVESTY THIS SHIT-HOLE STATE'S EVER SEEN.
C'MON, NITZ. DON'T GO BEIN'--
AND HERE'S TO ROBERT M. BAYER AND STEVE L. BERNTSON, THE FINEST FEDERAL AGENTS I'VE EVER KNOWN...
"...BOTH FAMILY MEN. BOTH GOOD GODDAMN CHRISTIANS.
"BOTH SHOT DOWN LIKE DOGS ON JUNE 16, 1975.
AND BY GOD, EITHER ONE OF 'EM WAS WORTH TEN TIMES MORE'N YA'LL...
...OR A HUNDRED OTHER NO-ACCOUNT, REDSKIN FUCKS JUST LIKE YA.
SHUNGKA SAPA!

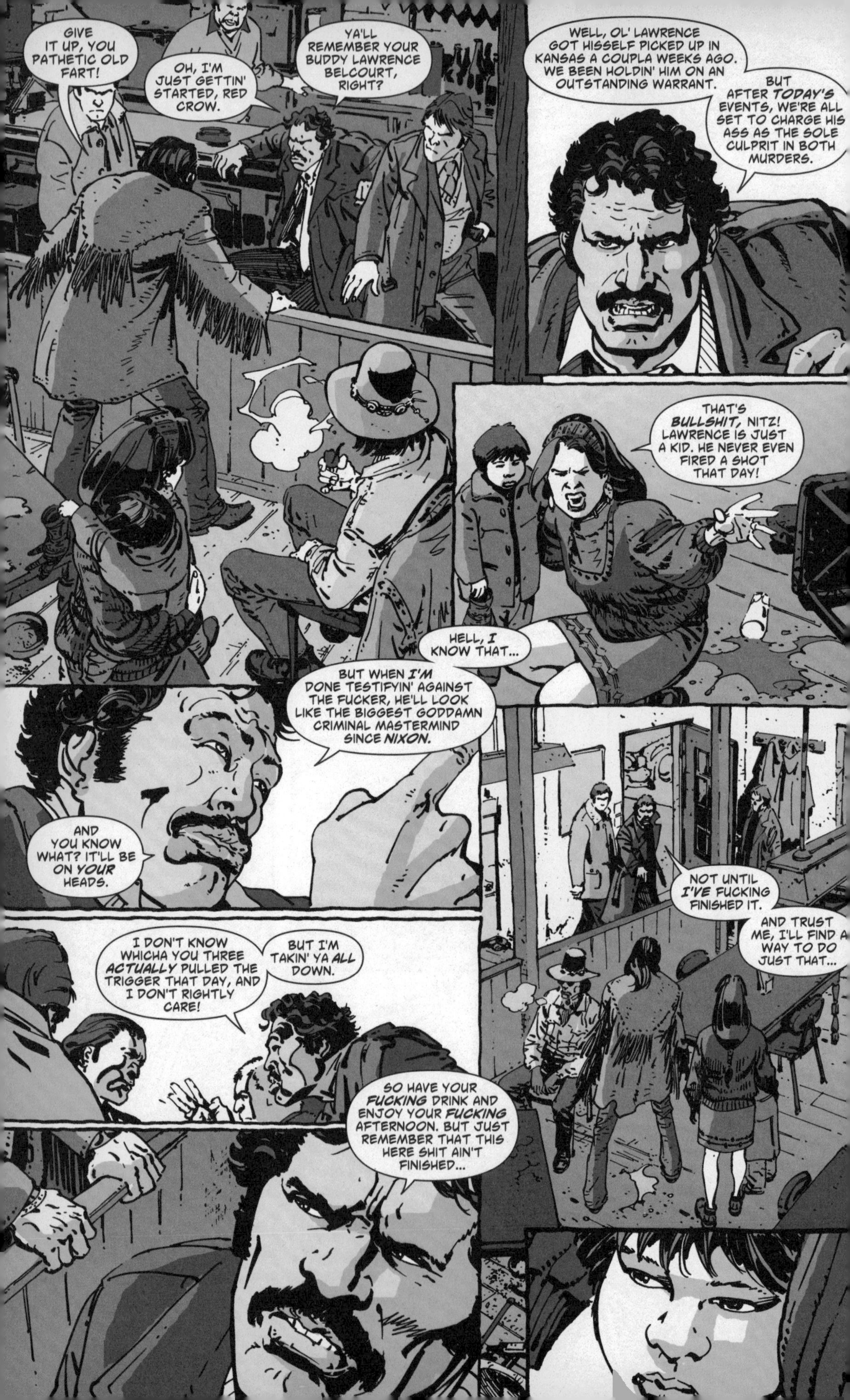
GIVE IT UP, YOU PATHETIC OLD FART!
OH, I'M JUST GETTIN' STARTED, RED CROW.
YA'LL REMEMBER YOUR BUDDY LAWRENCE BELCOURT, RIGHT?
WELL, OL' LAWRENCE GOT HISSELF PICKED UP IN KANSAS A COUPLA WEEKS AGO. WE BEEN HOLDIN' HIM ON AN OUTSTANDING WARRANT.
BUT AFTER *TODAY'S* EVENTS, WE'RE ALL SET TO CHARGE HIS ASS AS THE SOLE CULPRIT IN BOTH MURDERS.
THAT'S *BULLSHIT,* NITZ! LAWRENCE IS JUST A KID. HE NEVER EVEN FIRED A SHOT THAT DAY!
HELL, *I* KNOW THAT...
BUT WHEN *I'M* DONE TESTIFYIN' AGAINST THE FUCKER, HE'LL LOOK LIKE THE BIGGEST GODDAMN CRIMINAL MASTERMIND SINCE *NIXON.*
AND YOU KNOW WHAT? IT'LL BE ON *YOUR* HEADS.
I DON'T KNOW WHICHA YOU THREE *ACTUALLY* PULLED THE TRIGGER THAT DAY, AND I DON'T RIGHTLY CARE!
BUT I'M TAKIN' YA *ALL* DOWN.
SO HAVE YOUR *FUCKING* DRINK AND ENJOY YOUR *FUCKING* AFTERNOON. BUT JUST REMEMBER THAT THIS HERE SHIT AIN'T FINISHED...
NOT UNTIL *I'VE* FUCKING FINISHED IT.
AND TRUST ME, I'LL FIND A WAY TO DO JUST THAT...

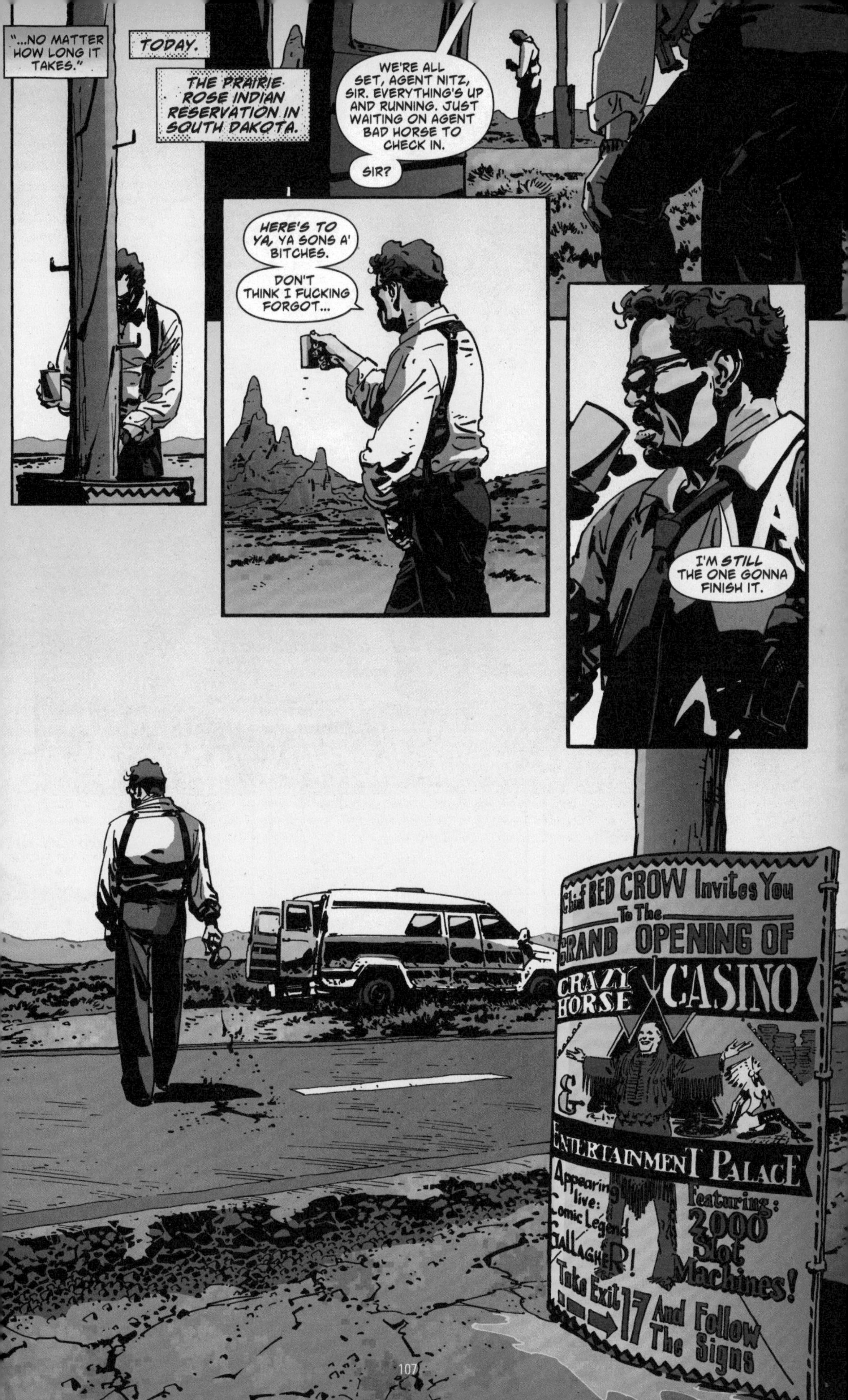
"...NO MATTER HOW LONG IT TAKES."
TODAY.
THE PRAIRIE ROSE INDIAN RESERVATION IN SOUTH DAKOTA.
WE'RE ALL SET, AGENT NITZ, SIR. EVERYTHING'S UP AND RUNNING. JUST WAITING ON AGENT BAD HORSE TO CHECK IN.
SIR?
HERE'S TO YA, YA SONS A' BITCHES.
DON'T THINK I FUCKING FORGOT...
I'M STILL THE ONE GONNA FINISH IT.
Chief RED CROW Invites You To The GRAND OPENING OF
CRAZY HORSE CASINO
& ENTERTAINMENT PALACE
Appearing live: Comic Legend GALLAGHER!
Featuring: 2000 Slot Machines!
Take Exit 17 And Follow The Signs

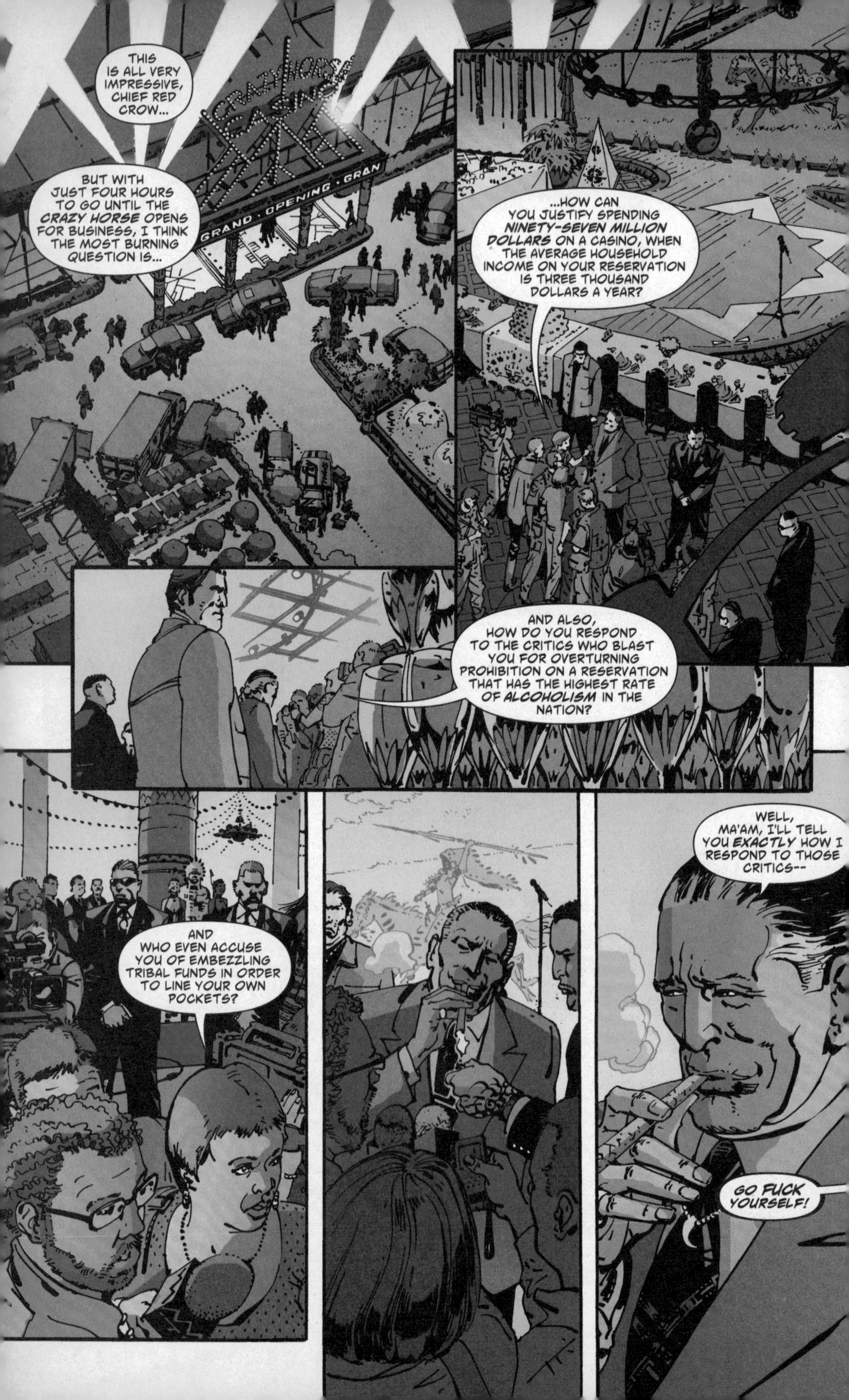
THIS IS ALL VERY IMPRESSIVE, CHIEF RED CROW...
CRAZY HORSE CASINO
GRAND · OPENING · GRAN
BUT WITH JUST FOUR HOURS TO GO UNTIL THE CRAZY HORSE OPENS FOR BUSINESS, I THINK THE MOST BURNING QUESTION IS...
...HOW CAN YOU JUSTIFY SPENDING NINETY-SEVEN MILLION DOLLARS ON A CASINO, WHEN THE AVERAGE HOUSEHOLD INCOME ON YOUR RESERVATION IS THREE THOUSAND DOLLARS A YEAR?
AND ALSO, HOW DO YOU RESPOND TO THE CRITICS WHO BLAST YOU FOR OVERTURNING PROHIBITION ON A RESERVATION THAT HAS THE HIGHEST RATE OF ALCOHOLISM IN THE NATION?
AND WHO EVEN ACCUSE YOU OF EMBEZZLING TRIBAL FUNDS IN ORDER TO LINE YOUR OWN POCKETS?
WELL, MA'AM, I'LL TELL YOU EXACTLY HOW I RESPOND TO THOSE CRITICS--
GO FUCK YOURSELF!

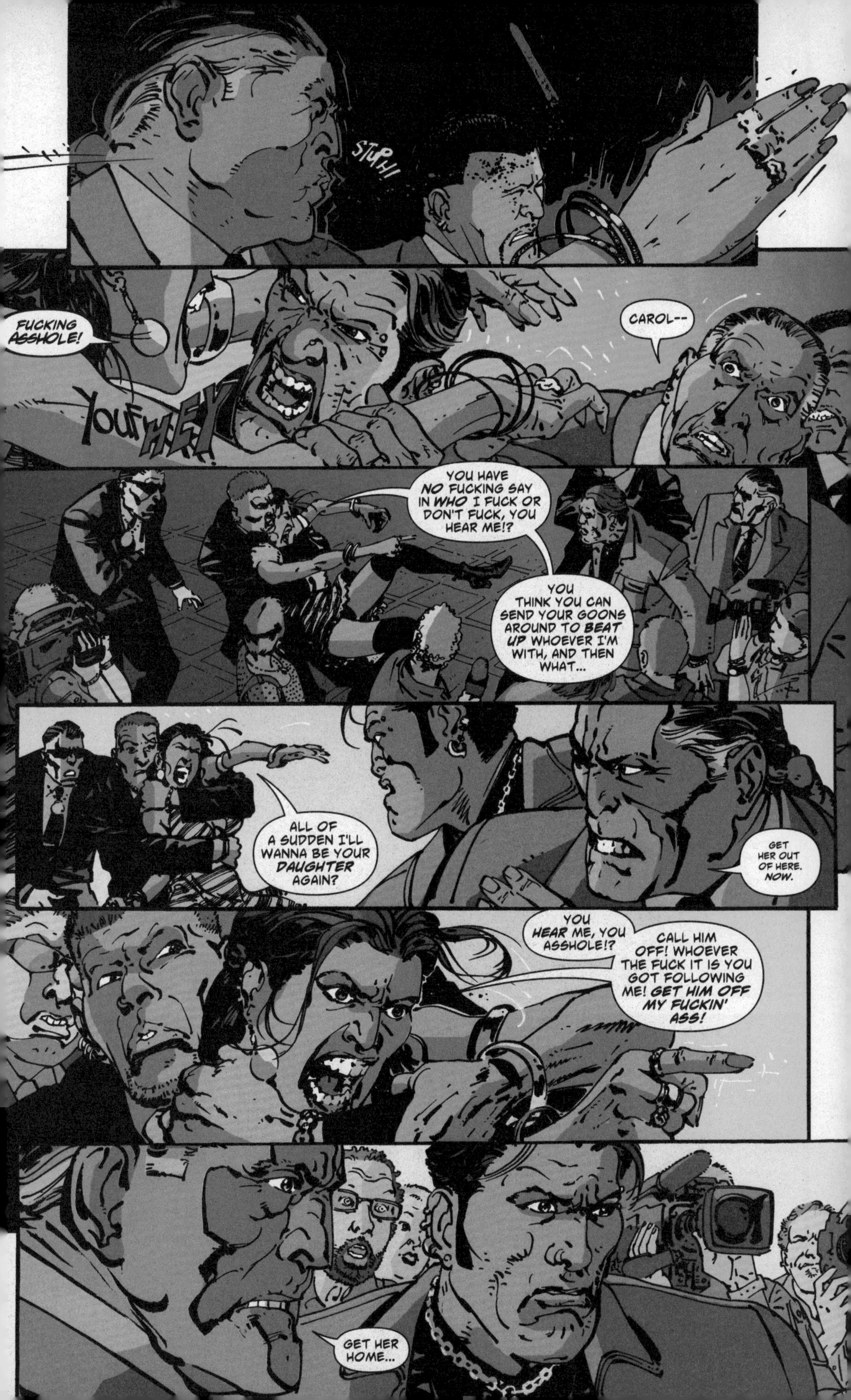
STUPH!
FUCKING ASSHOLE!
YOU! HEY
CAROL--
YOU HAVE NO FUCKING SAY IN WHO I FUCK OR DON'T FUCK, YOU HEAR ME!?
YOU THINK YOU CAN SEND YOUR GOONS AROUND TO BEAT UP WHOEVER I'M WITH, AND THEN WHAT...
ALL OF A SUDDEN I'LL WANNA BE YOUR DAUGHTER AGAIN?
GET HER OUT OF HERE. NOW.
YOU HEAR ME, YOU ASSHOLE!?
CALL HIM OFF! WHOEVER THE FUCK IT IS YOU GOT FOLLOWING ME! GET HIM OFF MY FUCKIN' ASS!
GET HER HOME...

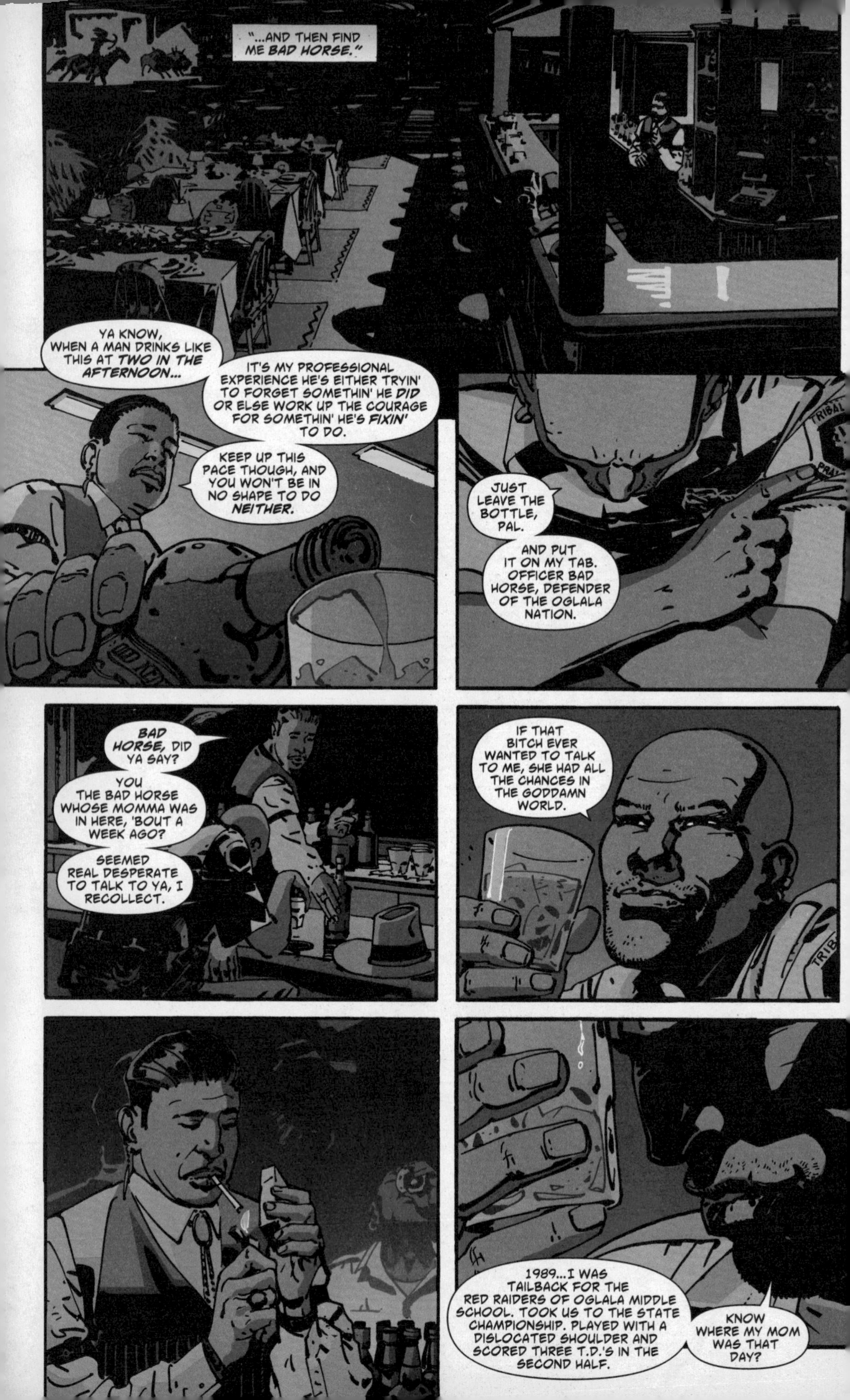
"...AND THEN FIND ME BAD HORSE."
YA KNOW, WHEN A MAN DRINKS LIKE THIS AT TWO IN THE AFTERNOON...
IT'S MY PROFESSIONAL EXPERIENCE HE'S EITHER TRYIN' TO FORGET SOMETHIN' HE DID OR ELSE WORK UP THE COURAGE FOR SOMETHIN' HE'S FIXIN' TO DO.
KEEP UP THIS PACE THOUGH, AND YOU WON'T BE IN NO SHAPE TO DO NEITHER.
JUST LEAVE THE BOTTLE, PAL.
AND PUT IT ON MY TAB. OFFICER BAD HORSE, DEFENDER OF THE OGLALA NATION.
BAD HORSE, DID YA SAY?
YOU THE BAD HORSE WHOSE MOMMA WAS IN HERE, 'BOUT A WEEK AGO?
SEEMED REAL DESPERATE TO TALK TO YA, I RECOLLECT.
IF THAT BITCH EVER WANTED TO TALK TO ME, SHE HAD ALL THE CHANCES IN THE GODDAMN WORLD.
1989...I WAS TAILBACK FOR THE RED RAIDERS OF OGLALA MIDDLE SCHOOL. TOOK US TO THE STATE CHAMPIONSHIP. PLAYED WITH A DISLOCATED SHOULDER AND SCORED THREE T.D.'S IN THE SECOND HALF.
KNOW WHERE MY MOM WAS THAT DAY?

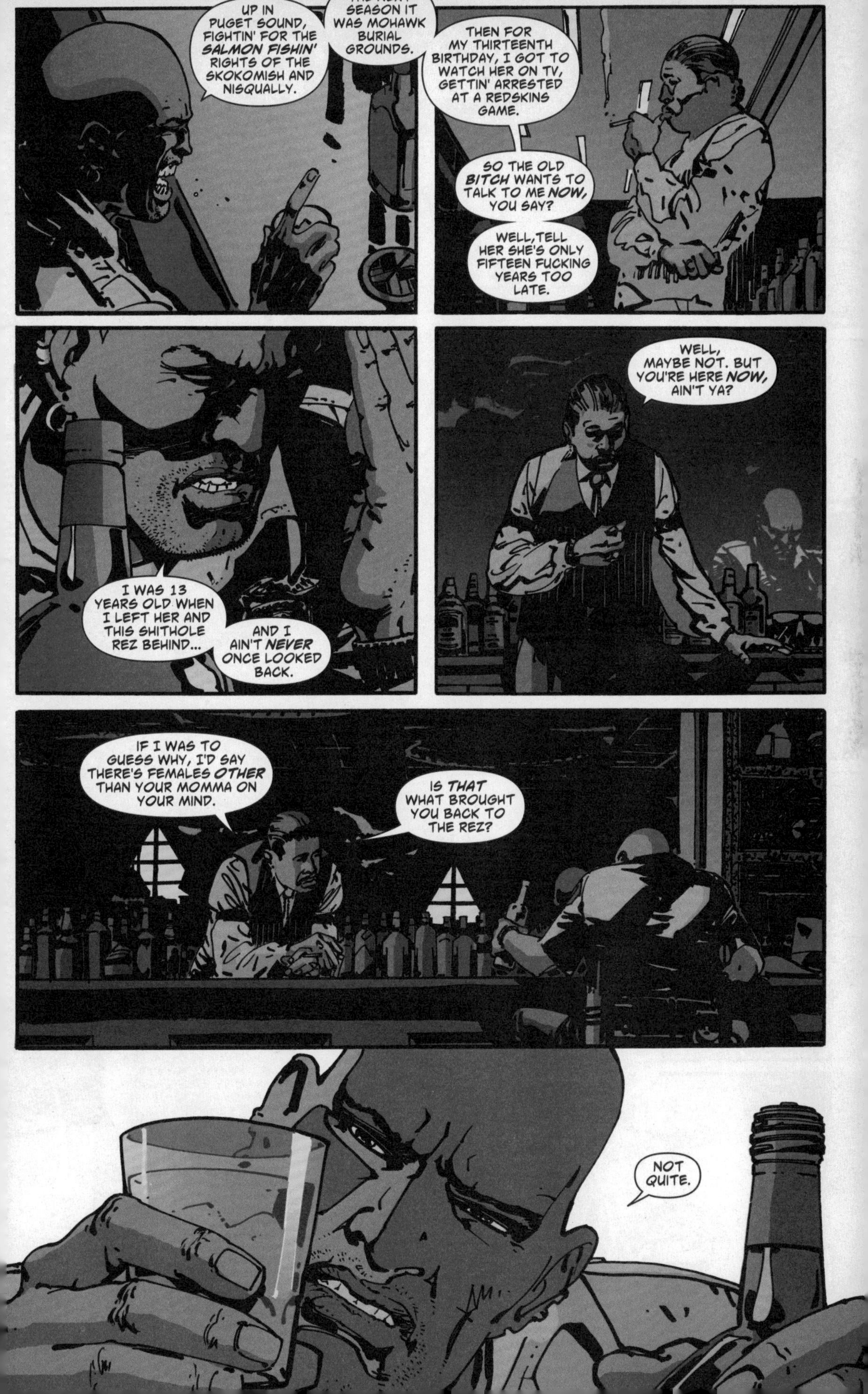

UP IN PUGET SOUND, FIGHTIN' FOR THE SALMON FISHIN' RIGHTS OF THE SKOKOMISH AND NISQUALLY.
THE NEXT SEASON IT WAS MOHAWK BURIAL GROUNDS.
THEN FOR MY THIRTEENTH BIRTHDAY, I GOT TO WATCH HER ON TV, GETTIN' ARRESTED AT A REDSKINS GAME.
SO THE OLD BITCH WANTS TO TALK TO ME NOW, YOU SAY?
WELL,TELL HER SHE'S ONLY FIFTEEN FUCKING YEARS TOO LATE.
I WAS 13 YEARS OLD WHEN I LEFT HER AND THIS SHITHOLE REZ BEHIND...
AND I AIN'T NEVER ONCE LOOKED BACK.
WELL, MAYBE NOT. BUT YOU'RE HERE NOW, AIN'T YA?
IF I WAS TO GUESS WHY, I'D SAY THERE'S FEMALES OTHER THAN YOUR MOMMA ON YOUR MIND.
IS THAT WHAT BROUGHT YOU BACK TO THE REZ?
NOT QUITE.

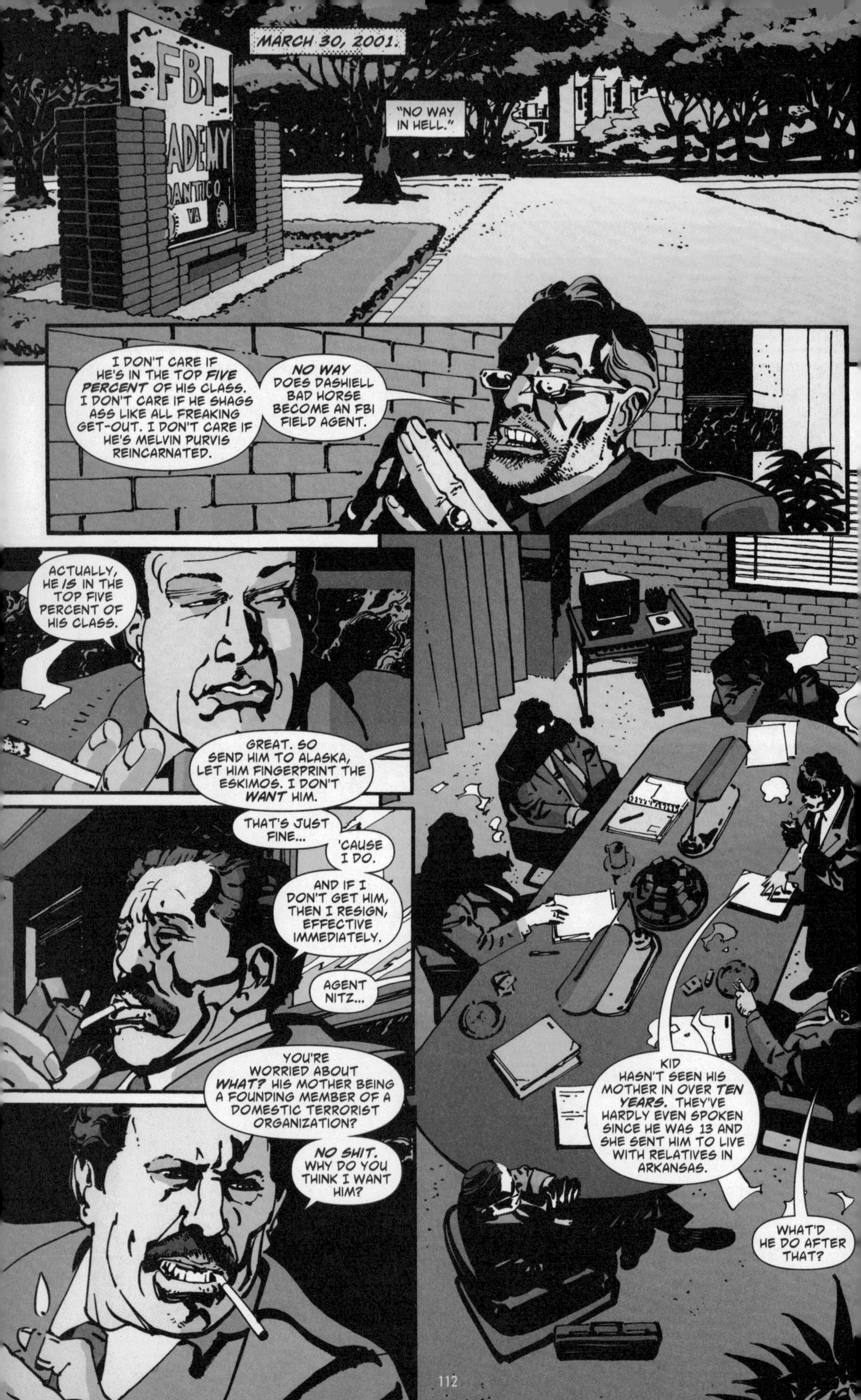
MARCH 30, 2001.
FBI
ADEMY
ANTICO
VA
"NO WAY IN HELL."
I DON'T CARE IF HE'S IN THE TOP FIVE PERCENT OF HIS CLASS. I DON'T CARE IF HE SHAGS ASS LIKE ALL FREAKING GET-OUT. I DON'T CARE IF HE'S MELVIN PURVIS REINCARNATED.
NO WAY DOES DASHIELL BAD HORSE BECOME AN FBI FIELD AGENT.
ACTUALLY, HE IS IN THE TOP FIVE PERCENT OF HIS CLASS.
GREAT. SO SEND HIM TO ALASKA, LET HIM FINGERPRINT THE ESKIMOS. I DON'T WANT HIM.
THAT'S JUST FINE...
'CAUSE I DO.
AND IF I DON'T GET HIM, THEN I RESIGN, EFFECTIVE IMMEDIATELY.
AGENT NITZ...
YOU'RE WORRIED ABOUT WHAT? HIS MOTHER BEING A FOUNDING MEMBER OF A DOMESTIC TERRORIST ORGANIZATION?
NO SHIT. WHY DO YOU THINK I WANT HIM?
KID HASN'T SEEN HIS MOTHER IN OVER TEN YEARS. THEY'VE HARDLY EVEN SPOKEN SINCE HE WAS 13 AND SHE SENT HIM TO LIVE WITH RELATIVES IN ARKANSAS.
WHAT'D HE DO AFTER THAT?

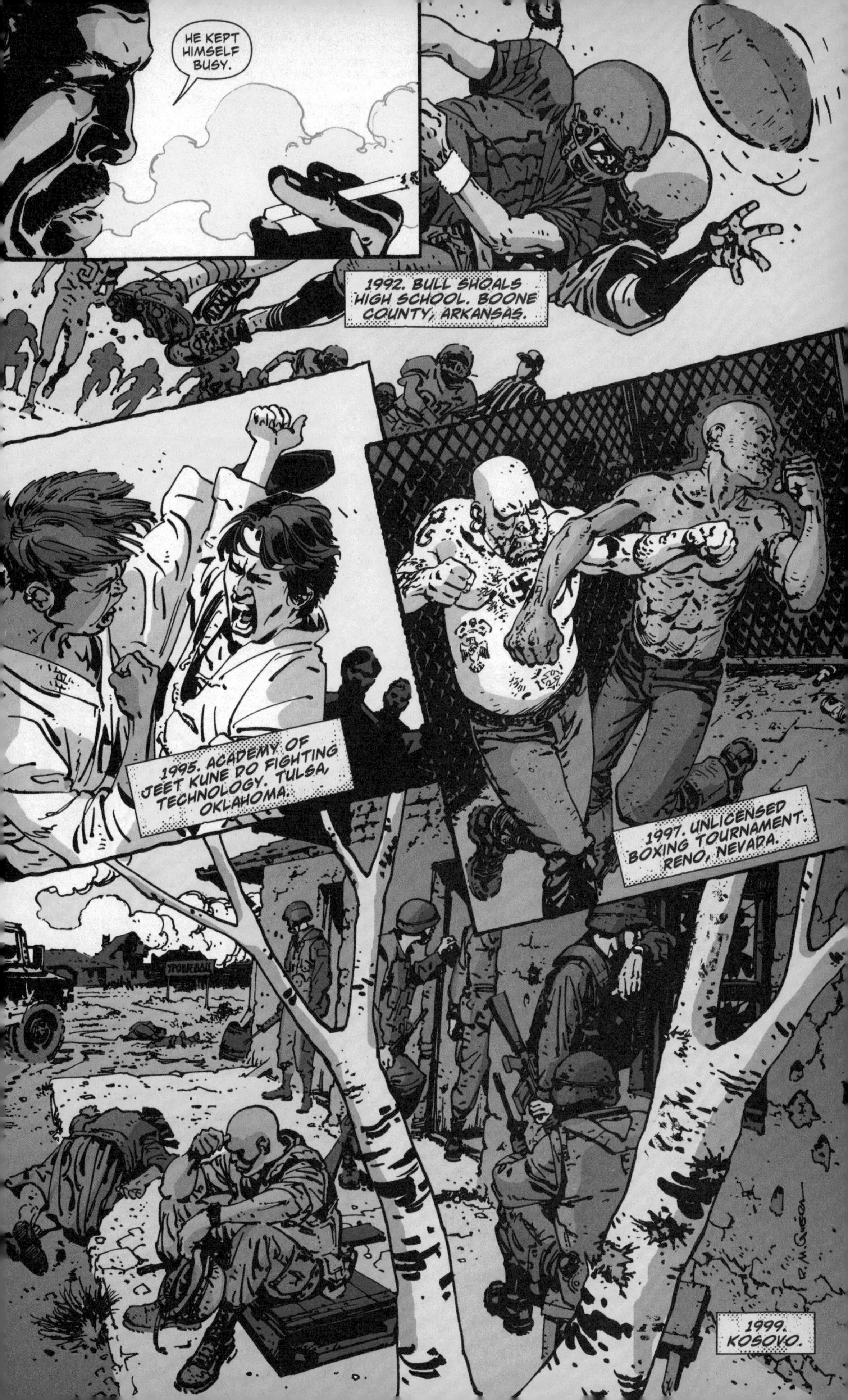
HE KEPT HIMSELF BUSY.
1992. BULL SHOALS HIGH SCHOOL. BOONE COUNTY, ARKANSAS.
1995. ACADEMY OF JEET KUNE DO FIGHTING TECHNOLOGY. TULSA, OKLAHOMA.
1997. UNLICENSED BOXING TOURNAMENT. RENO, NEVADA.
1999. KOSOVO.

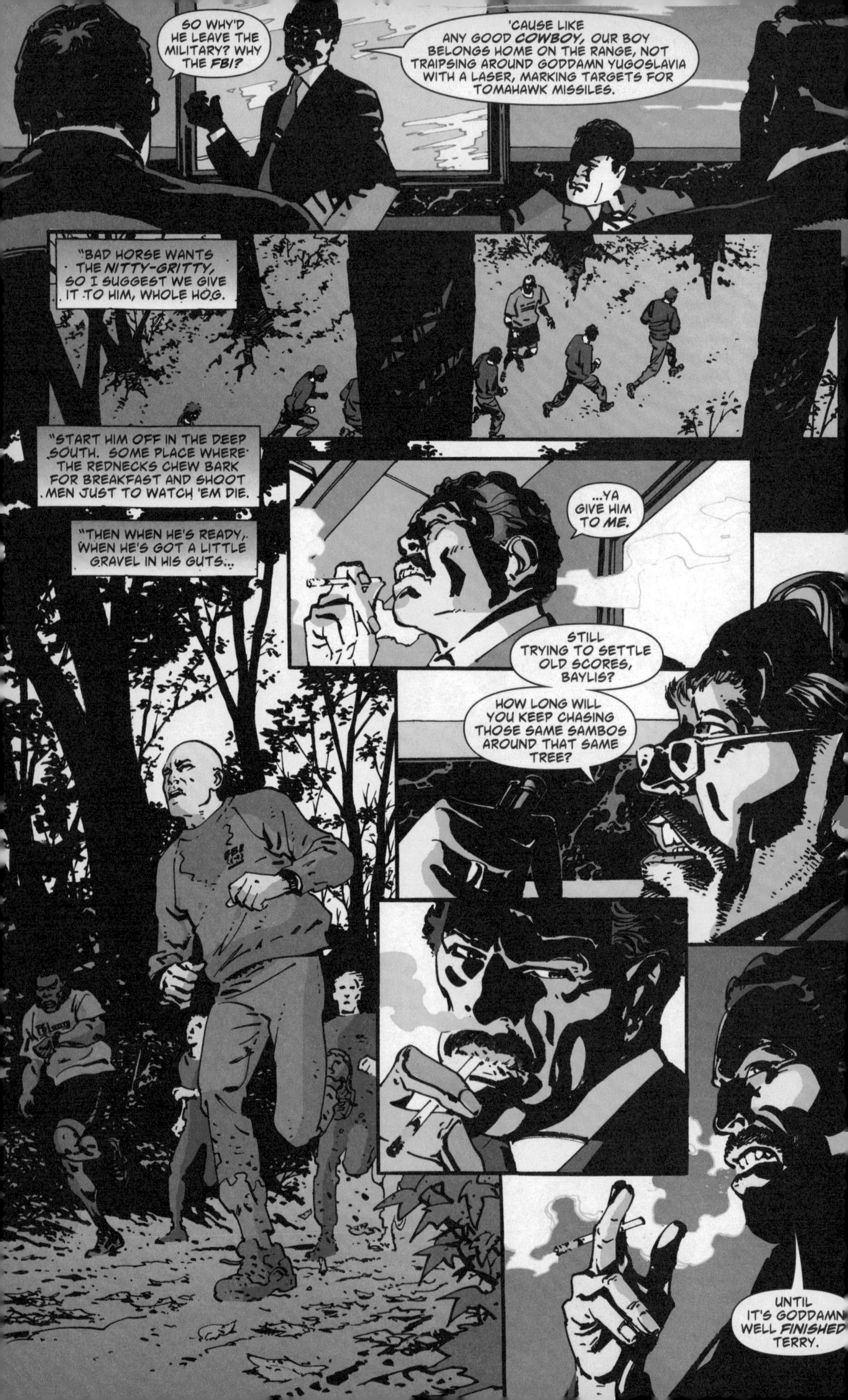
SO WHY'D HE LEAVE THE MILITARY? WHY THE FBI?
'CAUSE LIKE ANY GOOD COWBOY, OUR BOY BELONGS HOME ON THE RANGE, NOT TRAIPSING AROUND GODDAMN YUGOSLAVIA WITH A LASER, MARKING TARGETS FOR TOMAHAWK MISSILES.
"BAD HORSE WANTS THE NITTY-GRITTY, SO I SUGGEST WE GIVE IT TO HIM, WHOLE HOG.
"START HIM OFF IN THE DEEP SOUTH. SOME PLACE WHERE THE REDNECKS CHEW BARK FOR BREAKFAST AND SHOOT MEN JUST TO WATCH 'EM DIE.
"THEN WHEN HE'S READY, WHEN HE'S GOT A LITTLE GRAVEL IN HIS GUTS...
...YA GIVE HIM TO ME.
STILL TRYING TO SETTLE OLD SCORES, BAYLIS?
HOW LONG WILL YOU KEEP CHASING THOSE SAME SAMBOS AROUND THAT SAME TREE?
UNTIL IT'S GODDAMN WELL FINISHED TERRY.

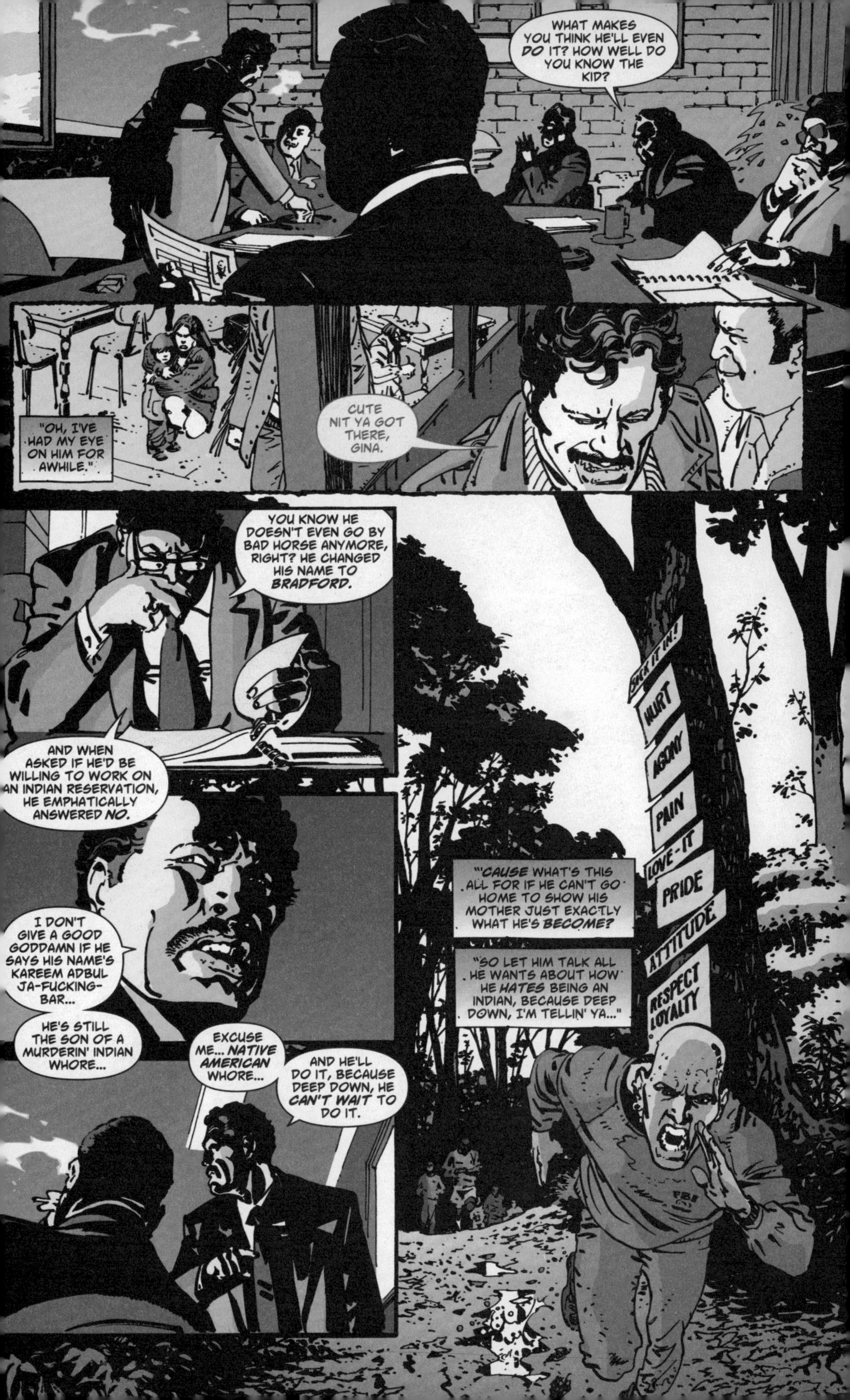

WHAT MAKES YOU THINK HE'LL EVEN DO IT? HOW WELL DO YOU KNOW THE KID?
"OH, I'VE HAD MY EYE ON HIM FOR AWHILE."
CUTE NIT YA GOT THERE, GINA.
YOU KNOW HE DOESN'T EVEN GO BY BAD HORSE ANYMORE, RIGHT? HE CHANGED HIS NAME TO BRADFORD.
AND WHEN ASKED IF HE'D BE WILLING TO WORK ON AN INDIAN RESERVATION, HE EMPHATICALLY ANSWERED NO.
I DON'T GIVE A GOOD GODDAMN IF HE SAYS HIS NAME'S KAREEM ADBUL JA-FUCKING-BAR...
HE'S STILL THE SON OF A MURDERIN' INDIAN WHORE...
EXCUSE ME... NATIVE AMERICAN WHORE...
AND HE'LL DO IT, BECAUSE DEEP DOWN, HE CAN'T WAIT TO DO IT.
"'CAUSE WHAT'S THIS ALL FOR IF HE CAN'T GO HOME TO SHOW HIS MOTHER JUST EXACTLY WHAT HE'S BECOME?
"SO LET HIM TALK ALL HE WANTS ABOUT HOW HE HATES BEING AN INDIAN, BECAUSE DEEP DOWN, I'M TELLIN' YA..."
SUCK IT IN!
HURT
AGONY
PAIN
LOVE-IT
PRIDE
ATTITUDE
RESPECT
LOYALTY
FBI

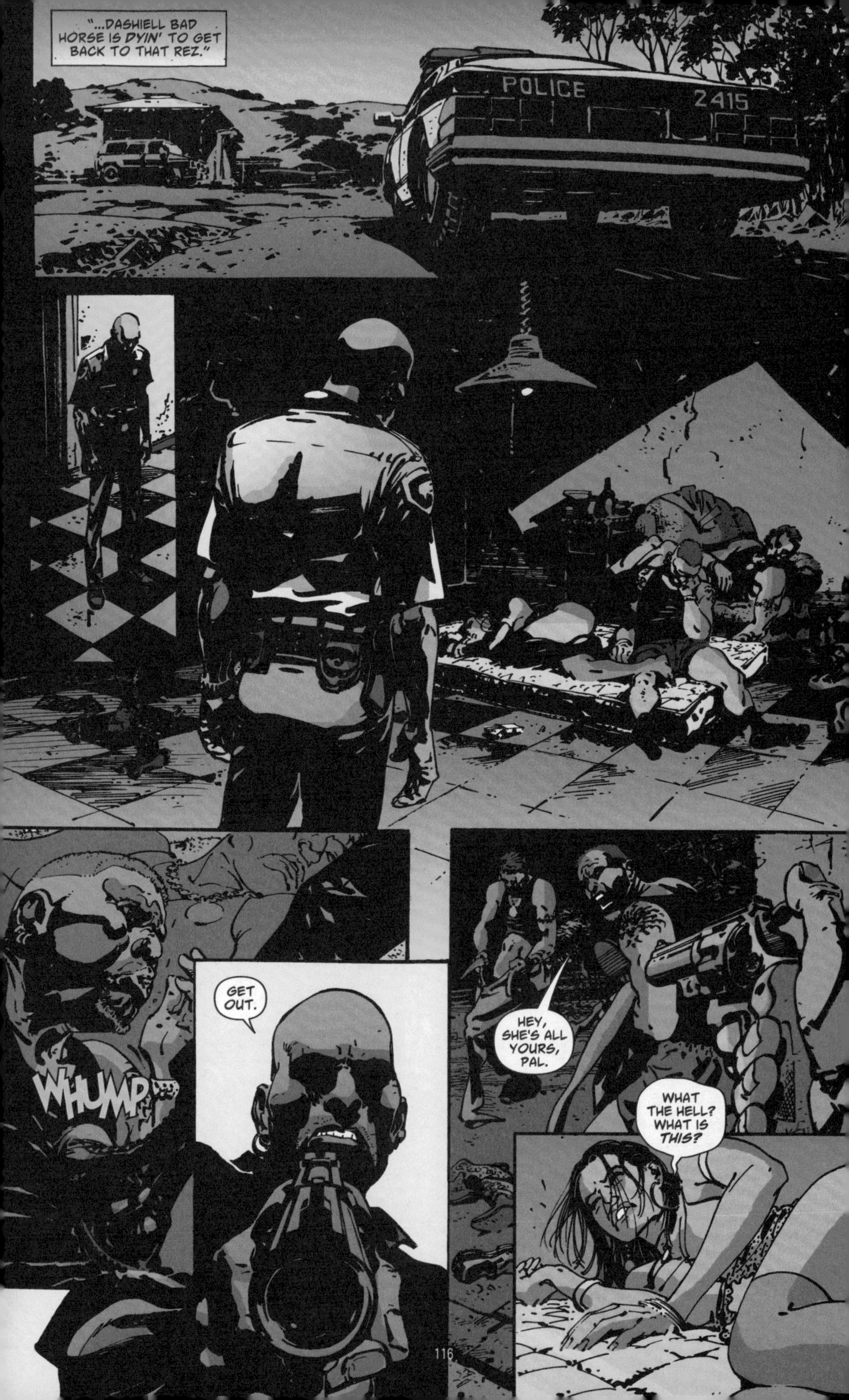
"...DASHIELL BAD HORSE IS DYIN' TO GET BACK TO THAT REZ."
POLICE
2415
WHUMP
GET OUT.
HEY, SHE'S ALL YOURS, PAL.
WHAT THE HELL? WHAT IS THIS?

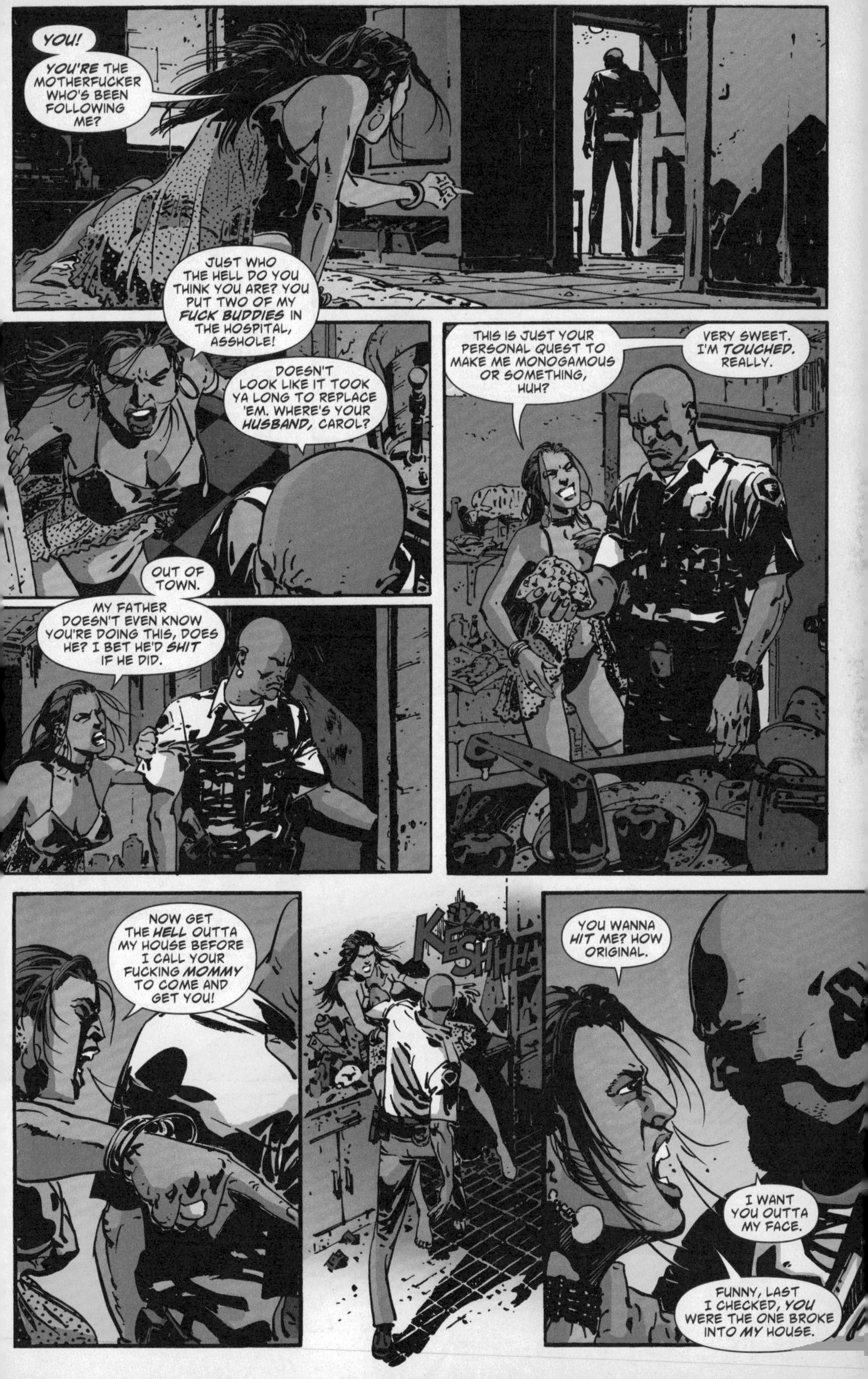
YOU!
YOU'RE THE MOTHERFUCKER WHO'S BEEN FOLLOWING ME?
JUST WHO THE HELL DO YOU THINK YOU ARE? YOU PUT TWO OF MY FUCK BUDDIES IN THE HOSPITAL, ASSHOLE!
DOESN'T LOOK LIKE IT TOOK YA LONG TO REPLACE 'EM. WHERE'S YOUR HUSBAND, CAROL?
OUT OF TOWN.
MY FATHER DOESN'T EVEN KNOW YOU'RE DOING THIS, DOES HE? I BET HE'D SHIT IF HE DID.
THIS IS JUST YOUR PERSONAL QUEST TO MAKE ME MONOGAMOUS OR SOMETHING, HUH?
VERY SWEET. I'M TOUCHED. REALLY.
NOW GET THE HELL OUTTA MY HOUSE BEFORE I CALL YOUR FUCKING MOMMY TO COME AND GET YOU!
KSHHH
YOU WANNA HIT ME? HOW ORIGINAL.
I WANT YOU OUTTA MY FACE.
FUNNY, LAST I CHECKED, YOU WERE THE ONE BROKE INTO MY HOUSE.

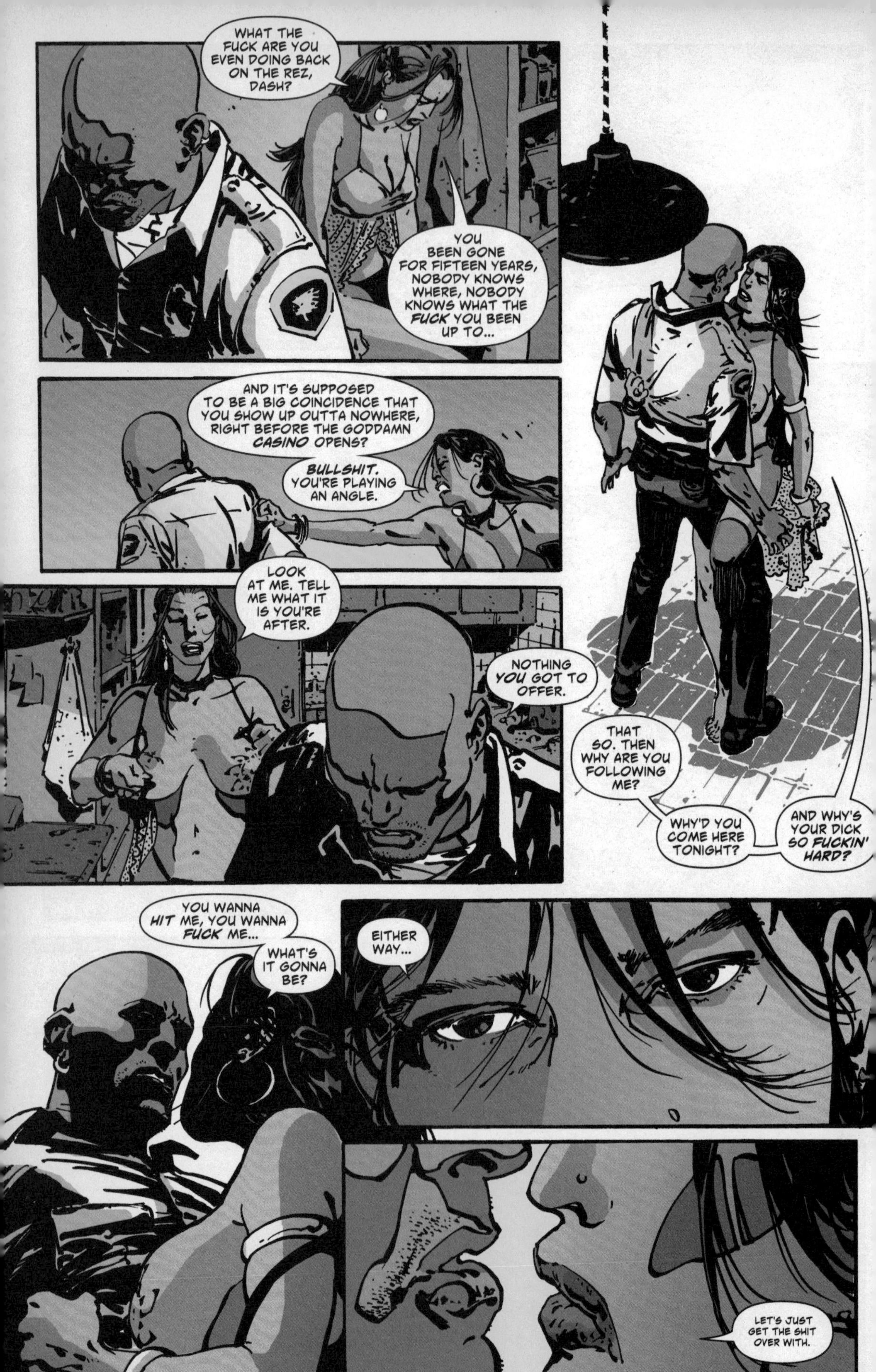
WHAT THE FUCK ARE YOU EVEN DOING BACK ON THE REZ, DASH?
YOU BEEN GONE FOR FIFTEEN YEARS, NOBODY KNOWS WHERE, NOBODY KNOWS WHAT THE FUCK YOU BEEN UP TO...
AND IT'S SUPPOSED TO BE A BIG COINCIDENCE THAT YOU SHOW UP OUTTA NOWHERE, RIGHT BEFORE THE GODDAMN CASINO OPENS?
BULLSHIT. YOU'RE PLAYING AN ANGLE.
LOOK AT ME. TELL ME WHAT IT IS YOU'RE AFTER.
NOTHING YOU GOT TO OFFER.
THAT SO. THEN WHY ARE YOU FOLLOWING ME?
WHY'D YOU COME HERE TONIGHT?
AND WHY'S YOUR DICK SO FUCKIN' HARD?
YOU WANNA HIT ME, YOU WANNA FUCK ME...
WHAT'S IT GONNA BE?
EITHER WAY...
LET'S JUST GET THE SHIT OVER WITH.

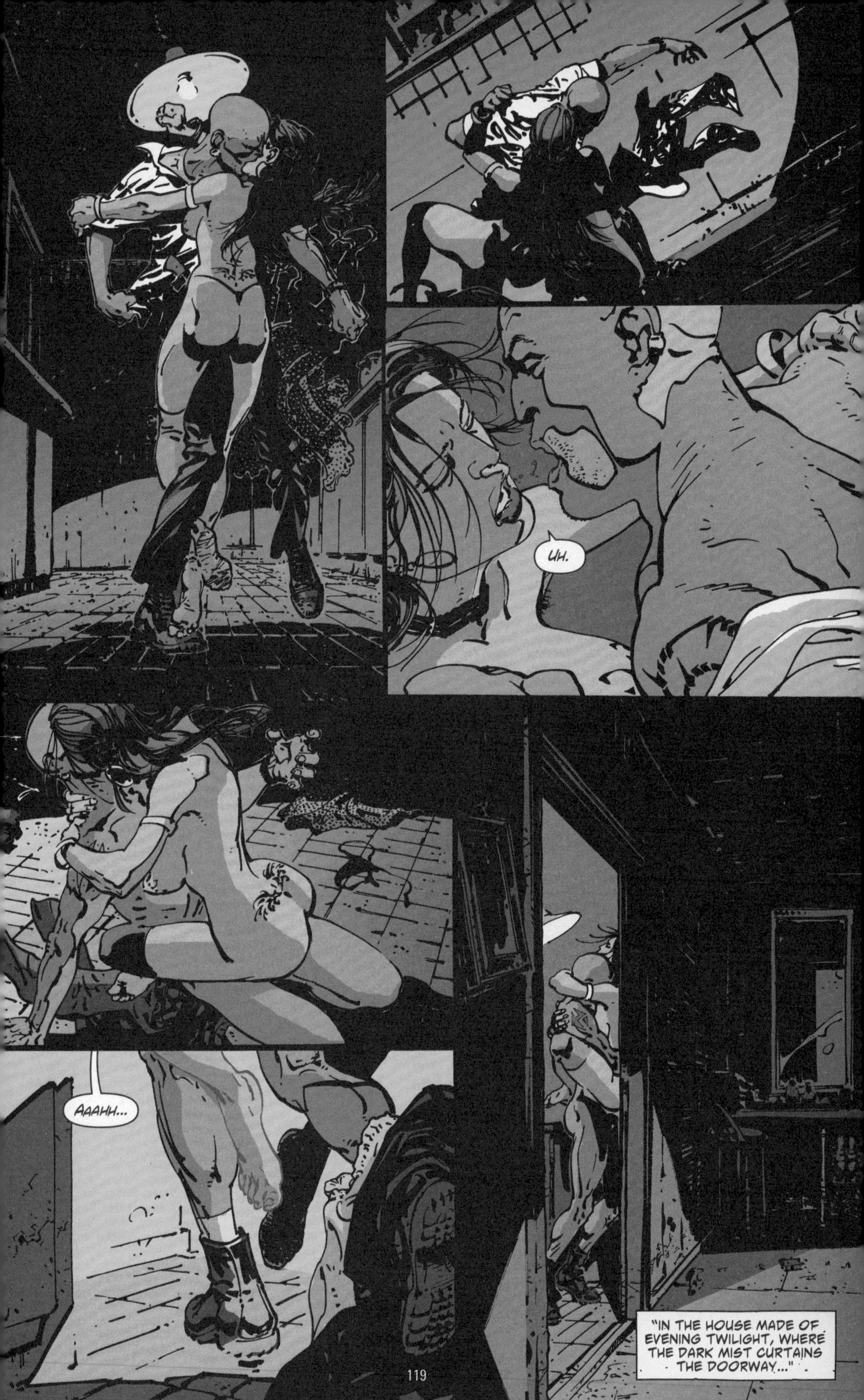
UH.
AAAHH...
"IN THE HOUSE MADE OF EVENING TWILIGHT, WHERE THE DARK MIST CURTAINS THE DOORWAY..."

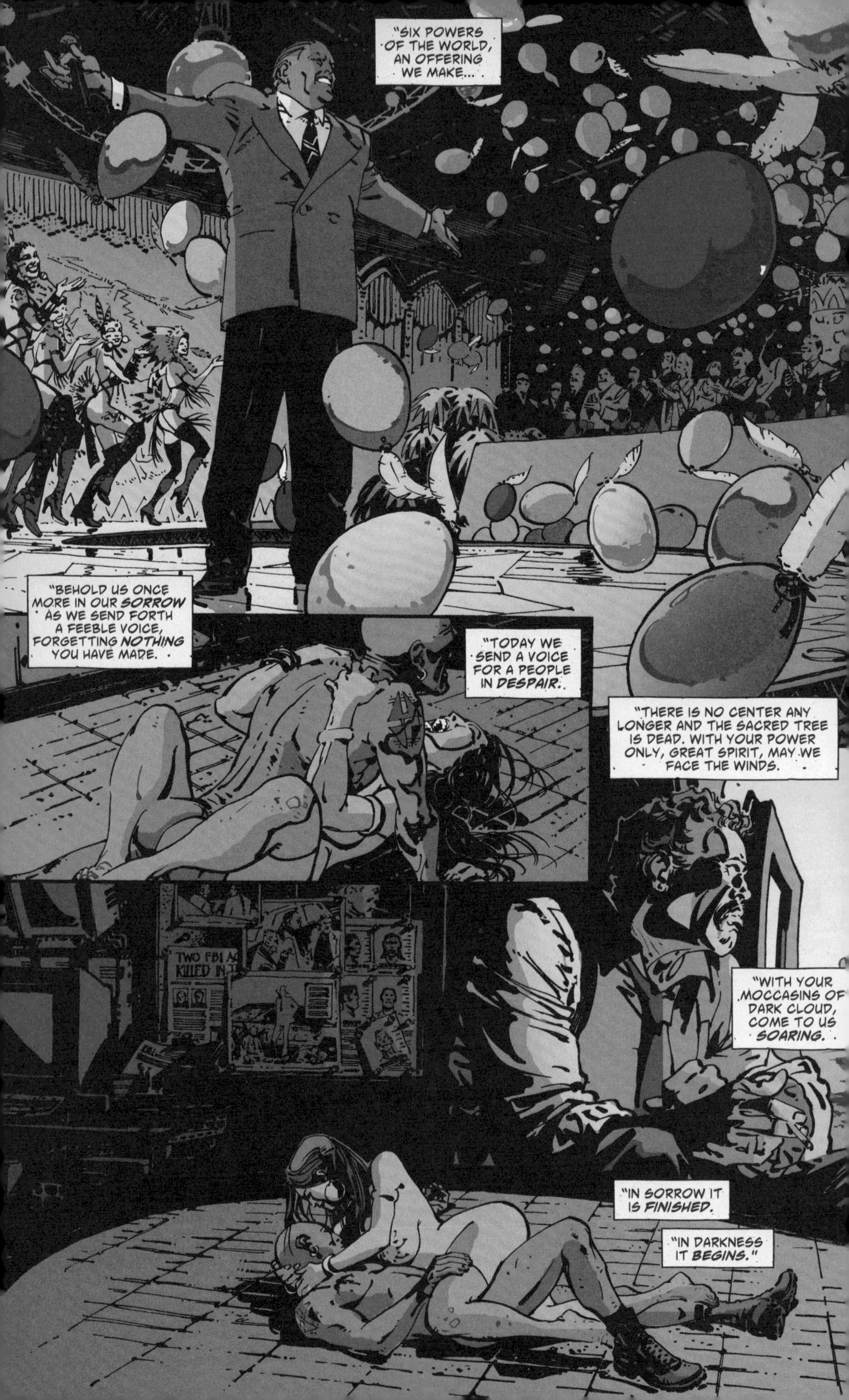
"SIX POWERS OF THE WORLD, AN OFFERING WE MAKE...
"BEHOLD US ONCE MORE IN OUR SORROW AS WE SEND FORTH A FEEBLE VOICE, FORGETTING NOTHING YOU HAVE MADE.
"TODAY WE SEND A VOICE FOR A PEOPLE IN DESPAIR.
"THERE IS NO CENTER ANY LONGER AND THE SACRED TREE IS DEAD. WITH YOUR POWER ONLY, GREAT SPIRIT, MAY WE FACE THE WINDS.
TWO FBI
KILLED IN
"WITH YOUR MOCCASINS OF DARK CLOUD, COME TO US SOARING.
"IN SORROW IT IS FINISHED.
"IN DARKNESS IT BEGINS."

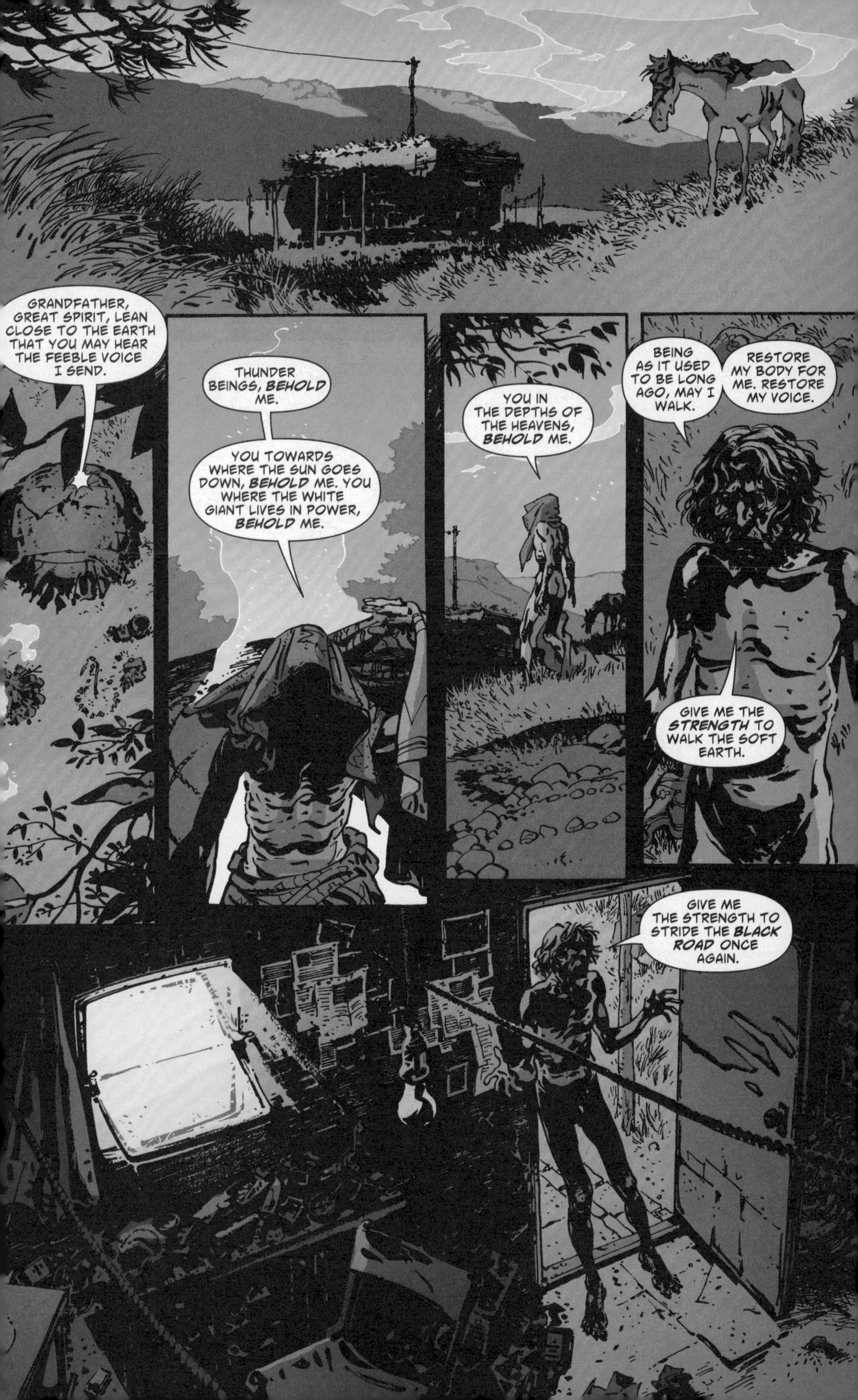
GRANDFATHER, GREAT SPIRIT, LEAN CLOSE TO THE EARTH THAT YOU MAY HEAR THE FEEBLE VOICE I SEND.
THUNDER BEINGS, BEHOLD ME.
YOU TOWARDS WHERE THE SUN GOES DOWN, BEHOLD ME. YOU WHERE THE WHITE GIANT LIVES IN POWER, BEHOLD ME.
YOU IN THE DEPTHS OF THE HEAVENS, BEHOLD ME.
BEING AS IT USED TO BE LONG AGO, MAY I WALK.
RESTORE MY BODY FOR ME. RESTORE MY VOICE.
GIVE ME THE STRENGTH TO WALK THE SOFT EARTH.
GIVE ME THE STRENGTH TO STRIDE THE BLACK ROAD ONCE AGAIN.

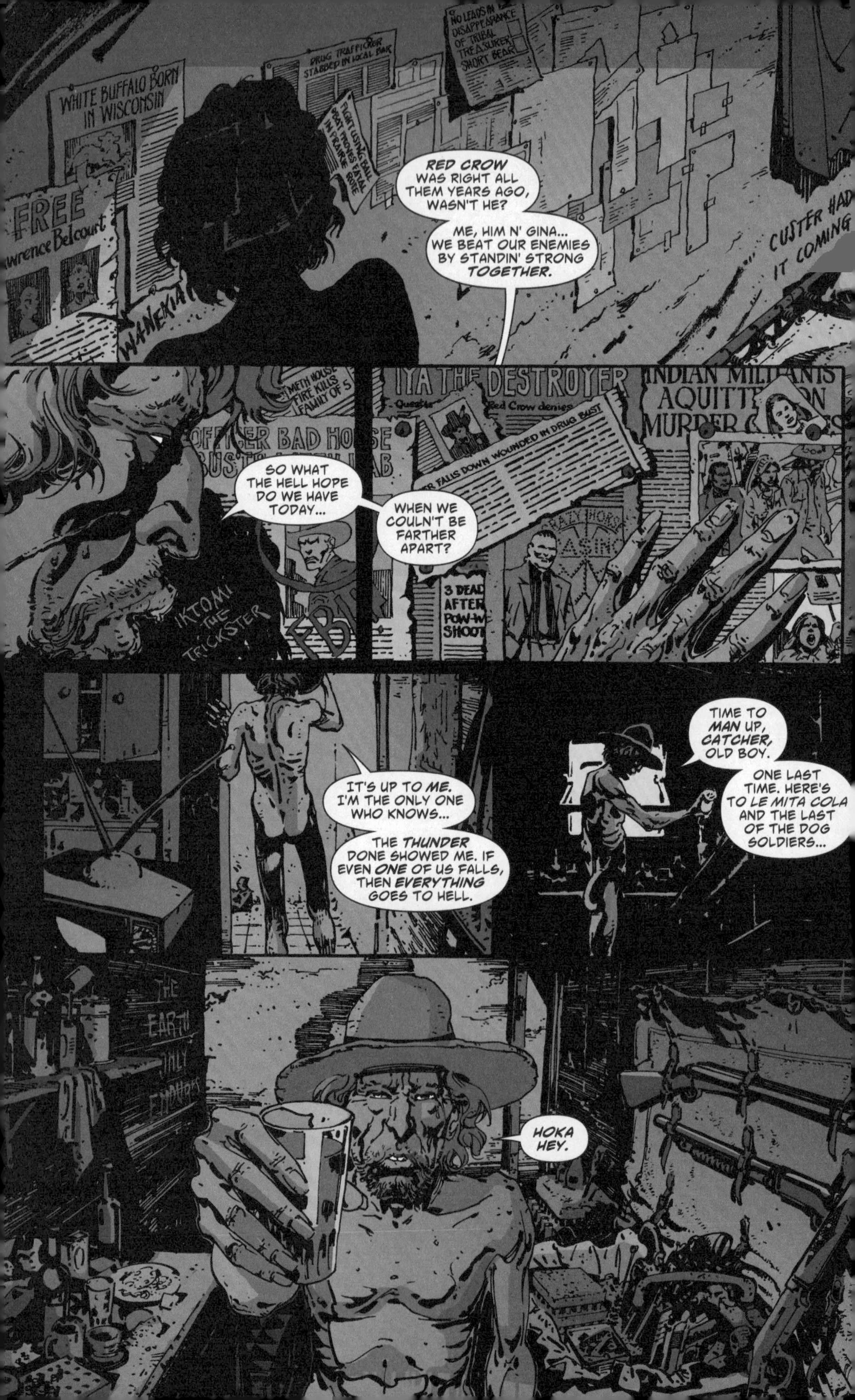
WHITE BUFFALO BORN IN WISCONSIN
DRUG TRAFFICKER STABBED IN LOCAL BAR
NO LEADS IN DISAPPEARANCE OF TRIBAL TREASURER SHORT BEAR
FREE
WANEKIA
RED CROW WAS RIGHT ALL THEM YEARS AGO, WASN'T HE?
ME, HIM N' GINA... WE BEAT OUR ENEMIES BY STANDIN' STRONG TOGETHER.
CUSTER HAD IT COMING
METH HOUSE FIRE KILLS FAMILY OF 5
IYA THE DESTROYER
Red Crow denies
SO WHAT THE HELL HOPE DO WE HAVE TODAY...
WHEN WE COULN'T BE FARTHER APART?
IKTOMI THE TRICKSTER
IT'S UP TO ME. I'M THE ONLY ONE WHO KNOWS...
THE THUNDER DONE SHOWED ME. IF EVEN ONE OF US FALLS, THEN EVERYTHING GOES TO HELL.
TIME TO MAN UP, CATCHER, OLD BOY.
ONE LAST TIME. HERE'S TO LE MITA COLA AND THE LAST OF THE DOG SOLDIERS...
HOKA HEY.

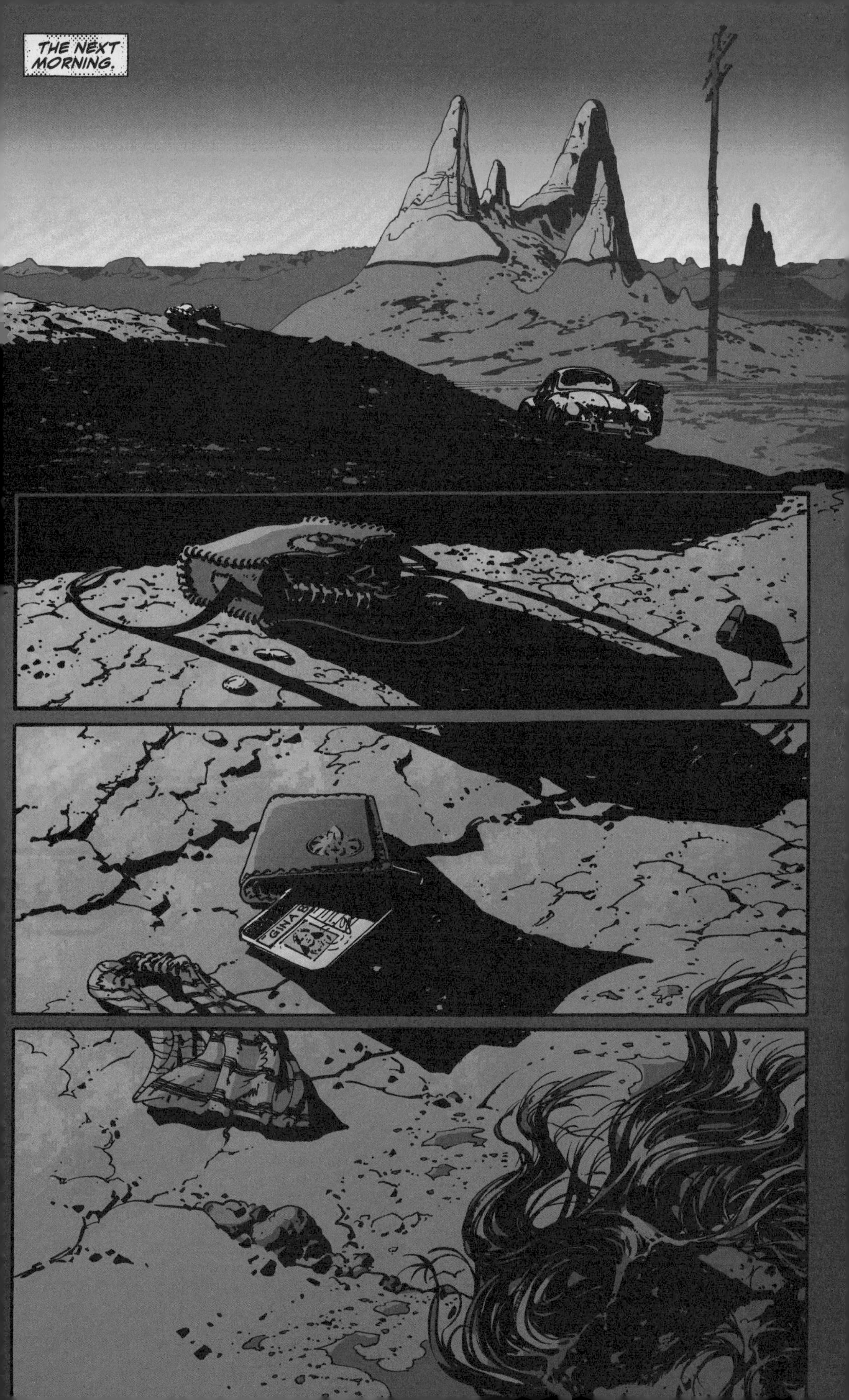
THE NEXT MORNING.

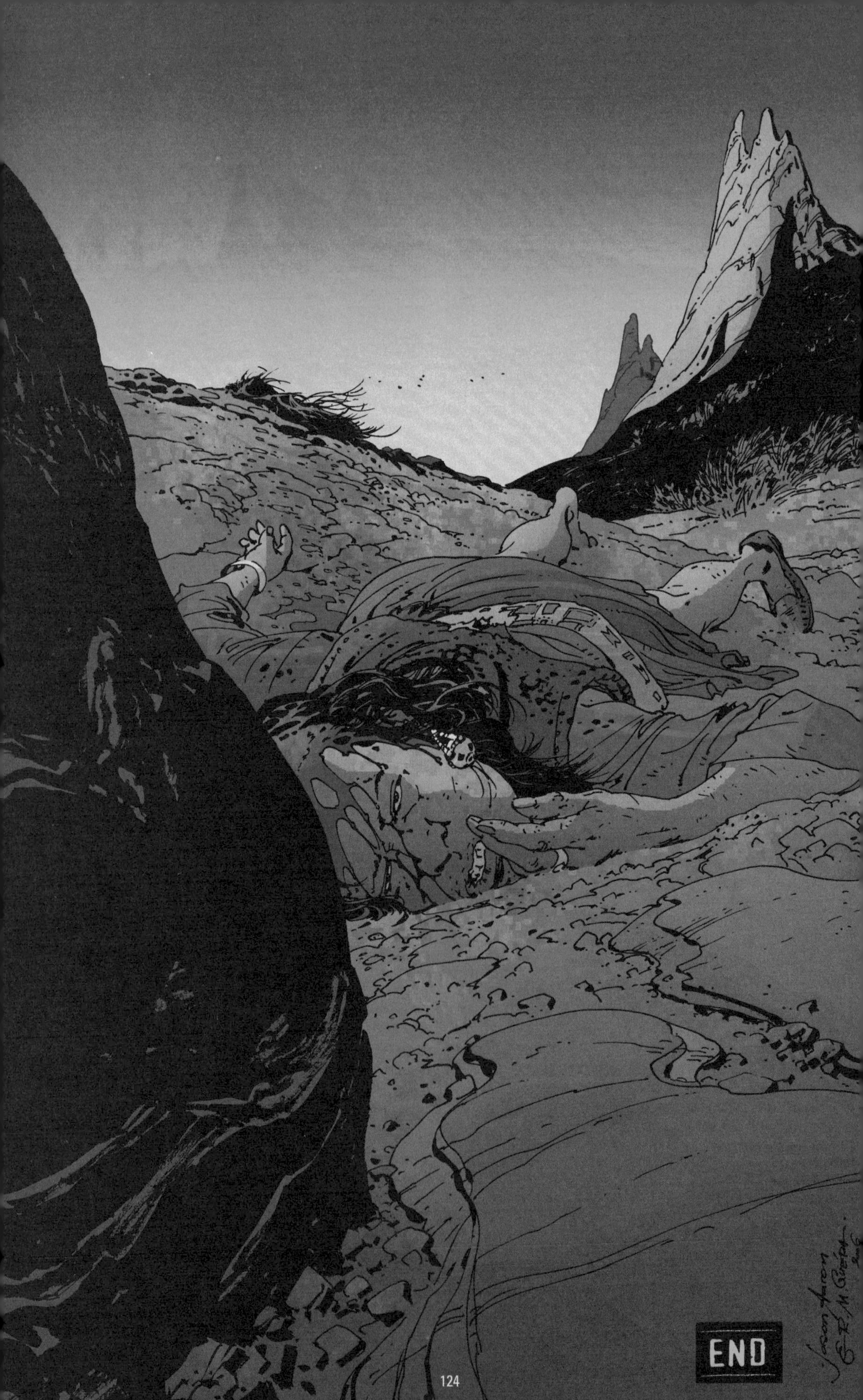
END

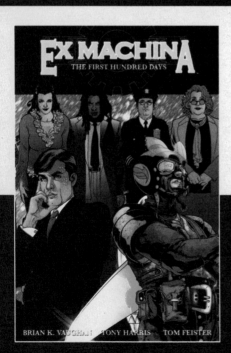

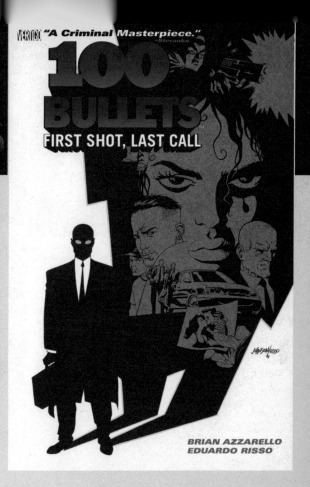

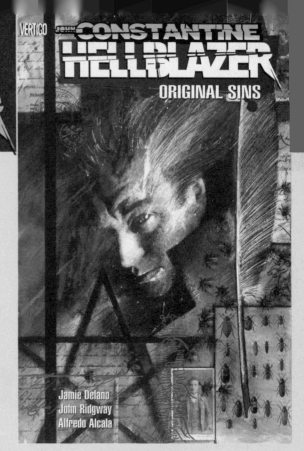